European Monographs in Social Psychology
Experiencing emotion
A cross-cultural study

European Monographs in Social Psychology

Executive Editors:
J. RICHARD EISER and KLAUS R. SCHERER
Sponsored by the European Association of Experimental Social Psychology

This series, first published by Academic Press (who will continue to distribute the numbered volumes), appeared under the joint imprint of Cambridge University Press and the Maison des Sciences de l'Homme in 1985 as an amalgamation of the Academic Press series and the European Studies in Social Psychology, published by Cambridge and the Maison in collaboration with the Laboratoire Européen de Psychologie Sociale of the Maison.

The original aims of the two series still very much apply today: to provide a forum for the best European research in different fields of social psychology and to foster the interchange of ideas between different developments and different traditions. The Executive Editors also expect that it will have an important role to play as a European forum for international work.

Other titles in this series:

Unemployment: its social psychological effects by Peter Kelvin and Joanna E. Jarrett.
National characteristics by Dean Peabody
Levels of explanation in social psychology by Willem Doise

Experiencing emotion

A cross-cultural study

Edited by

Klaus R. Scherer

Université de Genève and
Justus-Liebig-Universität, Giessen

Harald G. Wallbott

Justus-Liebig-Universität, Giessen

and

Angela B. Summerfield

Birkbeck College,
University of London

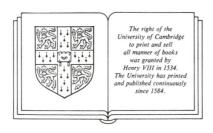

The right of the
University of Cambridge
to print and sell
all manner of books
was granted by
Henry VIII in 1534.
The University has printed
and published continuously
since 1584.

Cambridge University Press

Cambridge

London   New York   New Rochelle

Melbourne   Sydney

Editions de la Maison des Sciences de l'Homme

Paris

Published by the Press Syndicate of the University of Cambridge
The Pitt Building, Trumpington Street, Cambridge CB2 1RP
32 East 57th Street, New York, NY 10022, USA
10 Stamford Road, Oakleigh, Melbourne 3166, Australia
and Editions de la Maison des Sciences de l'Homme
54 Boulevard Raspail, 75270 Paris Cedex 06

First published 1986

Printed in Great Britain by the
University Press, Cambridge

British Library cataloguing in publication data
Experiencing emotion: a cross-cultural study. –
(European monographs in social psychology)
1. Emotions
I. Scherer, Klaus R.   II. Wallbott, Harald G.
III. Summerfield, Angela B.   IV. Series
152.4   BF531

Library of Congress cataloguing in publication data

Main entry under title:
Experiencing emotion.
(European monographs in social psychology)
Bibliography.
Includes index.
1. Emotions–Cross-cultural studies. 2. National
characteristics, European. I. Scherer, Klaus Rainer.
II. Wallbott, Harald G., 1952–   . III. Summerfield,
Angela B. IV. Series.
BF531.E96 1986   152.4   85-31382

ISBN 0 521 30427 X

ISBN 2 7351 0143 6 (France only)

Contents

Contributors

Aebischer, Verena   Maison des Sciences de l'Homme, Paris

Babad, Elisho Y.   Hebrew University of Jerusalem

Bänninger-Huber, Eva   Universität Zürich

Cosnier, Jacques   Universitè Lyon II

Dols, José M. F.   Universidad Autonoma de Madrid

Edelmann, Robert J.   University of Sheffield

Ellgring, Heiner   Max-Planck-Institut für Psychiatrie, München

Fernandez, Alfonso J.   Universidad Autonoma de Madrid

Giovannini, Dino   Università di Bologna

Green, Elizabeth J.   Medical Research Council, Clinical Research Centre, Harrow

Ricci-Bitti, Pio   Università di Bologna

Rimé, Bernard   Université Catholique de Louvain

Scherer, Klaus R.   Université de Genève and Justus-Liebig-Universität Giessen

Summerfield, Angela B.   University of London (Birkbeck College and United Medical and Dental Schools of Guy's and St. Thomas's Hospitals)

Wallbott, Harald G.   Justus-Liebig-Universität Giessen

Preface

This book was conceived in the summer of 1979, on the terrace of the Birkbeck College Senior Common Room, over some glasses of Macon Blanc. The occasion was a lunch-break during an international workshop on methods of non-verbal behaviour research. A number of the European researchers present felt strongly that laboratory research on the non-verbal expression of emotion will remain sterile unless it is informed by better knowledge about the day-to-day experience of emotion. Thus the plan was born to carry out a comparative questionnaire study between several European countries with the aim of attempting to assess the nature of the antecedents of, the reactions to, and the regulation of everyday emotional experiences. During the next four years, an international research group consisting of the contributors to this volume developed a research design, a free response questionnaire, and detailed coding schemes for antecedent situations and emotional reactions in various modalities; administered questionnaires to almost 800 student respondents in eight countries; and coded and analysed the responses. The results of this massive study, which was conducted with very little external funding, provides a fascinating account of the experience of emotion in European student cultures.

The present volume reports the most important findings from this cross-cultural questionnaire study. While an attempt is made to situate the results within some of the current concerns of the psychology of emotion, this is not a textbook on emotion nor a survey of research in the field. Consequently, while major sources are cited whenever appropriate, no attempt is made to review the relevant literature systematically. Given the steadily growing number of publications in this area, both in psychology and the related disciplines of sociology, ethology, and psychiatry, a comprehensive review of the literature would have vastly exceeded the space available in this monograph. Furthermore, it would have been almost impossible to cite all the work that has contributed to the explanatory principles mentioned in various parts of the manuscript. While it is tempting to relate some of the findings and interpretations to current work in various areas of psychology and the social and behavioural sciences, we had to refrain from such a broad approach, if only to keep the reader focussed on the major issues under investigation.

Chapter 1 provides an overview of four of the major issues of research into the psychology of emotion and tries to show how the data obtained in the present study can help to facilitate future empirical study of these issues. In addition, the specific questions that were addressed in this study are spelled out in detail. The details of the methodological procedure in designing and administering the questionnaire are described in Chapter 2, and the development of the various coding schemes for categorising the free responses and the reliability of the data in Chapter 3. Chapter 4 describes the antecedent categories and provides a first qualitative glimpse of the data. Chapter 5 systematically reviews the patterns of results on the antecedent situations that have provoked experiences of joy, sadness, fear, and anger in our student subjects. In addition, various characteristics of the emotion-eliciting situations are analysed. Chapter 6 is devoted to a review of the physiological symptoms reported for the different emotional reactions. An attempt is made to link these data to the predictions proposed early on in the history of the psychology of emotion by Lange. Chapter 7 reports the various non-verbal behaviour patterns that the subjects described as occurring during the emotion-eliciting incidents. In both Chapters 6 and 7 the question of the differential patterning of the four discrete emotions studied is highlighted. Chapter 8 examines the verbal reactions in the emotional episodes, both in terms of the subjects' recalled production during the incident and, on a meta-level, in terms of their written descriptions in the questionnaire.

In Chapter 9 an attempt is made to link the information on antecedents and reactions by examining the extent to which specific types of antecedents have differentially affected the intensity and duration of the emotional experience, as well as the physiological, non-verbal, and verbal behaviour patterns. Furthermore, the nature of attempts to control or regulate the emotional reaction, as reported by the subjects, is examined in terms of differences across emotions. The individual differences in emotional reactions are explored in Chapter 10, where groups of subjects are compared. A different level of analysis is chosen in Chapter 11. Here the data are examined in terms of the social situation in which the emotional experience was situated. A summary statement is provided in Chapter 12, the concluding chapter. Here an attempt is made to review the major patterns of our findings and formulate hypotheses for further empirical studies.

Because of the special nature of this large-scale research project, this monograph has somewhat more extensive Appendices than is customary. Appendix A consists of a number of 'country notes'. In these short contributions researchers who have been involved in this long-term cross-cultural study describe aspects of the data that are specific to the culture of their own individual countries, often comparing them to the overall pattern of the results. Given the latter situation, it has not always been possible to avoid some overlap of chapters. Furthermore, each of the contributors has been encouraged to develop his or her own theoretical perspective in trying to place the findings within a larger framework of the psychology of emotion.

The 'country notes' also provide an opportunity for the contributors to speculate, somewhat more freely than one would want to in a formal chapter, about the origin of some of the intercultural differences found. Given that we did not have any specific hypotheses concerning the possible differences between the inhabitants of the European countries involved before starting this research (apart from the common stereotypes concerning the emotionality of different nations), these notes might help to generate some ideas and clues for a more systematic set of questions to be asked in future studies. Consequently, while not essential for the reader interested in a general overview, they may provide interesting raw material for the specialist, particularly scholars involved in cross-cultural research. Since we had to limit the length of these notes to keep the size manageable, many of the original contributions were severely cut. Consequently, many ideas are only hinted at and in most cases there was not enough space to discuss issues exhaustively.

We consider it to be one of the strengths of this book that the different theoretical approaches that are apparent in the various contributions are as diverse as the countries of origin of the contributors. Consequently, a number of different orientations are presented, including rather different styles of presentation of data. In editing the volume, we have tried to preserve as much as possible the idiosyncrasies in theoretical and analytical approach without endangering the reader's ability to integrate the information presented.

Given the diverse approaches of the authors, we are counting on diverse interests of the readers. Given the many different traditions of data reporting in the social and behavioural sciences, we have tried to make this volume readable for a broad public. This required a reduction in the number of data tables, figures, and significance levels, all of which are dear to the hearts of experimental social psychologists, to a level that would be tolerable to readers from other disciplines. However, in order not to sacrifice scientific rigour, we reproduce the results of the statistical analyses in Appendix D (Appendixes B and C reproduce some of the major research materials), and in the text we have used the term 'significant' or 'significant difference' in those cases where the statistical analysis yielded a significance level of < 0.05; we talk of a 'tendency' or a 'trend' in a particular direction whenever that level was barely missed, that is the significance level was > 0.05 but < 0.1; and we use the term 'highly significant' or something similar when a significance level of < 0.01 was obtained. The fact that exact significance levels and the underlying statistical analyses are not reported in the individual chapters should not therefore be taken as an indication that no such tests have been performed. On the contrary, we have attempted to carry out a rather comprehensive analysis of the quantitative data and to use the significance levels to guard against the interpretation of trivial differences.

It remains to us to acknowledge the support we received from a large number of sources. Most particularly, we very gratefully acknowledge a research grant from the Délégation Genéral de la Recherche en Sciences et Technologie, a major governmental research funding agency in France. This grant was obtained within the framework of a research programme in the European Laboratory for Social Psychology (LEPS) at the Maison des Sciences de l'Homme in Paris, of which this project is a part. We are most grateful to Clemens Heller and Adriana Touraine for their continuing support and encouragement. We also greatly appreciate the hospitality and financial support given by the local institutions where the meetings of the participating scientists were held, in particular the Maison des Sciences de l'Homme, the University of Lyon, the University of Giessen and the *Giessener Hochschulgesellschaft*, the University of Bologna, and the Max-Planck-Institute for Psychiatry in Munich. Without this support this major research enterprise would have been entirely impossible.

Klaus R. Scherer and Harald G. Wallbott would like to thank Thomas Wehrsig, Susanne Ahrens, Christine Gürtler, Ute Klee, Elisabeth Gohl, and Ursula Hess for their help in coding the questionnaires and statistical analyses, and Heike Clasen and Ute Schönwetter for secretarial work. Angela B. Summerfield would like to thank The Economic and Social Research Council for financial support, J. P. Watson for his valuable comments and encouragement, Janet P. Oliver for translation and secretarial assistance, and Greta Cason and Susan C. Godfrey for secretarial assistance. Pio Ricci-Bitti and Dino Giovannini are grateful to Giannini Brighetti for his helpful assistance at many stages of the research. Eva Bänninger-Huber's research was conducted at the Institute of Psychology, Department of Clinical Psychology, University of Zurich. She would like to thank Ulrich Moser for generously providing the resources for her research and a productive research environment. Her thanks go also to Felix Steiner for his assistance in the statistical analyses of the data reported here, and to Barbara Hochweber, Christine Nelevic, and Liza Timmel for their help in submitting and coding the questionnaires. Elisha Babad is grateful to Ayala Ariav and Dorit Rosenblatt for their helpful assistance at all stages of this research. Jacques Cosnier thanks Gil Benejam for participating in the research.

Bernard Rimé extends his thanks to Claudia Ucros for her assistance in running the statistical analyses.

Finally, we thank Tony Manstead for critically reviewing some of the major chapters of this volume, and Louise Sanders for her excellent subediting of a difficult manuscript.

Giessen, March 1985   *Klaus R. Scherer*
                                         Harald G. Wallbott
                                         Angela B. Summerfield

Part I
Asking about emotional experiences: rationale and methods

1 Studying emotion empirically: issues and a paradigm for research

Klaus R. Scherer

In recent years, a number of psychologists have pointed out that the topic of emotion has been severely neglected in the past few decades (e.g. Plutchik, 1980; Scherer, 1981*b*; Averill, 1982). One reason for this neglect may be the current preference for rational models of man (which reached an apex with the 'cognitive revolution' in the 1970s) after irrational models of human nature had dominated psychology during the earlier part of the century. However, this may not have been the only reason why scholars in the social and behavioural sciences have been reluctant to devote themselves wholeheartedly to the study of emotion. The reluctance may also be based on a rather pessimistic evaluation of the likelihood of being able to settle some of the perennial difficulties in developing adequate theoretical models of emotion and to circumvent the serious problems faced by empirical research in this area.

Reading the history of emotional research is a somewhat frustrating experience. Most of the theoretical and research efforts have been directed toward a small number of controversies that have dominated the field: the centralist–peripheralist controversy (Cannon, James, Lange, Mandler, Schachter), the non-specific arousal versus discrete emotions controversy (Duffy, Izard, Tomkins), the disruption/disorganisation versus adaptational function controversy (Hebb, Plutchik, Wallon), and the universality versus cultural determinism of expression controversy (Ekman, Izard, La-Barre, Mead), to mention the most important ones. None of these controversies has been satisfactorily resolved so far, partly because the issues have not been defined with sufficient theoretical rigour to allow the design of critical experiments, and partly because of the many practical and ethical difficulties affecting empirical research on these issues.

1.1 Research issues in the psychology of emotion

Because of the almost exclusive concern of emotion theorists with these controversies, many other issues of equal if not greater importance have been overlooked. In a recent book, Ekman & Scherer (1984) have provided a catalogue of questions to be asked on emotion. These questions can be grouped into four main categories: What is the nature of the antecedent situation? Are there clearly differentiated reaction patterns accompanying different emotional states? Is there response specificity for different types of persons, in terms of both the nature of the antecedents eliciting emotion and the nature of the reaction? What is the role of social regulation, in terms of both the appropriateness of the emotional response for specific antecedents and the control of expressive reactions? These questions will now be discussed in turn.

Antecedent situation

Ever since antiquity, the nature of the situation or event considered likely to evoke a specific emotion has been treated as part of the definition of emotion. Aristotle, in attempting to teach orators to evoke specific emotions in their audiences wrote:

> Take, for instance, the emotion of anger: here we must discover (1) what the state of mind of angry people is, (2) whom the people are with whom they usually get angry, and (3) on what grounds they get angry with them. It is not enough to know one or even two of these points; unless we know all three we will be unable to arouse anger in anyone. The same is true of the other emotions. (Aristotle, Rhetoric, in McKeon, 1941, p. 1380)

The nature of the antecedent seems to play a major role in the naive psychology of emotion. For example, in evaluating the appropriateness of an emotional response, people will often compare an emotional reaction to how a 'normal person' would have reacted in a specific situation. Thus, there seem to be very clear rules about which kinds of reaction, including also the intensity, can be considered appropriate under given circumstances. Emotional reactions that exceed such normative expectations are often considered 'irrational'. Furthermore, it is one of the defining characteristics in the diagnosis of affect disturbances that the emotional reaction is habitually too extreme (mania) or too weak (flat affect) for various antecedent situations, or appears unrelated to it.

As with most other aspects of culturally shared knowledge, there seems to be considerable consensus on the adequacy of particular emotional reactions to specific antecedent situations, without the criteria for such judgments being explicit. One has little difficulty in eliciting a consensual opinion on how angry one ought to be in a concrete situation involving a frustrating experience. However, it would be difficult if not impossible to elicit an abstract definition of the necessary and sufficient antecedent conditions for anger in general.

Psychologists writing on emotion have been remarkably uninterested in the role of the antecedent elicitors of specific affects. Most theorists have been concerned with the nature of the consequences, that is the specific experimental or physiological reactions once a specific emotion could be said to have been elicited (see Fraisse, 1963, p. 102). This lack of interest in the antecedents of emotions is understandable from the vantage point of specific theoretical concerns. For example, if one equates emotion with non-specific arousal (Duffy, 1941), it would seem of little importance to study the factors producing such arousal since they can be considered to be more or less interchangeable. Similarly, cognitively orientated arousal theorists (e.g. Schachter & Singer, 1962) may consider the number of cognitive evaluations of different situational characteristics which modify the non-specific arousal to be almost endless and thus beyond systematic description. Even in discrete emotion theory, although there is interest in the nature of the elicitors (Tomkins, 1962/63), the issue seems of secondary importance since the theory postulates that once one of the discrete emotion systems has been triggered, an innate motor programme which is invariant and independent of different kinds of eliciting events will run its course. Given this assumption, the nature of the ancedent situation is of lesser importance for a number of questions conerning details of the reaction patterns. However, for cognitive evaluation or appraisal theories (e.g. Arnold, 1960; Lazarus, 1966) and for process theories which postulate that the nature of the reaction is closely tied to a sequence of evaluations of antecedent stimuli (e.g. Scherer, 1981*b*, 1984), the study of antecedent situations is of vital importance for understanding emotional experiences.

Quite apart from its relevance for psychological theories of emotion in a narrow sense, the study of antecedent situations which tend to elicit emotional reactions is of primary importance for a social psychological approach to emotion. Here the focus is not so much on the nature of the intrapsychic and intraorganismic processes that unfold in a particular emotion sequence as on the origin of emotional reactions in interactional events and the consequences of the reactions for interpersonal behaviour. Since, as mentioned above, in everyday life emotional reactions seem to be evaluated in the light of perceived situational antecedents, a social psychology of emotion needs to place major emphasis on the situational antecedents and the attribution processes that are involved.

Because emotional experiences are very much private events, we have very little *a priori* knowledge about their *actual incidence* and about the pattern of emotional reactions in *real life*. In other words, even our intuitive knowledge about emotional experience in other people is highly limited. Clearly, this lack of common knowledge strongly limits our capacity to draw up intelligent hypotheses that can be tested in empirical research.

In addition to not knowing much about the detailed processes of emotion, we know very little about the frequency with which people are emotionally aroused in everyday life and about which situational factors are most likely to evoke such emotions. The neglect of these antecedent conditions for emotional arousal has serious consequences for theorising about emotion. So far, it has not been empirically established that each discrete emotion is a homogeneous entity. It could be that the anger following a traffic incident where another car overtook in a very dangerous manner is rather different from the anger resulting from unreasonable behaviour shown by one's spouse. Also, we know very little about other situational factors and their role in evoking particular emotions. For example, does it make a difference for the type of emotional reaction whether we experience an emotional situation inside or outside buildings, in familiar surroundings, or in strange territory? Furthermore, what is the role of other interactants in the situation: is our emotion increased in intensity or modified if there are friends and/or strangers around?

Clearly, then, the systematic study of the nature of antecedent events or situations that elicit specific emotions must be considered one of the most pressing issues for future research.

Differentiated reactions

While the issue of the differentiation of the emotions in terms of specific reaction patterns has been much more central than the question of antecedents, the issue is far from resolved and, like many other topics in the psychology of emotion, suffers from a dearth of empirical data. There is little dissention about the differentiatedness of the subjective experience, that is the different feeling states, for various emotions. In fact, a number of theorists claim that this may be the only differentiated reaction, assuming that physiological arousal and maybe even expressive behaviour are either non-specific or culturally determined. The problem with empirical research in this area is, of course, that feeling states are not amenable to objective measurement. We have to rely on subjective reports from the person experiencing the state and thus of necessity have to use natural language categories for the description.

The differentiation in the physiological modality in different emotions is a matter of hot debate. Whereas there were some early empirical reports of differentiated hormonal and physiological reaction patterns (e.g. Ax, 1953), many subsequent studies have failed to replicate these findings and have thus encouraged the view that non-specific arousal is the accompaniment to differentiated subjective feeling states. This view has been strongly reinforced by the influential experiment by Schachter & Singer (1962), which showed that drug-induced non-specific arousal can, provided proper cognitive input, accompany a number of different emotions. Even though this study was hardly an ecologically valid model of normal emotional processes, and despite the fact that the results were rather weak, the impact of this work on the psychology of emotion has been extremely strong (see Mandler, 1975, 1984). Recently, criticism of the method employed by Schachter & Singer and of the interpretation of the results has been mounting (for summaries see Kemper, 1978; Reisenszein, 1983). Furthermore, a number of attempts at replication have produced data that are not consistent with the Schachter & Singer position (Erdmann & Janke, 1978; Marshall & Zimbardo, 1979; Maslach, 1979a, 1979b). Since a number of recent studies stemming from other traditions (Schwartz, Weinberger & Singer, 1981; Ekman, Levenson & Friesen, 1983) suggest rather clear differentiation in physiological response, the issue is again wide open and in urgent need of systematic study.

Another major modality of emotional reactivity is non-verbal expression in face, body and voice. Since everyday experience leaves little doubt about the degree to which non-verbal reaction in different emotional states is differentiated, and since a large number of studies have shown the ability of human observers to differentiate clearly between different emotions on the basis of a variety of expressive modes, the specificity of the reaction patterns seems rather well-established. However, as mentioned above, there has been some debate on whether these expressive patterns are biologically based or culturally determined (for reviews of this debate see Ekman, 1972, 1977). This is not a trivial point, particularly from a social psychological point of view, since the social origin and the strategic use of such expressive behaviours is of major importance in the study of interactive behaviour, deception, impression management, and other social psychological concerns. Furthermore, while there have been a rather large number of decoding studies, that is studies investigating the ability of judges to discriminate the emotions expressed in various non-verbal behaviour modalities accurately, there are very few encoding studies, that is studies investigating the natural occurrence of particular non-verbal behaviour patterns following specific emotional antecedents.

This brief discussion demonstrates that the study of the differentiated reaction patterns in various behavioural modalities is another central topic for empirical research in the psychology of emotion. As with the antecedent issue, the empirical data base is extremely small and in urgent need of broadening.

Besides specific symptoms and reactions for certain emotions, we also know very little about the relative frequency and general intensity of specific emotional reaction patterns under normal, day-to-day circumstances. We have all experienced examples of extreme emotions and the rather striking changes in expression, physiology, and overt behaviour that takes place. However, such cases have been rare. What is the average intensity of 'routine' anger? What are the physiological symptoms and the behavioural changes that the experiencing subject him- or herself observes? And, even more important, to what extent does he or she generally attempt to control these tell-tale signs of emotional arousal?

Response specificity

One of the most disheartening experiences in the history of behavioural research has been the realisation of the strength of individual differences in a large number of modalities of psychological reactivity. The phenomenon of response specificity in different individuals has been best demonstrated in psychophysiology (Lacey & Lacey, 1958). In many physiological studies, particularly in the area of stress research, researchers have to acknowledge that it is difficult if not impossible to find and then to replicate general effects of specific stimuli on human physiological responses. In many cases the response to a particular stimulus will differ according to the sex, the social background, the personality, or the coping style of the subjects studied (Asendorpf & Scherer, 1983; Scherer, Wallbott, Tolkmitt & Bergmann, 1985). Unfortunately, it does not seem to be the case that once one knows the characteristic response pattern for a particular type of person it is then possible to predict the behavioural reactivity across situation. On the contrary, there seems to be a strong interaction between person and situation characteristics, a topic which has dominated the psychology of personality for the past twenty years (see Endler & Magnusson, 1976). Interestingly, this has reawakened the interest in ideographic approaches to the study of individual differences (see the special issue of the *Journal of Personality*, Vol. 51, No. 3, 1983).

So far, the psychology of emotion has taken little cognisance of such person specificity. The assumption has been, particularly in the biologically oriented theories, that emotional response patterns are preprogrammed and should be observable in a very similar form in all of the subjects studied. However, it is now known that this is not the case. Process theories of emotion (Scherer, 1984) would predict that, as in many other areas of human functioning, there are major individual differences, not only in the nature of the reaction in the physiological, experiential, and non-verbal modalities, but also in the process of evaluating the antecedent situation. If this assumption is correct, it is easy to see why there have been so many difficulties in the past in replicating findings, particularly in studies using a very small number of subjects. If the patterns of information processing, as well as the reaction patterns, differ between subjects it would be almost impossible to replicate findings in studies using a small number of subjects without controlling for a number of central subject characteristics.

One of the major research needs for the future, then, is the inclusion of person-specific background factors in the study of both the antecedents and the reactions of emotion. It will be necessary to study much larger numbers of subjects than have been studied hitherto, in order to sample the various background factors mentioned above.

Social regulation and control

Again, we can cite Aristotle as an early, if certainly not the earliest source on the social regulation of emotion:

The man who is angry at the right things and with the right people, and, further, as he ought, when he ought, and as long as he ought, is praised...For the good-tempered man tends to be unperturbed and not to be led by passion, but to be angry in the manner, at the things, and for the length of time, that the rule dictates. (Aristotle, Nicomachean Ethics, in McKeon, 1941, p. 996)

Another example is Aristotle's 'how-to' treatment of the emotions in his Rhetoric: how to evoke certain emotions reliably in an audience to attain the desired persuasive effects. This is only one example of the ways in which emotion can be socially regulated and used for strategic purposes (see Elias, 1977; Vohwinkel, 1983; for historical surveys). Another important aspect is the control of experienced emotion and the accompanying reaction patterns for a variety of reasons such as prohibition of overt affect expression in a particular social group, or strategic purposes in interpersonal interaction.

Given the central function of non-verbal expression as the major medium of communication of emotional feeling (Darwin, 1872/1965), one would expect well-elaborated social prescriptions for what is allowable or desirable in terms of emotional expression under specific situational circumstances. As early as 1905 Wilhelm Wundt emphasised that: 'Civilised man attempts to control affect expression in line with the expectation of others, by whom he feels observed, through appropriate manipulation of his gestures and facial expression; trying to mask certain affects and to express others more strongly' (Wundt, 1905, p. 285; author translation). More recently, Ekman & Friesen (1969a) have coined the term 'display rules' for such sociocultural pressures on the manipulation and control of affective expression. The social regulation and control of expressive behaviour has been an important topic in anthropology (La-Barre, 1947; Birdwhistell, 1970), particularly with respect to the assumed cultural determination of the expressive patterns. But even theorists who lean more toward a biological view of emotional expression (Darwin, 1872/1965; Leyhausen, 1967; Izard, 1971, 1977; Ekman, 1972, 1984) have pointed out that there are cultural norms concerning the appropriateness of particular types of expression in specific situations.

Social regulation and control are not, however, only noticeable in the visible or audible manifestations of emotional reactions. If social control affected only the outwardly manifested signs of emotion, then one would presume that it is used exclusively for strategic purposes. However, this is clearly not the case. Apart from the control of outward expression, it is likely that social control exercises an influence on the appropriateness of experiencing an emotion privately even though no one else may be aware of it. Sociologists have highlighted the important social role of emotion regulation. Elias (1977) has even argued that the process of civilisation consists of an increasing control of 'primitive' affective reactions. Other sociologists have shown the importance of internalised patterns of emotion regulation in society (Hochschild, 1979, 1983).

There can be little doubt, then, that there are quite a number of internalised norms concerning the kinds of emotions that it is appropriate to experience in specific situations, these extending to physiological arousal as well as to subjective feeling states. Individuals noticing that an emotion they are beginning to experience (both in terms of subjective feeling and physiological arousal) deviates from what can be considered normal under the circumstances, will attempt to regulate their state in accordance with cultural prescription. Obviously, there can be major differences between individuals in terms of their notion of what is culturally appropriate and what is not, quite apart from differences arising from the self-concept, that is notions concerning the types of emotion that are acceptable to the ideal self in a particular situation.

While there is little debate concerning the important role of social and individual attempts at regulating or controlling emotional states, the empirical evidence for such control processes is again dismal. This is hardly surprising, since quite apart from the usual difficulties in studying emotion, repressed or controlled emotion is even more private and therefore more difficult to assess than overtly manifested emotion. This then is another area of high priority for emotion research.

1.2 Problems of empirical research on emotion

Apart from the problems that most of the above issues are not yet properly integrated into a theory of emotion – particularly since so far there is not even a consensual definition of emotion – empirical research is beset by serious conceptual and methodological difficulties. Contrary to the study of cognitive processes, where there are fairly clearly defined outcome criteria, such as solutions to problems as well as a number of powerful process variables such as latency time, much of emotion consists of internal phenomena, such as subjective experiences and physiological changes, which present formidable difficulties for objective measurement. Emotional expression, which is one of the few outwardly visible signs of affective processes, is often strictly regulated by cultural norms which may prescribe masking of emotional expression. In addition to these problems in obtaining the appropriate indicators for emotional processes, it is difficult to observe a sufficient number of incidences of emotion for systematic research. While results of cognitive processes are often public and even institutionalised, as in school settings, emotions are private experiences and are often carefully hidden from public exposure. Therefore, both lack of opportunity and ethical restraints hamper the emotion researchers' access to appropriate material for study. This is particularly true for the systematic production or manipulation of emotional states by using experimental techniques which have yielded rich results in cognitive science.

In this section, a number of major problems pertinent to the design and execution of studies designed to investigate some of the questions discussed above are described. The respective problems with experimental laboratory research on the one hand and naturalistic field studies on the other hand are treated separately.

Experimental laboratory research

The paradigm that is generally used in studies of this sort requires the experimental induction of specific emotional states by either creating antecedent events that are presumed to evoke specific emotions in the situation itself (spontaneous induction) or the use of techniques to induce subjects to recall antecedent situations or events that evoked particular emotions (recall induction). Examples of the former technique are the early Landis (1924, 1926) studies in which the antecedent events included the decapitation of mice right in front of the subjects, or stress studies in which participants are electroshocked, subjected to difficult arithmetic tasks or stressed in some other fashion. Even the threat of such treatment is a sufficient condition for the elicitation of particular emotions. Other techniques in this tradition are the creation of social situations, for example requiring a public speech, producing an embarrassing encounter, etc., to evoke social emotions. A modified form of such spontaneous induction is the presentation of audiovisual material, such as films or slides, in which emotion-producing events are depicted and the subjects experience the impact of the situation in question by identifying with the models displayed. Recall induction techniques, on the other hand, rely on the ability of the subjects to reproduce antecedent situations which have elicited particular emotions from them in the past. Using straight instruction or hypnotic techniques, the investigator requests the subject to think of such situations and to attempt to re-experience the emotional feeling that was felt at the time.

We shall now examine the usefulness of these laboratory techniques for the investigation of the major theoretical issues described above. Each of the four major issues listed is examined separately.

The antecedent situation. The spontaneous induction techniques are of little use in exploring the nature of the antecedent situations or events that elicit specific emotions. Any attempt at manipulation requires prior knowledge of the effect of the factors to be manipulated. Thus, knowledge of the situational factors that produce certain kinds of emotion needs to exist before these can be properly manipulated. Spontaneous induction via experimental manipulation techniques can be very useful in testing hypotheses about suspected antecedent factors but cannot be used to generate knowledge about such antecedents. Since we all have naive preconceptions of appropriate antecedent events for particular emotions, it is easy to design induction procedures which may indeed evoke the respective emotion. However, the problem with this procedure is that it is not based on a systematic and well-specified concept of the structure of the eliciting situation and of the contributing effects of the various aspects of such situations. Induction procedures that do not start from such systematic hypotheses about the effects of specific situational factors usually proceed via vague analogies between situations. Therefore, it is frequently impossible to test specific hypotheses concerning the relative effects of particular factors, or to ascertain whether the desired emotion has actually been obtained, particularly since there is no established criterion for the presence of a specific emotion. Thus P. Ekman (personal communication) has argued that many of the early spontaneous induction studies did not find differentiated responses to particular stimuli because they all seem to have evoked the same state, namely embarrassment, rather than different discrete emotions.

Recall induction techniques, as generally used, have also contributed little to the study of emotion antecedents. While the past situations and events that subjects are encouraged to recall can certainly be expected to contain emotion-eliciting factors, researchers using these techniques are rarely interested in studying those factors. They are usually content to have reproduced some of the original affect that the subjects experienced in the actual situation. Subjects are rarely questioned about the details of the situations they recall. Thus, in studies of this kind, the affective end result is important, not the process whereby it was originally evoked.

The experimental laboratory studies, then, seem to be of little use in developing systematic knowledge about the emotion-eliciting effects of specific situational antecedents. They can, however, play an important role, particularly those utilising the spontaneous induction techniques, once a systematic theory of antecedent effects has been developed, by enabling one to test some of the hypotheses generated by such a theory.

Differentiated reactions. Experimental laboratory studies using spontaneous or recall induction seem ideal for studying the patterning of reactions accompanying the various emotions. Complex physiological measurements can only be obtained in such laboratory settings. Furthermore, the experimental nature of the procedure makes it possible to obtain a series of measurements over time, including repeated assessments of subjective feeling states via self-rating methods. However, the very setting that enables the researcher to obtain systematic physiological and self-report measurements makes it difficult to study the behavioural reactions. This is partly an artefact of the physiological measurement methods, which require fixation of arms, legs, and head in order to avoid movement artefacts in the physiological response measurement, and partly an artefact of the highly impoverished nature of the laboratory situation. Thus, artificial reduction or limitation of one or several of those responses should have a severe impact on the unfolding of any of the others if, as is theoretically expected, there are strong relations between physiological response, behavioural manifestation, and subjective feeling state.

Another major problem for the measurement of the differentiatedness of emotional responses in laboratory studies is the near impossibility of inducing very intense emotions. Apart from the difficulties of creating the antecedent precursors for intense emotions in the laboratory (given that strong ego involvement seems to be required for the experience of intense emotion), the ethical code for modern behavioural research and the concerns of human subject committees clearly do not permit the researcher to produce intense emotion, particularly of a negative kind, in the laboratory. Thus, we are faced with a paradox: while the laboratory is optimally suited for the detailed study of complex differentiated reaction patterns, it is highly likely that the conditions in which such differentiated reaction patterns occur cannot be produced in the laboratory. The difficulty that psychologists have had in replicating some of the early findings of differentiated physiological responses could well be due to this problem. Similarly, in stress research, it seems likely that many failures to replicate results and the difficulty of finding generalisable patterns of stress reaction could be due to the fact that the emotional states induced were neither intense enough nor comparable enough over subjects. In other words, the stressors produced *different types of emotions* in different subjects.

Person specificity. In order to assess individual differences, in terms of both the processing of antecedent events and the differentiation of reaction patterns, the study of fairly large numbers of people is required. Furthermore, one would want to study different types or groups of persons with known characteristics and to assess additional background variables that may be relevant for differences in emotional responsivity. Both of these requirements are difficult to meet in experimental laboratory studies. Since only very few subjects can be run at any one time, and since subjects have to be brought into the laboratory, the procedure is very demanding in terms of time and expense. This makes the use of a large number of subjects prohibitive. Furthermore, since participation in experiments is largely voluntary, even though monetary inducements or course requirements can be used to encourage participation, the effect of self-selection can never be completely excluded. Thus, it is possible that those types of subjects that would be particularly interesting to study (e.g. those prone to react rather extremely in a variety of emotion-eliciting situations) are never available for study since they select out of experiments where there seems to be the slightest danger of emotional involvement. In addition, there is the problem of demand characteristics, experimenter effects, and social desirability factors (Orne, 1962; Rosenthal, 1966), which are likely to operate in emotion experiments just as much as in other types of experimental manipulation. These effects are likely to be particularly confounding in the study of person characteristics since it is possible that those groups that are particularly prone to demand characteristics or experimenter effects are also those that tend to use particular types of coping strategies in emotional situations (e.g. denying or sensitising) (Asendorpf & Scherer, 1983; Asendorpf, Wallbott & Scherer, 1983). While some of these factors may be less salient in the recall induction procedures, it is still the case that the particular nature of the laboratory situation may mask some of the person specificity that would be observable under more natural circumstances.

Social regulation and control. Laboratory experiments are by definition of very little use in the investigation of social regulation and control, since it is well known that the laboratory situation is a rather special social situation with a large number of very specific normative constraints. Thus, it is highly unlikely that the operation of normal social rules concerning both feeling and expression can be expected to occur in such a context. In addition, there may be strong differences in the way that subjects perceive the rules of the laboratory situation in studies involving emotion. Given the prevailing lore about psychology, it is possible that some subjects perceive the situation as a licence to let go, to engage in cathartic emotional flooding. Others may be worried by the psychologist's presumed ability to analyse their innermost secrets on the basis of their emotion display and may control their expressive behaviour even more strongly than they would under normal circumstances. Therefore, the laboratory situation is somewhat unsuitable for the study of social regulation and control.

Naturalistic field studies

A research strategy that is highly valued in many behavioural sciences, particularly in ethology and sociology, is the naturalistic study of behaviour as it occurs in the field. In terms of studies on emotion, this requires the identification of settings in which the occurrence of emotions is likely and can be observed. Since emotions are often private events that occur spontaneously, it is rather difficult to find settings in which emotional behaviour reliably occurs. However, there are such settings, for example leisure activities, achievement situations, and sports situations, in which naturally occurring emotions can be observed. Unfortunately, even though this seems to be the most promising method for studying emotions, there are a number of drawbacks for the study of the issues raised above.

The antecedent situation. As mentioned above, the naturalistic study of emotions in this field requires the identification of settings, the structural characteristics of which make it likely that a particular emotion will occur. Thus, there is already severe preselection in terms of the antecedents that can be studied. As in the case of laboratory experiments in which known antecedents are manipulated, the selection of known emotion-producing situations or settings for field studies limits the ability to sample systematically a large number of antecedent situations or events that are likely to elicit particular emotions. As in the experimental situation, and possibly even more so, the high investment in terms of time and money that is required for such field studies makes it prohibitive to sample more than a very few such settings. Thus, as in the case of the laboratory studies, the utility of field studies is primarily in the testing of specific hypotheses that need to be generated on the basis of more systematic knowledge about the nature of antecedent situations.

It is important to distinguish between field studies in which subjects are only observed, often without their knowledge, and studies in which experiencing subjects are also questioned with the help of interviews or questionnaires. This distinction has important consequences for the assessment of objective versus subjective situations. So far, in talking about the situational antecedents, we have not distinguished between the objective characteristics of a situational event, as they would be described by a researcher (e.g. using methods from ecological psychology; Barker, 1960; Barker *et al.*, 1978) or by the consensus of a group of observers, for example, and the subjective experience of these objective situational characteristics by the person involved.

As is now well known from many studies of social perception, the mapping of objective situational characteristics into subjective experience is less than perfect. The famous notion of the 'definition of the situation' (Thomas, 1928) has highlighted the fact that the subjectively experienced situation may be more like an active creation of the acting subject than a passive reflection of objective factors (see also Berger & Luckmann, 1969).

In many cases, the motivational state of a person, perceptual errors, or particular attribution tendencies in terms of causal inference can result in sizeable differences between the objective characteristics of a situation and their subjective experience by different people. Consequently, in many psychological traditions (see Koffka, 1935; Lewin, 1951; Murray, 1951; Bowers, 1973; Ekehammar, 1974; Endler & Magnusson, 1974) the subjective definition or experience of a situation is considered to be much more central than objective situation characteristics in determining behavioural consequences.

Since emotion seems to be primarily determined by the evaluation process, that is the specific processing of incoming information in each person (Arnold, 1960; Lazarus, 1966; Scherer, 1981b, 1984), the subjectively experienced situation is clearly more important for the understanding of the antecedents of emotion. These subjective evaluation processes cannot be directly observed in the field without questioning the persons observed. Therefore, studies relying exclusively on observation are of fairly limited value for the investigation of emotion antecedents unless there are very clear-cut relations between objective situation characteristics and subjective appraisal without interference from individual differences in subjective appraisal.

Differentiated reactions. For the study of differentiated reactions, observational studies in the field represent the opposite extreme from laboratory studies. While the likelihood of observing rather intense emotions with clearly differentiated reactions is very high in field studies, the ability to assess those reactions objectively is very limited indeed. In field observation studies only relatively gross behavioural patterns can be observed and coded without the help of audiovisual recording. A more molecular analysis allowing measurement of many of the non-verbal behaviours that seem to provide the bulk of emotional signals, particularly facial and vocal phenomena (Ekman, 1982; Scherer, 1982), can only be assessed with a high investment in audiovisual apparatus (see Wallbott, 1982a). Given the requirements in terms of recording quality for some of the analyses to be carried out, this may well become obtrusive to the point where the naturalness of the observation is no longer guaranteed.

Physiological responses in subjective feeling states cannot be assessed in naturalistic observations unless the experiencing subjects are actually interviewed. While this is possible in principle, in reality it is often difficult to interfere in an ongoing situation to obtain such self-reports. By the very definition of naturalistic field studies, such behaviour is embedded in an ongoing social context which often makes it difficult, if not impossible, to interrupt the proceedings for a research activity which is not pertinent to the social processes occurring at the time. Similarly, the use of telemetric measuring devices strongly limits the naturalness of the situation.

Person specificity. As in laboratory studies, it is demanding in terms of both organisation and resources to study large numbers of people, and particularly different types of people, with respect to their emotional responses in natural social situations. Apart from the time that it takes and the expense, it is often difficult to obtain access to particular settings, especially those where emotions are likely to occur (particularly emotions considered to be socially disadvantageous). Again, there may also be a strong self-selection in terms of the types of people who are willing actually to show emotions in public where they can be observed. It is likely that groups of people with particular types of coping strategies (such as repression) will rarely display emotional behaviour in public.

Social regulation and control. In principle, the observation of emotions actually occurring in the field should be an optimal setting for the study of social regulation and control. Indeed the setting should reveal those normative constraints which operate on what is considered appropriate as feeling and those which operate on what is allowed or required in terms of emotional expression. However, at our present state of knowledge, it seems to be very difficult to differentiate the prototypic aspects of emotional expression and those features that are produced by social regulation or control without actually asking the person observed. It is particularly difficult to decide which aspects of the social situation produce which constraints and how they are perceived by the experiencing subject.

This review of the problems inherent in the use of experimental laboratory research and naturalistic field observation for the study of theoretical issues central to the psychology of emotion leaves a rather bleak picture. Clearly, the two major research strategies of the behavioural sciences present a number of very serious drawbacks for the study of emotion antecedents, reactions, and regulation attempts. As mentioned before, it is rather likely that the frustration resulting from some of these difficulties has, at least in part, been responsible for the neglect of emotion as a topic of research in the social and behavioural sciences in the last decades. Yet, many of these techniques are highly useful for testing hypotheses once we have more systematic knowledge.

1.3 Emotion research by questionnaire

The use of self-report techniques

Given the problems connected with laboratory experiments and field observations of emotions and given the fact that emotions are to a large extent private experiences that are not easily subject to public scrutiny, it seems reasonable to attempt to make an assessment of emotion antecedents and emotional reactions by *asking* the person who experiences an emotion about it. There are many psychological phenomena that are amenable to study only by questioning an experiencing subject: preferences, attitudes, moral judgments, and problem-solving processes, to name just a few. The need to ask subjects about their internal responses is almost never questioned in those areas of research, since everybody realises that there is no other way, at least at present, to study internal processes objectively. For some strange reason the use of the same method to study emotional experience is often considered somewhat dubious, almost as if one should somehow trust subjects less in the reporting of their emotional experiences accurately than, say, in their moral judgments or problem-solving processes. While it is true that defence strategies may operate in the reporting of emotional experiences, given the important role of social norms and self-concept influences on emotion, this would seem to be no less true for their moral judgments, problem-solving skills, or preferences.

Thus, there can be no serious objection to the study of the subjective experience component of emotion by questioning the experiencing subject. In some cases, the questioning of subjects may be preferable even for the study of those components of emotion that *are* amenable to objective measurement, for example bodily and vocal expression or physiological reactivity. There are two reasons for this: (i) the subjective experience of expression and physiological response and the ability consciously to report this is an important area of study in its own right, particularly with regard to regulation attempts and the operation of feedback loops between the different components of emotion, and (ii) if self-reported expression and physiological responses were fairly accurate, it would be very economical and feasible to study emotions in naturalistic contexts by questioning the persons involved. While the evidence to date concerning the accuracy of self-reported expression and physiological symptoms is inconclusive, there is some indication that subjective reports of these behavioural modalities are not entirely invalid (see Cacioppo & Petty, 1982; Pennebaker, 1982).

The most useful tool for studying emotion by the questioning of subjects would seem to be the in-depth interview. However, there are a number of drawbacks. Apart from the high cost of this procedure, it is possible that subjects would respond less truthfully than in a more anonymous procedure, given that emotions are often connected to intimate events relevant to self-esteem and social standing. Thus, the use of more or less standardised questionnaires which can be administered in a very anonymous context may be more promising, at least in the initial stages of a research programme. Given the widespread use of questionnaire methods in the social and behavioural sciences, it is not surprising that some attempts at studying emotions by the use of questionnaires have been made in the past (see Averill, 1982, for a review). Unfortunately, these early attempts have rarely used the full potential of the questionnaire method and have rarely acknowledged its problems and limitations, and so have not had much impact on the field. Averill (1982), after reviewing the handful of previous surveys of the everyday experience of anger, concludes:

One reason for the paucity of surveys of the everyday experience of anger is the concern with the validity of self-report data. To a certain extent the concern is quite justified. It would seem, however, that a healthy scepticism and caution about self-report have resulted in an unhealthy form of self-censorship, in which psychologists have cut themselves off from some potentially useful sources of information. (Averill, 1982, p. 150)

This was basically our view when the researchers represented in this volume started the research reported here in 1979. We felt that there was very little empirical or *a priori* intuitive knowledge about emotional experience which could be used to develop theoretical models of emotion or promising experimental studies. Given that many components of the emotion process, including the evaluation of antecedent situations and the subjective feeling quality, of necessity require the questioning of the experiencing subject, we decided that it might be well worth the effort to conduct a large-scale questionnaire study in order to obtain some more systematic information on emotional experiences in real life.

Methodological issues in the use of questionnaires
We shall first explore some of the advantages and disadvantages of the questionnaire method for the study of the issues discussed above.

The antecedent situation. The questionnaire approach can yield information only about the subject's subjective perception on the situation. All of those features of a situational event that were not visible to the subject, or that, while visible, were not perceived at the time or were repressed later, cannot be assessed. However, since, as shown above, the subjectively experienced features of a situation or event are those that are likely to affect the emotional process, this would seem to be an asset rather than a drawback (except for repressed features which may have had an effect but are not reported). The subjective recall of an emotion-producing situation should not only contain those features of the situation that had an effect on the course of the emotion process but also reflect the weighting, that is, the relative importance, of the different features. Thus, in asking a subject to recall and describe a situation or event that produced a certain emotion, we should be able to obtain an indication not only of what the situation was like but also of the process, in terms of the subjective evaluation or event, that produced the emotion.

In order to obtain this information, an open-ended questionnaire format seems indicated. This allows sufficient flexibility for the subject to describe the essential features of the situation as recalled and to indicate the sequence in which these features were evaluated. In order to avoid the operation of selective memory which may lead to the exclusion of specific aspects of the situation, it is possible to combine the open-ended response format with a cueing format in which subjects are reminded of specific important aspects of the situation such as: who was involved, where it took place, what exactly happened, and so on.

Differentiated reactions. Since people seem to be well-aware of many aspects of their emotional responses in the different modalities, at least of the more extreme responses, the use of the questionnaire method seems to be quite suitable for the study of how differentiated the responses are in different emotional states. Here it is more difficult to decide whether one should use an open-ended format or a closed format with precoded responses. One of the major problems of the latter is that it may have a 'cueing' effect in that subjects may be motivated to indicate a specific response which they consider appropriate and likely under the circumstances but which they may not exactly remember to have experienced. In this research we have opted for an open-ended format in order to ensure that subjects would only record those responses which they remembered very vividly. In order to remind them of the various modalities, that is non-verbal expressions and physiological responses, some of these were detailed in the question. Clearly, the use of an open-ended format will result in a sizeable reduction in the number of responses as compared to a forced-choice format or a tick-mark format which lends itself much more easily to the recording of many responses. It is likely, then, that in our research we are assessing only the more extreme responses, that is those which are likely to have been accessible to awareness.

Person specificity. Since questionnaire methods are highly economical, it is feasible to study a large number of people and to assess a wide range of background factors allowing the formation of groups of respondents with specific characteristics. In addition, personality tests can be easily combined with questionnaires in order to obtain an indication of personality differences in emotional reactivity.

Social regulation and control. The study of social regulation is one of the most difficult issues in this area of research. As mentioned above, the operation of social constraints or attempts at regulation produced by self-esteem considerations are often not observable directly in the response patterns of the subject. Therefore, the use of a questionnaire method to ask directly for such tendencies seems promising. Whereas it is possible that a number of regulation and control attempts are not consciously experienced by the subject, one will at least obtain information about those regulation and control attempts that have been experienced as such. Furthermore, it is possible to use other information obtained in the questionnaire to assess indirectly the operation of such control factors. For example, by analysing the responses in terms of some of the social characteristics of the antecedent situation, such as the nature of the setting or the number and types of people present, it becomes possible to generate hypotheses about the operation of social control factors.

The validity of the questionnaire method
On the whole, a questionnaire method seems to be well-suited to the study of the issues listed above. It is the only alternative for assessing those aspects of the emotional response that are related to subjective experience, that is the feeling component itself, and the subjective impression of the expressive and physiological reactions. As far as the objectively measurable components of emotion are concerned, the use of the questionnaire method will at least allow us to develop a number of hypotheses which can then be studied more specifically in laboratory experiments and field settings, thereby enabling future research to concentrate resources on those issues that seem most promising to study on the basis of prior evidence.

Questionnaire methods have a large number of drawbacks too, of course. We know that self-reports are subject to many artefacts such as response distortion due to ego-defence tendencies or social desirability effects. Furthermore, apart from such strategies designed to protect or enhance the self, it is known that self-reports are often affected by stereotypes, that is subjects reporting that they behaved in a way corresponding to their preconceptions about the response requirements in a specific situation. This presumably reflects the fact that common notions about the most likely response overpower the recall of the actual response.

The problem of memory is of course also important, particularly in a research situation in which subjects are asked to recall past emotional events rather than to report on impressions they had in the immediate past (as in spontaneous induction studies). Some potential sources of artefacts like, for example, defence strategies and stereotypical responses, are inherent in the use of any self-report technique of natural events, independently of whether questionnaires or interviewing techniques are used. They also plague self-reports that are obtained in controlled laboratory studies or field observation. Thus, ego defence strategies and stereotypical response tendencies can only be avoided if one decides to do without self-report altogether. The choice of this alternative, however, as has been shown above, would make it altogether impossible to study the subjective experience of the emotional response.

While it would be unrealistic to assume that one can avoid these potential artefacts altogether, there are a number of ways of minimising their effects. The questionnaire method seems to be well-suited for this purpose. For example, the obvious anonymity of the questionnaire format, particularly in group administration, would tend to reduce the likelihood of conscious ego defence strategies. By avoiding closed formats with standardised response alternatives, one can avoid encouraging stereotypical response patterns. Memory problems can be reduced if subjects are asked to recall events that are not too far in the past, that is if one restricts the period for recall to about a month or so.

The problem of artefacts is brought up again in the conclusion to this volume, where an attempt is made to assess the likelihood of response distortion on the basis of some of the results.

Other studies using questionnaires in research on emotion

Despite the fact that the use of questionnaires for obtaining information is widespread in the social and behavioural sciences, there were not many studies that had used questionnaires to obtain self-report data on emotional situations when we began this project in 1979. However, given the change in research on emotion referred to earlier, our group has not been surprised to learn of other, similar studies since then.

Like our study, quite a few of these studies were directed at gathering information about the types of situations or events that elicit specific emotions, in some cases with the idea of developing a classification or taxonomy of such situations. Only a few of these studies have been directed toward more than one emotion, however. In most cases the eliciting events for specific types of emotion were investigated, for example the causes of anxiety and fear (Hall, 1899; Geer, 1965; Bernstein & Allen, 1969; Magnusson & Stattin, 1981; Rose & Ditto, 1983; Stattin & Magnusson, 1983), stress situations (McGrath, 1982), jealousy (Hupka, 1981), anger (Averill, 1982), or shame (Wicker, Payne & Morgan, 1983). Similar techniques for gathering information about situations and events that affect positive or negative mood or the well-being of a person have been extensively reported in the area of life event research (Bradburn, 1969; Dohrenwend & Dohrenwend, 1974; Warr & Payne, 1982).

While respondents in most of these studies have been asked for events that they actually experienced, there are quite a few studies in which subjects were asked about stereotypical social situations that are likely to evoke certain emotions (e.g. Schwartz & Weinberger, 1980; Boucher & Brandt, 1981). In such studies, the major purpose was to assess to what extent subjects will report similar reaction patterns when asked to imagine that they experience similar situations.

Questionnaire approaches have also been used in recent years for the study of subjectively experienced physiological arousal (Pennebaker, 1982). In addition a number of studies in the area of self-awareness and self-attribution may provide relevant material for interpreting the results reported in this volume (see section II.D. in Cacioppo & Petty, 1983).

Whenever possible and appropriate, the results of these other studies are compared to our findings in the various chapters below.

Furthermore, a number of research groups, particularly in the United States, have started to gather information about emotional experience using questionnaire methods (G. L. Clore & H. Ortony, personal communication; I. Roseman, personal communication; P. Shaver, personal communication; Smith & Ellsworth, 1985). Most of these researchers are interested in developing a taxonomy or classification of emotions and emotion-provoking situations on the basis of the cognitive factors involved in the elicitation of specific and discrete emotions.

1.4 A paradigm for research

Given the scarce research so far and the problems discussed above, our research plan was dominated by two major considerations. First, we wanted to ask the respondents to report *salient emotional episodes* which they had experienced in the last few weeks and at the same time to get as much detail as possible on the nature of the antecedents, the reactions, and the potential regulation or control attempts. In order to render the responses more comparable, we asked the respondents to think of one episode each for four major emotions: joy, sadness, fear, and anger. Second, from the outset, the study was planned as a cross-cultural investigation. The phenomenon of emotion is characterised by a complex interweaving of biological and cultural factors, an aspect which has frequently led to fruitless debates about the relative importance of these factors, particularly in terms of expressive behaviour. Comparative studies across cultures are mandatory in order to settle some of these theoretical differences and we wanted to make a modest contribution to this end. Cross-cultural comparison is especially important in trying to assess social regulation and control attempts. While it is possible to ask subjects about control attempts and their perception of the rules governing emotional experience in expression, it is likely that at least some of the prescriptions are so much taken for granted in a particular culture that they are not easily amenable to conscious analysis and verbalisation. A comparison of the reported reaction patterns across cultures may yield some hypotheses as to the operation of such unconscious control or regulation attempts. More specifically, we were hoping to obtain preliminary answers to several questions we had concerning the issues discussed above, for the reasons detailed below.

The antecedent situation
Which types of situations or events elicit different emotions?
The questionnaire responses on this question were to serve as the basis for attempts to develop a classification or categorisation system for emotion-eliciting situations. Clearly, this has important implications for theory development in the psychology of emotion, particularly with respect to the critical differential features or characteristics of situations that determine the resulting emotion.

Which types of situations are more frequent, salient, or powerful in eliciting specific emotions?
To some extent, this is an actuarial question. The information about the relative frequency with which specific antecedent situations elicit certain emotions and how intensely and how long these emotional episodes are experienced is important for a number of practical research issues, such as identifying the situational factors one might want to select for experimental studies with maximal ecological validity, quite apart from the general interest value of such data.

What is the nature of the social settings in which salient emotional episodes are situated?
Apart from the actuarial importance of this question, the answer may yield interesting insights into mediating variables or conditions which may strengthen or weaken the likelihood that a particular emotion is elicited. The social setting may also affect the nature of the response, and, particularly, the regulation attempts.

Do different types of persons encounter specific situations more frequently?
To some extent, this is part of the person specificity issue. Given the importance of the subjective evaluation of situations and events, it seems

likely that particular types of processing modes are related to cognitive style and affect the likelihood that certain types of events or situations serve as elicitors for emotions. Furthermore, it is possible that certain personality traits predispose some people to encounter specific situations more frequently, for example danger situations for sensation seekers, frustration situations for hysterics, etc.

Differentiated actions

We intended to study the emotional responses as comprehensively as possible, including behavioural tendencies, verbal behaviour, non-verbal behaviour, and physiological symptoms.

Are differential reaction patterns reported for different emotions?
This, of course, is one of the oldest issues in the psychology of emotion. Given the scarce evidence from experimental studies, it would seem important to gather some data in terms of the subjective experience of the reaction pattern differences. More specifically, one could attempt to examine some of the theoretical predictions about expressive and physiological responses that are found in the literature.

Are there differences between the reported reaction patterns for specific classes of antecedent situations within a particular emotion?
This question is particularly important for the theoretical notion of specific responses for different emotions, as postulated by the discrete emotion theorists. Similarly, it is important to know whether specific types of situations have a powerful effect in producing specific types of reaction, or more intense reactions.

What are the interrelationships between different responses?
This question is particularly important for the topic of response patterning, that is the question of whether emotional reactions are elicited independently of each other or in the form of coordinated patterns. The answer to this question is of major importance for the theoretical analysis of the emotion mechanism.

What is the relative importance or salience of different response patterns?
Again, this question has actuarial value. Which types of reactions are more frequently experienced and/or remembered? This may yield important insights into the ability to monitor one's bodily reactions during emotional episodes and the likelihood of the occurrence of regulation or control attempts.

Are there individual differences in reaction patterns?
Again, this question is relevant to response specificity. Given the evidence from physiological psychology, it seems highly likely that one would encounter rather strong individual differences in terms of emotional reactivity. In part, this could be due to individual differences in the reporting of emotional behaviours and symptoms, although this possibility is difficult to address in questionnaire data.

Person specificity
To some extent, the issue of individual response stereotype cuts across the other issues and it has already been mentioned in connection with some of the questions mentioned above. For antecedents, reactions, and regulation, one would want to know to what extent there are differences between individuals as a function of sex, age, social background, and occupation or field of study, as well as of personality. Since the scope of the present study did not allow us to carry out extensive personality tests, we restricted our questions to some of the major background variables that are typically used in questionnaire studies.

Social regulation and control
'Regulation' and 'control' are frequently mentioned in conjunction with each other in this volume and may therefore appear to be interchangeable. However, although this distinction is not rigidly made in the pages to follow, by *regulation* we mean an individual's attempts, conscious or unconscious, actually to change the emotion (e.g. getting out of an emotion), whereas *control* implies attempts to hide or mask an ongoing emotional reaction *vis à vis* the social environment.

Are there differences between emotions in terms of the amount of regulation or control reported?
This question reflects the interesting issue of whether particular emotions are more or less acceptable in social life or in terms of the individual's self-concept.

Are there relationships between specific types of antecedents and regulation or control?
As before, it is possible that different types of antecedent situations have a differential effect on coping attempts. This may be particularly relevant in relation to social versus non-social types of antecedent situations.

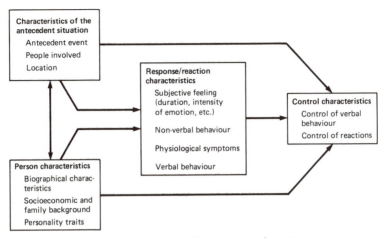

Figure 1.1   Relationships between the different aspects of emotion

Are there any individual differences in the frequency and degree of regulation and control attempts?
The literature on coping strategies, particularly repression–sensitisation, seems to suggest that there may well be rather strong individual differences in this respect. It would be particularly interesting to know whether these individual differences are more or less pronounced for certain types of emotion and/or classes of antecedent events.

Because they have been listed one by one, it may seem that the issues we have identified are unconnected. However, we anticipated strong relationships, including cause-and-effect ones, between our theoretical constructs (and therefore between the variables we measured). The detailed analysis of these relationships is the central task of the chapters reporting the results of the study. Figure 1.1 presents a schematic overview of the hypothesised relationships between the different aspects of the emotion process assessed in the questionnaire.

In the intercultural study reported in this volume an attempt is made to collect data pertaining to some of the questions mentioned above. Apart from the hope of obtaining information that would allow the formulation of hypotheses for further empirical, particularly experimental, studies, we hoped that this study would serve the more mundane function of providing actuarial information about the incidence of particular patterns of emotional reactions in different countries. In other words, we wanted to create a rich data-base with examples of emotional situations and the most frequent reaction patterns that could serve as a more ecologically valid starting-point for psychological theories of emotion than the private experience or imagination of individual theorists.

2 Measuring emotional experiences: questionnaire design and procedure, and the nature of the sample

Verena Aebischer and Harald G. Wallbott

2.1 The questionnaire approach

Our interest in emotions from the point of view of their antecedent determinants, their physiological, verbal and non-verbal aspects and the subsequent coping strategies used have been discussed in Chapter 1, together with an evaluation of the advantages and problems of a questionnaire approach to the study of emotional experiences. We now turn to the description of the methods and procedures used in this large-scale inter-cultural study.

The questionnaire approach involves some inherent limitations and problems of which researchers need to be aware. These limitations are discussed in Chapter 1 and thus are only summarised here. Self-reports are subject to sources of distortion. Even if people are willing to answer as faithfully as possible, are they really able to remember the required information? Indeed, the bigger the time lag between the event and the report of it, the more likely it is that the outcome is a rationalisation and an interpretation: the event has been integrated in the meantime into the social reality of the individual who is likely to describe those items of the event that are most compatible with his own frames of reference.

Another, and important, source of distortion is the verbal description of the event. Indeed, an emotional situation is characterised by subjective, cognitive, and eventually non-verbal and physiological components. A transformation of these experiences into words might change the salience of some aspects, for instance in cases where no handy verbal labels are available to describe components of the experience. Thus, with a questionnaire we collect subjective representations of emotional experiences mediated by the process of verbalisation, not an objective representation of emotional situations. And, last but not least, are subjects willing to report all aspects of the event, or are there perhaps reasons for them to deceive or to lie, or to report pure nonsense?

Even if individuals are willing and able to answer the questions as faithfully as possible, their self-report is rarely an objective reflection of the real behaviour (see the discussion in Chapter 1). The researcher has to rely on self-perception and, knowing the possible sources of distortion, can never be sure that the situations reported have really happened the way they are now remembered and described, notwithstanding the tendency of most individuals to present themselves in a socially desirable way (Crowne & Marlowe, 1960).

These introductory considerations hint at some problems inherent in the questionnaire approach in general. When discussing the questionnaire approach used here and the questionnaire finally developed we shall have to return to these potential sources of distortion and describe remedies used to prevent most of these sources of error.

Before we give a detailed description of the different procedures, a word concerning the process of research used in this cross-cultural project may be in order. All of the development of the questionnaires and coding systems (see Chapter 3) was done jointly by the members of the research groups from the eight participating countries. The questionnaire and coding formats were discussed, pretested, and changed in a series of meetings, until the final form presented here emerged. A major pilot study with a slightly different questionnaire was conducted in five of the countries. The results of this pilot study are not reported in this monograph as they are published elsewhere (Scherer, Summerfield, & Wallbott, 1983). The experience gathered in this pilot study also contributed to the final versions of both the questionnaire and the coding systems.

One important problem in doing cross-cultural research concerns the equivalence of the question wording in the different languages involved. In order to guarantee equivalence as far as possible the questionnaire was originally developed in English, then the researchers from the different countries translated it into their respective languages, and finally a back-translation into English was compared with the original English version. As some of the participants of this study are multi-lingual, the results of this process could be checked further during the meetings.

The project was started in 1979. As a first step, semi-structured interviews were conducted in West Germany to elicit descriptions of emotional situations and to gather information on which aspects of these situations had to be included in the questionnaire. Out of the experiences gained from these interviews a first elicitation questionnaire and a first version of the coding systems to code especially the free answers concerning antecedents and reactions (see Chapter 3) was developed.

At the time it was planned to represent the different emotions by pictorial representations of facial expressions in order to avoid problems with translation of emotion terms. The (largely) unsuccessful attempts at this are reported below (Section 2.2). After these attempts it was decided to use verbal labels for the emotions which again called for translations and back-translations of the emotion terms to be used. The equivalence of the terms decided upon was also discussed at our various meetings. With the preliminary form of the questionnaire thus developed the above-mentioned pilot study was conducted (Scherer *et al.*, 1983).

The results obtained and further experience gained during the pilot study led to further changes in the questionnaire and to changes in the coding systems developed. The final version of the questionnaire is described below (Section 2.3).

2.2 The choice of emotion types and their presentation

The most important initial choice we had to make concerned the types of emotions to study and how to represent them. Different emotion theories discuss various basic emotions which are often conceptualised as discrete phenomena (Ekman, 1972: Izard, 1977). To these one may add blends and mixed emotions, which were not taken into consideration in this study. Looking at theories of discrete emotions, the four emotions joy, sadness, fear, and anger appear to be the most basic and universal, because they are mentioned in nearly all theories. Other emotions such as disgust, shame, or surprise are not mentioned in all theories, as they may be far more dependent on cultural interpretations. The choice of four emotions only, joy, sadness, fear, and anger, was motivated by theoretical and practical reasons (the number of emotions to be remembered had to be limited). The way of introducing these emotions to the subjects, however, presented a whole series of problems.

Ekman, in his studies, used photographs which, among other emotions, presented joyful, sad, fearful, or angry faces. Generally, he obtained satisfactory identification of the emotions which the photographs were supposed to represent (Ekman, 1972). Our pretests for this study, however, using the same photographs, were not conclusive, especially in France. Subjects did not reliably recognise the emotion presented on the photograph and inferred and ascribed various other types of states of mind to the person photographed. Furthermore, these photographs represent emotional states of relatively high intensity, which in a study such as ours may have led subjects to describe only emotional stituations of very high intensity. This was not intended, because one aim of our study was to collect representative examples of emotional situations occurring in everyday life, not just of very extreme emotional states. Thus, it was decided not to use photographic representations of the emotions.

A next attempt at introducing these emotions was to use neutral stimuli in the form of four sets of drawings each representing, like a scale, various degrees of intensity of the emotions. These drawings were done by an artist

Table 2.1. *The two verbal labels per emotion used in each country*

Emotion	Belgium/ France	Great Britain	Israel	Italy	Spain	Switzerland/ West Germany
			Country			
Joy	joie/ bonheur	joy/ happiness	simcha	gioia/ felicita	alegria/ felicidad	Freude/ Glück
Sadness	tristesse/ chagrin	sadness/ grief	etzev/ tza'ar	tristezza/ dolore	tristeza/ pesar	Trauer/ Kummer
Fear	peur/ frayeur	fear/ fright	pachad	paura/ timore	miedo/ susto	Furcht/ Angst
Anger	colère/ fureur	anger/ rage	ka'as	rabbia/ collera	colera/ rabia	Ärger/ Wut

whose task it was to draw the facial expressions from the Ekman photographs, on which the muscles characterising the specific emotions had been marked to stress the important facial features following Ekman & Friesen's 'Facial Action Coding System' (Ekman & Friesen, 1978). The artist had to draw four neutral faces and four faces representing the four emotions with high intensity, and then had to fill in three grades of emotional intensity for each of the emotions by stressing or lessening the pictorial representations of the facial muscles involved. The resulting four series of drawings representing the four emotions, each with five intensities, were given to subjects in Germany, France, and Great Britain; they were asked to judge the emotion depicted and its respective intensity. This yielded far more satisfactory results than the judgement of the original photographs. The identification of the correct emotion was better using the artist's drawings than using Ekman's photographs. The attempted variations in intensity of the emotions, however, were not reflected in the subjects' judgements. While too small in some cases, they were too large in some others. Therefore, unfortunately, these non-linguistic facial scales representing the emotions at different degrees of intensity also had to be discarded as a means of representing emotions.

For our pilot study, then (see Scherer *et al.*, 1983), we kept only the four drawings representing an emotion at its peak and associated it with a string of verbal labels adumbrating the emotion under study: joy – happiness and pleasure; sadness – sorrow and unhappiness; fear – fright and terror; anger – bad temper and rage.

This combination of two types of stimuli, that is verbal and pictorial, was designed to introduce the emotion under study to the subjects in a very open way. Unfortunately, experiences in this pilot study indicated that subjects did not respond to these representations as expected. Subjects to some degree were confused by the drawings, because often in their view they did not really represent the emotion labelled verbally. Thus, for the final study to be reported here it was decided to drop the drawings altogether and just to represent the four emotions by two verbal labels per emotion (see Table 2. 1). These labels were first decided upon in the English language, then translated into the respective other languages, and finally back-translated to guarantee equivalence across countries. Thus we tried to be sufficiently precise about the kind of emotion to be evoked.

2.3 Questionnaire content and format

As discussed in Chapter 1, we were interested in the antecedents and determinants of reported emotional situations; in the non-verbal reactions, the physiological symptoms, and the verbal reactions of the subjects confronted with these situations; in the amount of control and coping the subjects used to control their physiological, non-verbal, and verbal reactions; and finally, in the coping techniques the subjects used to achieve this.

The questions we asked therefore had to be formulated in such a way as to obtain information on all three topics, that is antecedents, reactions, and symptoms, and on coping and control processes. First, in order to obtain information on determinants and antecedents, we had to collect detailed descriptions of emotional situations, especially descriptions of what had really happened, who was involved in a situation, where the situation took place, when it happened, and how long it lasted.

Second, in order to give us information about symptoms and reactions, subjects had to report on their non-verbal reactions (i.e. facial expressions, gestures, body posture changes, changes in voice and speech, etc.), on their physiological symptoms and sensations, and finally, on what they had said in the situation, for example whether they had said nothing (as probably in some fear situations), whether they had uttered an affect exclamation (in fear, or anger, for instance) or whether they had talked a lot, and if so, what they had said. Finally, subjects had to report on the amount of control or coping they had used in the situation to control their reactions and their verbal behaviour, and on the type of control mechanisms they had used (i.e. what they did to control).

Type of questions and answers
For each of the types of information we wanted the subjects to give, we basically had the choice between three options: open-ended questions allowing the subjects to write down whatever they wanted in their own terms; closed questions with a list of possible answers for the subjects to

choose from; and rating scales for answers to be given in the form of a numeric value.

Open-answer possibilities allow the subjects the greatest freedom in answering. This may result in more representative situation descriptions in much more detail than can be obtained when using closed-answer alternatives or even rating scales. On the other hand, one often finds subjects who find it particularly hard and difficult to answer open questions, because they are not sure what information they are supposed to give and/or may have problems in formulating their feelings and thoughts verbally (this may be especially important if subjects from different social classes are to be compared). Furthermore, open answers have to be transferred into statistically manageable numbers via coding systems, whereas answer alternatives and rating scales are already in a form allowing statistical operations. The coding systems for open answers (see Chapter 3) have to be devised and tested, and their reliability has to be established.

The exclusive use of answer alternatives and rating scales (to get round the disadvantages of open answers) also has severe limitations, at least in our approach. To be able to use answer alternatives and rating scales one has to know beforehand which aspects are important in describing emotional situations, so that the respective answer alternatives and scales can be formulated. Thus, at present, the usage of alternatives and scales might be at best misleading. Certainly, important aspects of the emotional situations would be missed. And at least part of the results would be determined by the selection criteria and, in the present state of knowledge, probably by naive assumptions of the researchers selecting potential answer alternatives. Therefore, we decided to use a combination of open questions and rating scales for variables such as intensity of emotion that can be easily reported in this form.

Instructions and procedure

The exact instructions with the questionnaire can be found in the English version of the questionnaire in Appendix B. Basically, the instructions stated that the study was concerned with the investigation of events and situations that provoke emotional arousal. Subjects were instructed to describe situations or events that led to emotional arousal for the four different emotions and preferably to describe situations that they had experienced within the last four weeks. Furthermore, the cueing questions to be asked later were introduced and specified; they were questions such as 'What happened?', 'Who was present?', 'Where did it happen?', and 'How did you react?'. The subjects were told that they should not only recall situations in which emotional arousal was very obvious, but also recall events in which they were emotionally aroused without anybody noticing it. The main questionnaire was followed by a personal information sheet eliciting information about the subject's national, linguistic, and academic background. In some countries (e.g. West Germany and Switzerland; see Appendix A3 and A5) some personality questionnaires were also used, in order to study probable person-specific descriptions of emotional situations and reactions.

The procedure for distributing the questionnaires was standardised across cultures as much as possible. First of all, we decided that the subjects should not take the questionnaires home and fill them out there, but instead that the questionnaires should be filled out in the presence of an experimenter, either by a subject alone or in groups depending on time schedules etc. We did not want the subjects to talk about the task when working on the questionnaire or to pass the questionnaire to friends and relatives. If any questions arose after having read the instructions, the experimenters tried to answer them without giving information on the aim of the project and other topics which might have directed the attention of the subjects into special directions. After questions were answered in that way, the subjects started to work on the questionnaires, taking as much time as they wanted to. The experimenter did not mention any time limitations, that is the subjects were not put under any time pressure, allowing them to think about their answers and to answer the questions in as much detail as they wanted to.

To ensure that subjects were motivated to work on the questionnaire, a page was given to them before they read the instructions assuring them of anonymity, and asking them to answer all the questions carefully and in detail. The complete task of answering the questionnaire took between thirty minutes and about two hours for the subjects, depending on the length of the descriptions given and the time the subjects needed to think about, formulate, and write down their descriptions. After the task was completed, subjects were again assured that all the information they had given would remain anonymous and that no information would be published in any form that might allow identification of the subject.

To summarise, we tried to overcome potential problems with a question-naire approach as discussed in Chapter 1 and in the first part of this chapter by: using an open-ended questionnaire format including cueing questions to focus the subjects' attention on important aspects of the situation to be described; using rating scales where appropriate (as for the reported intensity of the experienced emotion or the amount of control attempts of verbal behaviour or non-verbal reactions and physiological symptoms); guaranteeing full anonymity for subjects; trying to reduce memory effects by focussing the subjects' attention on situations that had happened within the last four weeks; and ensuring equivalence of the questionnaires and the emotion labels in the different languages.

2.4 The subjects

It was first necessary to decide whether the subjects should be paid for their participation or not. Unpaid subjects are usually less affected by social desirability tendencies, etc. because they have volunteered to participate. However, this willingness to participate without receiving something for it might result in an artificial non-representative sample, because volunteer subjects might differ from other subjects in terms of personality traits or attitudes, thus probably also producing non-representative situation descriptions. On the other hand, problems might also arise from paying subjects. Paid subjects might tend to follow experimental demands (Orne, 1962) and feel they have to 'give something' for the money they receive, such as descriptions they think the experimenter might want to hear from them. Thus, stereotyped reports may result.

We decided on balance to leave the decision about payment to the researchers in the various countries. If subjects were to be paid, it was decided that for each sample the amount of payment should follow the local habits, that is no fixed amount was determined for all samples but instead a particular amount of money was selected for each group of subjects.

When studying descriptions of emotional situations, demographic characteristics of the subject sample are somewhat important. For example, married subjects might experience and thus report different emotional situations from unmarried subjects, male subjects might experience different situations from female subjects, or students might experience different situations from, for instance, blue-collar workers. Thus, sample characteristics had to be defined according to such criteria.

Furthermore, sample characteristics influence not only the type of situations reported, but also the verbal report itself, especially if open descriptions are called for. Students, for instance, usually have fewer difficulties with a questionnaire in general and with open questions in particular, than blue-collar workers, who are not used to describing their emotional experiences verbally and are especially not used to writing them down. The same argument might even be true for students from different faculties. Psychology students might be more used to introspection and verbal description of feelings and situations, which is essential for answering the questionnaire used in our study, than students of natural sciences and medicine, or of engineering.

Following these arguments, some rules were set up concerning the demographic characteristics of all samples. The researchers in the different countries tried to follow these criteria as far as possible. The first and most important decision was that all subjects should be students, with representative samples from different faculties. It was decided on a proportion of about 50% psychology students and about 50% students from other faculties, these again subdivided into about 25% from philosophical and social sciences (except psychology) and about 25% from medicine and natural sciences. Concerning the age range, subjects were to be from about 18 to about 35 years of age, with not more than 50% older than 25 years. The samples were to contain about 50% male and 50% female subjects with a possible extreme ratio of 30% to 70% at the most.

We thus tried, by using student subjects, to include only subjects who were used to questionnaires, and whose ability to verbalise emotional experiences could be considered relatively homogeneous. Furthermore, an attempt was made to make samples comparable across cultures by defining the standards and selection criteria as discussed above. Some of these criteria turned out to be very difficult to meet in some of the samples. We report on the demographic characteristics of the samples studied for the elicitation questionnaire below (Section 2.5).

2.5 The final samples

Subjects were undergraduate students in the University of Louvain-la-Neuve (Belgian sample), in the universities of Paris VII, Paris X, Lyon I, and Lyon II (French sample), in the University of London and other institutions of higher education in the London area (British sample), and in the Universities of Tel Aviv (Israeli sample), of Bologna (Italian sample), of Madrid (Spanish sample), of Zürich (Swiss sample), and of Giessen (West German sample). The most important sample characteristics are reported in Table 2.2.

The final samples had the following characteristics, after elimination of some non-student subjects, subjects who were either younger than 18 years or older than 35 years, and subjects whose background data indicated that they had not lived for most of their lives in the countries in which they answered the questionnaire. With the exception of the Italian sample more female than male students were questioned (the extreme is the British sample where only 34% were male subjects). This was above all due to the fact that more women than men enroll at university in the fields of psychology and the social sciences.

The average age for all the samples was roughly comparable, with a range from about 21 years for the Spanish sample to about 24 years for the Israeli sample. About half of the subjects were psychology students (as intended) and many of the others were social sciences students. Exceptions to this generalisation arose in the French sample, where humanities versus natural sciences were about equally represented, the Belgian sample, where it turned out to be impossible to collect questionnaires from social sciences and natural sciences students, and the Italian sample, where natural sciences

Table 2.2. *The most important sample characteristics for each country* (*in* %)

Sample characteristics	Belgium	France	Great Britain	Israel	Italy	Spain	Switzerland	West Germany
Sex								
Male	42	37	34	38	50	44	47	42
Female	58	63	66	62	50	56	53	58
Age group								
18–20	33	35	30	4	47	50	10	20
21–23	57	43	25	47	38	42	48	35
24–35	10	22	45	49	15	8	42	45
Average age (years)	21.7	21.9	23.9	24.2	21.5	20.7	23.8	23.2
Field of study								
Psychology	99	47	41	46	50	42	47	52
Social sciences	—	2	21	41	50	27	14	23
Natural sciences	1	51	38	13	—	31	39	25
No. of years spent at the university								
Up to 1	7	21	52	26	46	15	40	41
2–4	80	68	40	65	42	78	52	33
5–9	13	11	8	9	12	7	8	26
Full-time students	96	83	98	12	100	92	98	100
Social class								
White collar	89	84	66	69	70	68	78	76
Blue collar	11	16	34	31	30	32	22	24
Area grew up in								
Rural area	41	14	23	7	27	3	31	18
Town	36	35	41	34	45	10	43	57
City	23	51	36	59	28	87	26	25
Average number of siblings	2.3	2.3	2.2	2.3	1.6	3.0	2.3	1.9
Total of no. of subjects	77	149	64	102	100	106	91	90

were not represented. Except for the Israeli students, who often work as well as study, most of the students questioned were full-time students.

On average, the subjects had spent two or four years at university. The large majority of them were of urban, white-collar origin with about equal distributions for all samples. In the French, Israeli, and Spanish samples most of the subjects grew up in large cities; only in the Belgian sample did most subjects report that they grew up in rural areas, while for all other samples most subjects came from smaller cities or towns. The average number of siblings was also roughly comparable, ranging from a low of 1.6 for the Italian sample to a high of 3.0 for the Spanish sample. The total number of subjects in the different samples was fairly constant. We had aimed at about 100 subjects per sample. This goal was nearly reached with the exceptions of the Belgian and the British samples, which were a little smaller, and the French sample, which was larger than the others, because sub-samples were collected in Paris and in Lyon.

Thus we tried to achieve similarity not only in terms of the questionnaires used and in the procedures used for questionnaire administration, but also as far as possible in terms of sample characteristics.

3 The coding of reported emotional experiences: antecedents and reactions

Heiner Ellgring and Eva Bänninger-Huber

3.1 Introduction

One of the general aims of this study was to determine whether there are specific kinds of situations which elicit emotional reactions and what sort of non-verbal and bodily reactions are experienced in relation to these emotions. As described above (Section 2.3), open-ended questions were used to obtain as much information as possible on these issues and to avoid biassing subjects toward stereotypical or socially desirable answers. While this procedure yielded rich information, coding of the qualitative descriptions of antecedents and consequences was required to allow quantitative data analysis. In this chapter, the development, nature, and application of coding systems used for this purpose are described. This includes description of the general rationale behind the coding, of the construction principles used, and of the reliability of coding.

Investigation of antecedent situations and behavioural reactions to emotions touches two quite different areas within social psychology which have both received increasing attention in recent discussions: the concept of situation as a determinant of behaviour and the concept of non-verbal behaviour as an expression of emotion. Since both aspects each require a different approach, the coding of antecedent situations and of reactions to emotions will be described separately. In the following sections, the coding of situations as antecedents of emotions is described first, followed by the coding of non-verbal and physiological reactions. Since they were developed together, most of the construction principles apply to both codes. It should be noted that these codes cover only the free descriptions given by the subjects. Rating scales and other categories used in the questionnaire are described in Chapter 2.

3.2 Antecedent situations

Given the impact that is ascribed to social situations in various theories of personality, behaviour, and emotions, surprisingly little effort has been made to systematise it. So, when in 1979 we began the investigation of which kinds of situations elicit emotions, we had to develop a procedure that allowed their description and quantitative comparison.

A taxonomy of emotion-eliciting situations can only partly rely on objective characteristics. Situations are evaluated and defined by the individual (McHugh, 1968). Moreover, as is discussed in Chapter 1, the subjective definition of the situation is the chief determinant of the resulting emotion. Furthermore, a classification using only a few dimensions is likely to be insufficient, since such situations are highly complex in nature.

The literature was of only partial use in relation to achieving our goal. Situational aspects are dealt with, especially in connection with 'interactional' personality theories (e.g. Endler & Magnusson, 1976; see also contributions in Magnusson, 1981). According to these theories the situation has more influence in determining cognitions and behaviours than do the traits of an individual. The social episode theory (e.g. Bowers, 1973; Forgas, 1979) sees situations as cognitive representations of events that people experience in their everyday lives. Diaries of daily events are used here, as sources of information. The problem for quantification lies in defining the unit of analysis, that is in deciding when an episode is finished or when it starts, etc. No general classification of situations has emerged from this approach up to now.

Since the completion of our analysis, some procedures that take into account different classes of emotional situations have been published. In most cases, situations are presented to the subject in order that subjective and physiological reactions may be recorded (Schwartz & Weinberger, 1980; Averill, 1982; Boucher, 1983). Quite frequently, stress or anxiety-provoking situations are used in this way (Sells, 1970; Magnusson & Stattin, 1981; McGrath, 1982). In a recent publication, Brandstätter (1983) presents data on situations which were taken from diaries of subjects. Besides being often based on small samples of respondents or restricted to stress/anxiety concepts, these approaches are mostly not representative because of content restrictions. It is not possible to tell which situational aspects are recalled as eliciting agents for the various emotions.

For emotion-related situational features, then, there have been, up to now, no generally accepted classifications available which are broad enough to cover a variety of emotions and are sufficiently empirically validated. This might be due to the lack of a general theory of situations or their relevant dimensions. A theory-guided selection or construction of situations or situational components is therefore only partly possible. At this stage in our knowledge, an inductive empirical procedure had to be applied to the situations described by the subjects in their free responses in order to classify and quantify this information.

A somewhat eclectic approach seems justified at the point where we first have to gather information about what kinds of events are reported as eliciting discrete emotions. Some of the situational aspects clearly need to be defined on *a priori* grounds. One of these is the social aspect of the emotional experience. From a situational point of view it is important to know about other people who are involved, for instance how many are there and what is their relationship to the subject. The main question, however, concerns the content and the qualitative characteristics of the situations.

The construction of the codes

The final version of the coding scheme emerged from an interactive process whereby categories were developed on the basis of theoretical considerations and modified during the first attempts to apply the coding to the material available. The codes changed again after an extensive pilot study. Another stage of this process was the combining of categories in order to summarise the actual content. So, inductive as well as more theoretical strategies were used in the construction. The inductive procedure proved to be particularly necessary for coding the content of situational descriptions.

There were four stages of construction. First, a German sample of 20 subjects took part in a semi-structured interview. A rough content analysis of situation descriptions as a first approach to category construction was then carried out. Second, in a pilot study, 20 subjects completed a preliminary version of a questionnaire and a coding schema for situational aspects and behavioural reactions was developed. It proved necessary to add to the categories derived from the content of those categories which had not appeared yet, but which were of theoretical importance.

In a first study, described by Scherer, Summerfield & Wallbott (1983), this code was applied to 626 questionnaires of subjects from five countries (France, Great Britain, Italy, Switzerland, and West Germany). Some categories were added in order to include some country-specific aspects. For example, 'fear of supernatural events' occurred in the British sample and thus made an additional category necessary. The experience from this pilot study led to the present version of the code.

In a third stage, for the final version, the new form of the coding schema was applied to a small sample of 20 interviews. Again, the schema was expanded with a few categories which appeared necessary to cover as many elements from the answers as possible. Categories were made as comparable as possible for the different emotions. Code 01, for instance, always indicated news in the immediate social context, code 02 indicated news in the mass media, code 12 indicated situations in which strangers were involved, and so on. This kind of code applied to each of the four emotions.

The final version was then used to code the whole sample of questionnaires after reliability checks had been successfully completed. For this final version, translations into all of the six languages that were involved in the study were available, that is French, English, Hebrew, Italian, Spanish, and German.

After the coding of all the questionnaires was completed some of the codes were combined for data analysis. A single code was put together with another one if it had a very low frequency of occurrence and was similar in content.

The situation code

For each emotion, there was a situation or 'antecedent' code containing a varying number of categories. For joy, there were 20, for sadness, 19, for fear, 25, and for anger, 21 categories. In order to allow comparisons between emotions, a set of similar categories was used for all of the four emotions. The categories 'good news' (01, 02) for joy, for example, are comparable with the categories 'bad news' (01, 02) for sadness, fear, and anger. In addition, emotion-specific codes like 'fear of traffic' (17) were used, resulting in different numbers of categories for each emotion. For each emotion, there was also a category for 'uncodable situations'. A detailed description of all coding categories used is provided in Appendix C. Coders were instructed always to code the most specific category with the least degree of inference. Double coding was allowed in complex situations where at least two elements were present in the situation itself.

The frequencies of single categories, especially for joy, fear, and anger, show markedly skewed distributions (for details see Chapter 5). For four of the respective categories, relative frequencies were 10% and more. These four categories cover more than half of the codings: 61% for joy, 57% for fear, and 68% for anger. The remaining categories were used for only 1–4% of the situation descriptions. A few of the categories rarely or never appear: 2 of the categories for joy, 3 for fear, and 5 for anger.

In the case of sadness, the situation is somewhat different. Only two of the categories had a relative frequency of 10% or more. The distribution of relative frequencies over the categories is not as skewed as for the other emotions, that is 67% of the codings are distributed over 18 categories. Thus, nearly all of the categories were used quite frequently for coding antecedent situations for sadness. It should be noted that only 1–3% of the situations were uncodable within this framework.

From these findings, the question arises as to whether the different frequency distributions result from the differing resolution power of the categories. When, for example, 'relationships with friends' occurs in 22% of cases as an antecedent of the emotion 'joy', the category might not be sufficiently specific. Rather, different situations might be being included in this aspect. This would lead to a more frequent coding of broad categories than of specific ones.For example, the category 'relationships with friends' (especially for joy) covers a relatively broad spectrum of different emotion-releasing situations and thus results in a frequent coding.

This argument does not hold for the other emotion codes, however. For fear, for example, the category 'fear of traffic' (17) was the most frequent although it is quite a specific one. From this it might be concluded that the skewed distributions observed here are due to emotion-specific effects rather than to the insufficient resolution power of single categories.

It is not clear why a few of the categories appeared very rarely or not at all. Emotion-specific effects may play a role in the sense that these situations were of little or no relevance for these emotions.

Reliability of the final code

The coding was performed by trained coders in the respective universities. Training included practice trials with the coding procedure and discussion with the staff in order to establish inter-coder reliability. The number of paid student coders used in the various countries varied from two to six.

As an important criterion for the quality of the coding procedure, inter-coder reliability was assessed at different stages independently for situational and reaction codes.

In an 'international reliability study on antecedents', 10 randomly selected situations for each emotion, that is 40 situations, were coded by two coders in each country. Double coding was allowed. Reliability (% agreement) between the two coders in each country was established as well as agreement of the coders with a criterion coding. The latter agreement was averaged over the two coders in each country. The criterion coding was established during a meeting of the study group where 40 situation descriptions were coded and discussed. In cases of criterion double coding, agreement on both codes was scored '1', agreement on only one code was scored '1/2'. The percentage agreement between coders was calculated as:

$$p = N_{agreement}/\text{Total number of situations presented.}$$

Table 3.1 gives the corresponding figures.

Generally, coder agreement was reasonably high for the antecedent codes. The average agreement *between coders* varied very little between emotions (p = 76–78%) whereas between countries the variation was somewhat stronger (p = 63–90%) (Table 3. 1a). As an index of the validity of the codings with reference to a standard, the agreement of the coders with the criterion coding was determined. Values were similarly high for the average like agreement between coders with similar variability (between emotions, p = 70–81%; between countries, p = 66–86%). An average agreement of 76% can be considered an acceptable level of reliability for the coding of

Table 3.1. *Reliability of the antecedent code (percentage agreement between coders)*

(a) *Agreement* between coders *in each country*

| Country | Emotion | | | | |
	Joy	Sadness	Fear	Anger	Average
Belgium/France	70	70	80	60	70
Great Britain	65	80	85	70	75
Israel	90	80	75	80	81
Italy	80	70	50	50	63
Spain	70	80	90	90	83
Switzerland	75	100	85	100	90
West Germany	80	65	65	95	76
Average	76	78	76	78	77

(b) *Agreement* of coders with criterion

| Country | Emotion | | | | |
	Joy	Sadness	Fear	Anger	Average
Belgium/France	80	75	60	70	71
Great Britain	70	75	65	55	66
Israel	80	68	63	73	71
Italy	80	75	70	75	75
Spain	80	70	75	75	75
Switzerland	88	85	80	80	83
West Germany	88	83	75	98	86
Average	81	76	70	75	75

situational aspects, particularly given the variability and complexity of the situation reports.

The final version of the code reflects a process during which several modifications were made. This was mainly due to the rich and complex information given by the subjects. Our goal of enabling quantitative comparisons of content to be made could have led to the definition of rather abstract classes. However, a high amount of specific content information was retained in the coding schema of the final version.

3.3 Behavioural and physiological reactions

The emotional response, besides the subjective feeling state, is accompanied by non-verbal behaviours, physiological symptoms, and/or verbal behaviour. Quite apart from theoretical views about the order of occurrence of these reactions, they are most probably regarded by the individual as being a consequence of emotion which he or she may also attempt to control or reduce.

Non-verbal behaviour has attracted researchers as a possible indicator of discrete emotions for a long time. The expression of emotion on the face has been studied since Darwin (1872) (for a recent study see Ekman, Friesen & Ancoli, 1980). The voice has been examined by Scherer (1982) and other bodily movements have been studied by Wallbott (1982a).

Non-verbal behaviour can be measured in a variety of ways (see Scherer & Ekman, 1982). From the various methods reported in the literature it would be possible to adopt categories in order to classify behavioural reactions described by the subjects. Reports on physiological reactions may be classified in a similar way. Such a method was proposed independently after the completion of this study by Pennebaker (1982).

When describing non-verbal and physiological reactions, it should be kept in mind that the reports on these behaviours and sensations reflect only the subjectively remembered aspects which come into the consciousness of the individual. Thus, fewer behavioural changes may be reported than actually happened. It therefore seems sufficient to use relatively broad categories for these reactions rather than specific or differentiated behavioural descriptions as would emerge from applying codes similar to elements of the Facial Action Coding System (Ekman & Friesen, 1978).

The construction of the code

The procedure for coding non-verbal behaviour, physiological symptoms, and verbal behaviour, as in the case of the coding of antecedent events, has to be adapted to the material reported by the subjects. The method of categorising should be as open as possible in order to make use of all the types of information given. Similar strategies to those used for coding antecedent events were therefore used in constructing a coding schema for non-verbal behaviour and physiological reactions to emotions.

Reactions to emotional experiences were coded with regard to four general areas: (a) vocal behaviour, (b) non-verbal visible behaviour, (c) behavioural tendencies, and (d) sensations and vegetative symptoms. Within this 'symptom code', these aspects were assessed by means of categories which either could be generally applied, like 'experienced emotional quality', or were specific to the particular behaviour, like 'harsh voice'. Table 3.2 gives an overview of the code, which is described in detail in Appendix C.

As can be seen from Table 3.2 most of the categories were concerned with the description of vegetative sensations and symptoms (9), movements and postures of bodily parts (5), and behavioural tendencies (7). The area of cognitive symptoms will not be analysed further, since these symptoms were hardly ever reported.

Table 3.2. *Number of categories in the non-verbal behaviour and bodily reaction code*

Categories	
Vocal behaviour	
1. Speech	3
2. Voice	7
Non-verbal visible behaviour	
3. Facial expression	13
4. Gaze	5
5. Movement and posture of bodily parts	24
6. Body movement, displacement, and posture	10
Behavioural tendencies and intentions	
7. Behavioural tendencies	22
Sensations and vegetative symptoms	
8. General symptoms	4
9. Vegetative sensations and symptoms	34
10. Cognitive symptoms	3

For reaction classes 1 (speech) to 6 (body movement, displacement, and posture), an emotional qualifier (Experienced Subjective Quality, ESQ) could be coded, if it was mentioned explicitly. The ESQ was coded when a general description was given, such as 'my face became calm and quiet' (code 315 = decreased facial activity) or 'no muscle in my face moved' (code 316 = controlled). Coders were told, however, to check for the possibility of more specific codes (like 'smile', or 'painful smile') first. Thus, ESQ was coded for non-specific qualitative changes of specific bodily areas, for speech, and for voice. It was coded according to the following categories: normal, aroused positive or negative ('tight, nervous, tense'), increase ('fast, much, strong') or decrease ('slow, little, weak'), controlled, and changed (unspecified).

Associated emotions (happiness, sadness, etc.) could also be coded if explicitly mentioned by the subject. This was the case if, for example, a person reported that he or she reacted with a 'happy', 'angry', 'sad', etc. face, gaze, or other behaviours. For the vegetative sensations and symptoms, metaphors like 'butterflies in the stomach' were also accounted for (code 973). Multiple coding was permitted within this code.

For data analyses, a combined code was defined in order to compare the reaction tendencies across the various emotions (see Appendix C). The combination was done firstly according to low frequency and secondly according to comparable content. With these combinations the mere occurrence or mention of speech symptoms, face reactions, muscular reactions, etc. was counted without differentiating between specific codes.

The results are discussed in detail in Chapters 6 and 7. We report here only briefly on the general frequency of the different categories.

All the non-verbal reactions were distributed on 27% vocal reactions, 38% face and gaze reactions, and 27% bodily movements. Most of the vocal reactions occurred for voice (21%), especially in the case of anger. Laughing and smiling were found, as would be expected, together with joy (41%), whereas crying was mainly connected with sadness. Non-specific face reactions occurred in 15% of the situations, predominantly in association with negative emotions.

Physiological symptoms were mainly reported as muscular reactions (21%), stomach reactions (12%), a rise in blood pressure (10%), and temperature changes (10%). Non-specific unpleasant sensations were also quite frequent (14%).

Non-verbal reactions were reported on average in 65% of the situations and physiological symptoms in 81% of the situations. This may indicate some higher sensitivity with respect to physiological reactions. It is not possible to say, on the basis of the self-reported reactions, whether non-verbal reactions – as a consequence of stronger control tendencies – occur less often than physiological reactions in emotional situations.

Reliability of the symptom/reaction code

Inter-coder agreement was calculated for the detailed as well as for the combined code (see below). In order to assess reliability, 20 descriptions, 5 for each emotion, were coded independently by two coders in four countries. (Owing to organisational constraints, this reliability study could not be conducted in all countries.) The situations were chosen according to representativeness of symptoms. Reliability was assessed for each country independently.

It was to be expected that combined codes would give a higher agreement since the combination was calculated after the original coding had been done. Table 3.3 gives the reliability (percentage agreement) of the bodily reaction code for the different emotions and the different countries. Agreement was calculated according to $p = 2 \times N$ agreements (N of coder $1 + N$ of coder 2) where N is the number of coded symptoms. The average agreement of the coding of non-verbal behaviour and bodily reactions ranged from 69% to 86% for the detailed code. Reactions to sadness and anger were coded with somewhat less agreement than reactions to joy and fear. Considering the complexity of the phenomena coded, inter-coder agreement appears to be sufficiently high. The variability of the average agreement between countries was low enough to warrant comparable use of the coding schema across the cultures.

Table 3.3. *Reliability of the non-verbal behaviour and bodily reaction code (percentage agreement between coders)*

| Country | Emotion | | | | |
	Joy	Sadness	Fear	Anger	Average
Italy	69	81	78	68	74
Spain	91	58	100	44	71
Switzerland	86	68	93	100	86
West Germany	64	64	74	75	69
Average	78	68	86	72	75

From the general results reported in this section it can be seen that the code allows a reliable and differentiated categorising of a broad range of symptoms. The description of non-verbal and physiological reactions by the subject obviously does not tell us anything about the actual behaviour. This has to be assessed separately by observational methods and physiological measurement. The validity of the information gained in this way can, therefore, only refer to the subjective experience associated with an emotion. This, on the other hand, is important when there are attempts to control the emotion and its features.

3.4 Conclusions

The task of classifying and quantifying situational descriptions and non-verbal and physiological reactions was a difficult one given the complexity and richness of the qualitative information. Nevertheless, this task appears to have been successfully accomplished by means of the two coding systems developed here.

In order to evaluate the quality of coding systems like these, formal and content criteria have to be fulfilled. As formal criteria, the reliability and validity of the coding have to be established. In our study, the same procedures have been applied to material of a highly complex content that was gathered under quite different cultural conditions. Reliability expressed as inter-coder agreement can be regarded as being sufficiently high given the complexity of the material to be coded and the inter-cultural setting.

The validity of the coding system is much more difficult to determine. As mentioned before, subjective reports cannot be equalled to behavioural or physiological measures. However, validity can be inferred from comparisons described in the following chapters. As one criterion, values derived from these procedures should be able to differentiate between emotions and individuals (see especially Chapters 5, 6, 7, and 10). As is described in the following chapters, the system proved to be valid in this sense.

Content criteria are even more difficult to evaluate. Our general strategy was to build up the coding system primarily in an inductive way, that is we were guided by the material given by the subjects. Experience from two preliminary studies, especially the pilot study with over 600 subjects, was used for the compilation of the final form. Thus, the broadness of contents seems to be sufficiently accounted for in the code. As a quantitative criterion, the low percentage of 'uncodable' information may also be regarded as supporting evidence. For some aspects, however, a further split of categories might yield more differentiated information. A situation code like 'meeting friends' as an elicitor of joy is probably too broad a category containing too many divergent aspects. A further task would be to define some of the categories more finely, with more examples for coding. Inter-coder reliability could be improved by refined definitions as well as by more extensive training of the coders.

Generally, the coding schemata are tools which can also be used in other studies. Translation into six languages and their examination in eight countries make them applicable in different cultural contexts. In our study, the coding system gives access to antecedents and consequences of emotions. Differing from traditional questionnaire approaches, the categories developed take up and quantify not only predetermined answer possibilities but also highly complex information given by the individual in a free response.

4 Categories of emotion-eliciting events: a qualitative overview

Angela B. Summerfield and Elizabeth J. Green

4.1 Introduction

This chapter occupies a position in the grey area between the methods and the results part of this monograph. The primary aim is to describe in greater detail the categories of antecedent situations into which we sorted the experiences reported by our subjects. In Chapter 3 the emphasis is on describing our manner of proceeding in developing the antecedent situation code and our attempts at establishing the reliability of the situation coding across the research personnel in the different countries. In this chapter we attempt to provide the reader with a better insight into the nature of the categories by using examples from the questionnaires. This seems all the more necessary since a number of the labels which we have chosen for these categories are often shorthand references to rather complex patterns of situational features.

A further aim of this chapter is to justify and illustrate the combination of individual categories into more superordinate classes or clusters of antecedent situations. The major reason for this is that even though the number of respondents in this study is fairly high, the actual incidence of particular categories is often quite small. In order to allow quantitative statistical analyses, which are reported in the following part of the monograph, we therefore decided to combine those categories that seemed to share common dimensions.

Since most of the results in the remainder of this volume are based on these combined categories, we decided to report the frequencies for the individual categories in this chapter. Also, we occasionally mention differences between the various countries studied that have appeared to us to be rather striking in looking at the raw data. This first glimpse at the data is of a very qualitative nature. Contrary to the more quantitative report on the nature of the antecedent situations given in Chapter 5, which is mainly organised around specific aspects of the antecedent situation, we focus here on the individual emotions, with emphasis on the antecedents that are specific to the particular emotions.

Before starting to describe the categories of emotion antecedent situations in detail, we need briefly to address the issue of what it is that is represented by the situation descriptions that our respondents wrote down in the questionnaire.

First, it is important, as Magnusson & Stattin (1981) suggest (see also Chapter 1), to discriminate between the objective characteristics of a situation and the subjective experience of it. Many studies have mixed items from both categories indiscriminately, as in the composition of fear survey schedules (Geer, 1965). The subjective experience is likely to be particularly sensitive to the effects of socialisation and represents the efforts of the individual within the context of the culture to attribute meaning to a physical stimulus or objective event. Second, the phrasing of the questions on a questionnaire may influence the extent to which subjects emphasise actual concrete events and stimuli as antecedents in contrast to their feelings and cognitions. Subjects may experience a range of emotions elicited by their internal mental world which are not tapped by the particular questions asked. While it is legitimate for investigations to emphasise either actual or subjective aspects, the characteristics of a particular study should be clearly stated.

In the written instructions given at the beginning of our questionnaire, we clearly emphasised actual events as sources of emotion. By specifically requesting information about what had happened, where it had happened, who was present, etc., we biassed our respondents toward reporting event-based emotional experience. While we did get occasional reports of sadness 'for no reason', these were relatively rare. Similarly, subjects fairly infrequently reported events that were based on spontaneous cognitive processes or memories.

While the focus in this study was thus on actual events, our coding, or categorisation, of the nature of these situations was clearly not restricted to the objective characteristics of these events. In each case, subjects, without having to be prompted, reported essential subjective cognitions, mostly evaluations, that could serve to render their emotion understandable to an observer. Take the following example:

> 'My wife cooked meat and noodles for dinner. I noticed that she had decorated the noodles with some kind of bread crumbs. This, and the general care with which she had laid the table, made me very glad and I suppose I felt something like happiness for a moment.'

The sheer fact of a wife putting a dish of noodles on a table laid for dinner would not have been sufficient to allow us to categorise this situation in terms of the essential feature that produced this specific emotion (in this case joy or happiness). Thus, the basis for the categorisation of the emotional situations reported by our respondents has been the subjective evaluation of particular aspects of actual events, as highlighted in the situation reports. We now turn toward the detailed examination of these categories for the individual emotions.

4.2 Antecedents of joy

Table 4.1 lists the individual categories that were used to categorise situations which had given rise to joy or happiness as well as the frequency with which the respective category occurred, averaged across all of the cultural groups studied and separately for each sample. Only categories which occurred in at least 2.5% of all questionnaires are reported (all categories originally defined are listed in Appendix C).

On average, the most frequent antecedents of joy/happiness were situations in which 'relationships with friends' were important, indicating that friends, not relatives or strangers, are the social partners who are most often a source of happiness or joy. A wide variety of situations were described, ranging from 'visits of friends' and 'the return of a loved partner' to 'nice parties' and other leisure activities. Some examples are:

> 'During a conversation I told my friend that I loved him. Initially he was stunned. Then to my surprise he said he loved me too. The emotion lasted for weeks. I told him how hurt I had been thinking that he might not be interested in me and how foolish we both had been.'

> 'A friend sent me pictures of my last holiday where I had met her. This was completely unexpected. I had expected nothing more than the usual exchange of addresses.'

> '...at the beach. A guy was present, we were lying on the beach, sunbathing, taking photographs, and saying nice words to each other...'

> 'I met a friend for the first time outside the university lecture rooms. In our discussions we had noticed how incredibly close our views were. After only a few hours we felt as if we had known each other for a long time. I particularly remember the feeling I had when he said it would be wonderful to have a child with me and to stay with me forever.'

'Meeting friends' (i.e. usually short and often unexpected encounters with friends or lovers) was another frequent source of joyful experiences:

> 'By sheer chance I met in my old village some acquaintances with whom I have a pleasant, and friendly relationship. My sister was with me. We sat together until 3.00 a.m. and had a pleasant party.'

> 'I was lying in bed, reading. Suddenly the phone rang. It was after midnight. At first I could not make out who was on the other end. The name meant nothing to me. I was curious, my heart beat a little faster.

Table 4.1. *Major antecedents of joy/happiness and the percentage frequency of their occurrence*[a]

					Country				
Category	Belgium	France	Great Britain	Israel	Italy	Spain	Switzerland	West Germany	Total sample
03 Relationships with friends	9	20	22	9	32	13	28	45	22
06 Meeting friends	22	9	6	11	10	27	23	9	15
15 Success experiences	12	14	16	21	17	18	10	7	15
19 Natural, non-cultural pleasures	8	12	23	7	7	5	11	6	10
01 Good news – social context	9	8	8	13	6	8	8	6	8
16 Acquiring something material	7	5	3	7	3	3	4	4	5
10 Acquiring new friends	4	4	—	1	2	6	6	5	4
14 New experiences	3	3	2	4	7	6	—	1	3
04 Relationships with relatives	3	3	13	2	1	2	1	5	3
11 Acquiring new family members	1	2	—	11	—	3	2	5	3

[a] Categories occurring with a frequency of < 2.5% are not shown.

'Then I remembered that I had met him at a party. I was happy because I never expected him to call me after this chance meeting.'

'I had not met Andrea for about a month and our relationship at our last meeting was rather tense. Then, I ran into her in a restaurant. We sat down and talked together, and both felt at ease, because we again could talk openly to each other.'

However, friends were not the only cause of joy; success experiences in achievement situations were also very important. These success experiences were usually centred on topics like 'passing an important exam at the university' or 'getting the driver's licence' (it should be borne in mind that all the subjects were students!).

'I was successful in a public competition for working in a bank and it changed my family situation.'

'I had to take a test for a driving licence. I was terribly nervous beforehand. At the end of the test I stopped the car and the expert calmly said: 'That went very well.' He handed me the driving licence, and I was able to drive home by myself.'

'Three weeks ago in the departmental director's office, I asked the director for a dissertation and to my surprise he gave it to me without any problem.'

A fourth antecedent category mentioned rather frequently was 'natural, non-cultural pleasures', describing situations governed by the fairly 'basic' drives or needs of human beings, like 'eating and drinking' or 'sexual experiences'. Two examples are:

'I had prepared several litres of cold tea so as to have something to drink when coming home in the evening after training. When he returned from swimming and surfing, we were very thirsty and happy to have the tea.'

'We talked, laughed, ate, made love, slept…'

Some national variation was displayed in the importance accorded to these major antecedents of joy, and to some of the other categories (these differences are discussed in more detail in later chapters; see especially Chapter 5). Israeli subjects, for example, quite often reported good news in their immediate social environment as an antecedent of joy, and a reasonable proportion of them noted the acquisition of new family members. Basic pleasures were mentioned relatively often by British subjects, and to some extent by French and Swiss respondents, but by very few others.

4.3 Antecedents of sadness

The antecedent categories used to code experiences of sadness and the associated frequencies are listed in Table 4.2. Two categories were mentioned with a frequency of more than 10% in the total sample, namely 'problems with friends' (the equivalent to 'relationships with friends', which was the most important antecedent of joy) and 'death of friends'. Again, friends were generally more important than other people, but relatives also played a major role in evoking sadness ('death of relatives' and 'problems with relatives'). In general, the antecedents of sadness were quite evenly distributed across categories, with only the two categories mentioned above reaching frequencies of more than 10%.

Examples of reports on 'problems with friends' are:

'I was at a friend's home and some friends were there. My friend stammers. He was ignored and then molested by the others.'

'I had invited friends and acquaintances to a party I wanted to give, but only a few of them showed up.'

'I met with a friend for lunch to talk a little, when a friend of both of us appeared. I had to share my attention between both of them. Because of that situation the first friend, whom I wanted to talk to left very early.'

The second most common antecedent was 'the death of friends', being most often mentioned in Israel and Britain:

'I was thinking about something which triggered off a memory of a schoolfriend who was killed in a great road-accident. He was a brilliant scholar and a wonderful personality. His life wasted and for what?'

'A friend died under terrible pain, but fully conscious, because of cancer.'

Similar situations were described for 'death of relatives' (predominantly the death of parents and grandparents) and for 'problems with relatives', like the following:

'I moved out of my parents' house a few years ago. I no longer have a key. My parents were going on holidays, so I asked them to give me a key, so I could go to their house now and then. I did not receive a key and my mother informed me, through my father, that she did not want me to go into the house, when they were not there.'

Sickness (either one's own or that of people close to one) was another cause of sadness that was mentioned quite frequently:

'I was sitting in a train. A woman accompanied by two pretty 15-year-old girls entered the carriage and showed these girls the places opposite me without saying a word. I realised that the girls were deaf and dumb. After

Table 4.2. *Major antecedents of sadness/grief and the percentage frequency of their occurrence*[a]

					Country				
Category	Belgium	France	Great Britain	Israel	Italy	Spain	Switzerland	West Germany	Total sample
03 Problems with friends	33	18	14	3	18	22	21	27	19
10 Death of friends	9	16	17	21	14	8	13	6	13
19 Sickness (own or others)	11	8	3	8	11	9	10	9	9
11 Death of relatives	4	12	8	9	4	10	3	9	8
08 Permanent separation from friends	16	5	6	8	3	5	14	8	8
04 Problems with relatives	4	8	8	3	6	2	17	11	7
15 Failure in achievement situations	5	3	8	6	12	13	4	4	7
01 Bad news – social context	8	5	6	7	2	1	2	7	5
02 Bad news – mass media	3	5	8	10	2	2	–	–	4
06 Temporary separation from friends	–	9	5	–	2	3	3	4	4
13 Solitude	1	3	2	2	5	5	1	3	3
14 End of pleasurable experience	–	1	5	1	1	11	1	2	3
23 General depression	3	3	2	–	6	3	2	1	3

[a] Categories occurring with a frequency of < 2.5% are not shown.

the journey I was in a pensive mood. The situation had caused me to think a lot...'

'Psychosis of my girlfriend: After a three-month manic phase of depression I brought her to the clinic. Standing in the hall, she looked lost. When I said good-bye to her, she hardly seemed to notice.'

Again, there were some national differences in the frequency of reporting of these categories (see Chapter 5). For example, Israeli subjects were not as concerned with problems with friends as with the death of friends and sadness induced by bad news via the mass media; this may be due to the special political situation in Israel (see Appendix A8). 'Permanent separation from friends' seems to have been a particular problem in Switzerland and Belgium, while achievement failure was noted mostly by Italian and Spanish subjects.

4.4 Antecedents of fear

The individual categories used to code fear situations and their frequencies of occurrence across the cultures and for each sample are listed in Table 4.3. Four main antecedent categories resulted in the expression of feelings of fear by 10% or more of the overall sample. The first of these was traffic, and this was referred to by every fifth subject. The reports and the relative frequencies from the different countries (except Israel, where other antecedents of fear dominate) were very similar:

'Two months ago, in a car. Four friends were present. We were trying to change lanes. Another car crashed into us.'

'I crossed the street, when I suddenly got a glimpse of a car approaching at a very high speed.'

'I drove with a friend on the motorway at night. The friend was a little drunk and the street was wet because it had rained.'

Many subjects reported fear of physical aggression by others; this seemed to be especially important in Great Britain, Israel, and Spain:

'It was a dark night. A robber threatened me with a gun and tried to jerk my handbag away from me. We struggled for a few moments. I shouted and a plain-clothes policeman appeared.'

'About three weeks ago, in a demonstration. A large number of opponents started teasing and cursing us. They later became more violent.'

Other subjects were afraid of non-specific things, where the cause of fear was not exactly specified:

Table 4.3. *Major antecedents of fear/fright and the percentage frequency of their occurrence*[a]

					Country				
Category	Belgium	France	Great Britain	Israel	Italy	Spain	Switzerland	West Germany	Total sample
17 Traffic	25	29	20	12	18	18	14	19	20
12 Physical aggression	13	16	20	19	8	17	10	11	14
14 The unknown	9	10	13	13	28	5	12	17	13
15 Failure in achievement situations	17	8	20	10	10	9	11	17	12
19 Sickness	5	1	—	8	7	6	7	3	5
25 Risk-taking	8	6	2	3	—	6	8	3	5
11 Death of relatives	5	4	2	4	2	4	3	4	4
27 External forces	4	5	3	4	4	4	3	1	4
24 The supernatural	4	5	—	2	1	13	—	2	4
03 Problems with friends	—	1	2	—	7	1	7	9	3

[a] Categories occurring with a frequency of < 2.5% are not shown.

'The period of anxiety was over several weeks during the revision and actual examination period. It's hard to describe exactly what happened as it was not a particular event, but rather a period of uncertainty and pressure.'

'I walked home in the dark and had to pass through a badly illuminated lonely street. Nobody was to be seen.'

'I was at home alone. Since our house was about to be painted, there was scaffolding outside, by which anybody could climb to our floor. I kept hearing noises and thought that somebody might try to enter our flat.'

A fairly large proportion of respondents were afraid of situations involving the need for achievement, primarily examination situations:

'Some months ago, in the university, just before an exam. I always panic before exams because I think I am going to fail.'

'I had decided on a theme for my diploma work and the professor had agreed on that theme. When I started working on the topic, I realised that most of the important references I needed were not readily available.'

But also:

'I had to give a speech, which is something I do not like doing. I was very nervous at the beginning, especially when people entered the room and took their seats.'

National samples showed remarkable consistency with respect to the sample as a whole. The notable exception was fear of the supernatural, which was more common in Spain than in the other countries:

'I had seen a television programme about parapsychological phenomena and spiritual apparitions. I was at home at night and I was frightened of seeing an apparition.'

4.5 Antecedents of anger

The categories used to code the incidences of anger, and the frequencies with which they occurred are given in Table 4. 4. The most prevalent antecedent of anger was the failure of friends to conform to social norms. Other subjects mentioned similar behaviour by relatives. Anger at others (strangers) and inappropriate rewards to self were also mentioned by a large proportion of subjects. Most of the antecedents of anger thus centred around situations in which somebody had violated an explicit or implicit norm or rule or where the person answering the questionnaire felt unjustly or unfairly treated by others. Examples of statements for the 'failure' categories, where the agents of 'failure to conform to social norms and rules' were either friends, or relatives, or strangers, are the following:

Table 4.4. *Major antecedents of anger/rage and the percentage frequency of their occurrence*[a]

			Country						
Category	Belgium	France	Great Britain	Israel	Italy	Spain	Switzerland	West Germany	Total Sample
03 Failure of friends	36	25	17	8	20	25	28	37	24
12 Failure of strangers	18	18	23	25	5	22	21	12	18
28 Inappropriate rewards	20	14	16	26	16	16	18	20	18
04 Failure of relatives	14	16	5	6	18	15	12	10	13
30 Inconvenience	5	3	8	7	12	2	8	7	6
15 Failure to reach goals	4	8	—	6	10	10	1	2	6

[a] Categories occurring with a frequency of < 2.5% are not shown.

'I had an appointment with my friend at a specific time. I waited for hours and hours, until she finally arrived without having an explanation for her being late.'

'I was in the cinema with my friends. Three people behind us kept making totally idiotic comments during the whole show.'

'I was going to spend a day with my friend. But two other persons also present disturbed our conversation with rude jokes and inconsiderate behaviour.'

'I had worked until late night on a paper I had to present. I finally got some sleep, when early in the morning another person living in my place went for a walk with his dog. The dog was barking all the time and his owner did not try to stop him. I was not able to sleep any more.'

'A boy, whom I met at a party, phoned to arrange a date. Some days later he cancelled the date, because he was going out again with his old girlfriend.'

'My mother and my brother were present. My brother kept some things belonging to me, and my mother supported him wholeheartedly.'

Examples of statements concerning inconvenience and inappropriate treatment are the following:

'I had parked my motorcycle in the centre of the town in the morning. When I came to collect it at 5.00 p.m. I noticed that the basket which had been fixed to it lay in the street and that there was no air in the tyres.'

'Together with a friend I had prepared a paper for a seminar. When we had to present this paper, the friend did not show up. I had to read his part too and it was criticised heavily by the professor and the other students. Because I had not written that part, I felt I did not deserve this negative criticism.'

'I had failed an exam which I had expected to pass. A lecturer showed me what I had done, but I could still see no reason for the failure.'

'The last available ticket for a concert was snatched away right under my nose, because the ticket agent 'overlooked' me though it would have been my turn.'

As for the other emotions, national variation in reported antecedents of anger proved to be quite small (see Chapter 5).

4.6 Combination of categories

So far we have described the original categories used to code the material collected in the different countries. Tables 4.1–4.4 indicate that although some categories were mentioned quite frequently, most of them were not (as described in Chapter 3, originally there were 20–30 categories for each emotion). These relatively low frequencies called for a combination of categories into larger groups, in order to allow for quantitative statistical treatment of the data. The decisions as to which codes to combine (see list in Appendix C) were arrived at by consensual agreement of the participating researchers with respect to underlying common features of the categories.

Thus, for example, the 'news' categories ('news – immediate social context' and 'news – mass media') were combined into one category 'news', because this seemed to be the important characteristic of both categories. Similarly, a 'relationship' category was introduced by combining 'relationships/problems with friends' and 'relationships/problems with relatives' for all emotions, thus considering the aspect of relationship as more important than the type of relationship involved. A similar rationale was used for 'temporary meeting/separation' and 'permanent separation', where categories involving either friends or relatives were combined. Some other categories were not combined with others, because of their high frequency of occurrence and their distinctive content, for example, 'achievement' situations.

It was necessary to retain some of the original categories which were specific for particular emotions, especially for anger and fear, since comparable categories for the other emotions did not exist. For anger, we kept 'inappropriate rewards' and 'unnecessary inconvenience' as separate categories. For fear, 'fear of traffic', 'fear of novel, unknown situations', and 'fear of supernatural events' were kept, because these categories have a very distinctive content, while 'fear of risk-taking', 'fear of phobias' and 'fear of adverse effects and external forces' were combined to form a larger category, 'fear of risk-taking and external forces'. Most of the data in the following chapters are based on these combined categories.

4.7 Discussion

As is shown in the results section of this monograph, the present findings are quite consistent with results from earlier studies, including our own prior study (Scherer, Summerfield & Wallbott, 1983). The conclusion seems warranted, then, even at this early point in the discussion of our data, that the categories which we developed in the form of a coding system are not only reliable but also valid in describing the essential features of events and situations that provoke particular types of emotions.

In concluding, we would like to raise an issue that concerns the discussion of both methods and results. This is the point concerning the time delay between the happening of the actual event and the report of the event in

Table 4.5. *How long ago did the event happen? Data presented as percentage frequency of occurrence of time delay*

Category	Belgium	France	Great Britain	Israel	Italy	Spain	Switzerland	West Germany	Total sample
Joy									
Today or yesterday	16	12	10	6	6	4	17	10	10
Up to a month ago	57	41	70	66	61	72	73	64	62
Longer ago	27	47	20	28	33	24	10	26	28
Sadness									
Today or yesterday	12	11	3	5	4	8	10	8	8
Up to a month ago	46	41	72	46	67	53	56	59	54
Longer ago	42	48	25	49	29	29	34	33	38
Fear									
Today or yesterday	20	12	10	9	7	6	4	15	10
Up to a month ago	37	41	70	52	60	51	69	52	53
Longer ago	43	47	20	39	33	43	27	33	37
Anger									
Today or yesterday	13	12	11	11	15	8	12	16	12
Up to a month ago	57	53	73	60	63	75	74	63	64
Longer ago	30	35	16	29	22	17	14	21	24

the questionnaire. As we have seen throughout the qualitative reports in this chapter, there was quite a bit of variability in terms of how long ago the event had happened. To some extent, this was a violation of our instructions since we had asked that only events that had occurred during the past four weeks were to be reported. However, quite uniformally, respondents in the various cultures went back much further in time, in some cases even years, in order to find an emotional incident that they deemed worthy of reporting as an example of feeling a specific emotion. Obviously, this raises a number of interesting questions concerning the actual incidence of particular antecedent situations as well as the nature of specific emotions. Table 4.5 shows the percentage frequencies for the different time periods of reporting for each emotion separately.

For events of the most immediate past, anger tended to be recalled more frequently than sadness, with joy and fear coming in between. Although the differences in immediacy of recall were slight when pooled across the sample as a whole, the question of time delay of recall raises interesting possibilities for further research and insights into the different nature and quality of the various emotions. Alternatively, sadness may simply be an emotion that is experienced more rarely than anger, thus necessitating a longer time period for its recall. Certainly, sadness was the emotion for which the antecedent situations were distributed over the largest number of categories. However, it is not clear whether this is a reflection of difficulty in recalling the experience of sadness or whether it is due to some other factor. Turning to national differences in antecedents, Israeli subjects were distinguished from all others by the emphasis by some subjects on future rather than past events. It is not clear whether this is a reflection of the beliefs and hopes of Jewish culture or whether it is related to the development of a much newer country than those otherwise studied.

More generally, national variation was not very systematic. The reporting of joy, where the British displayed an atypical involvement in basic pleasures and the Israelis in good news from their social environment, can be contrasted with the high incidence of the reporting of the death of friends by both groups as causing sadness. Much more minor variations were evident for fear and anger. It could be argued that those national differences in antecedents that do exist are overshadowed by the homogeneity of student culture. The subjects in this study were for the most part yet untouched by the distinctive cultural traditions of marriage and child-rearing and work which have been documented by social scientists for the countries in question. As we discuss in the following chapters, even where significant cultural differences did emerge, the interpretation must remain speculative.

This chapter has provided a rather qualitative overview of the antecedent categories used to code the four emotions studied, both to provide the reader with actual examples given by the subjects and to give a first descriptive overview of the incidence and distribution of the different antecedents. In the following chapters we adopt a more quantitative approach to the data on antecedents and other characteristics of emotion-eliciting situations.

Part II
Patterns of results across cultures

5 The antecedents of emotional experiences

Harald G. Wallbott and Klaus R. Scherer

As mentioned in Chapter 1, the characteristics of the situations that evoke particular types of emotional experiences have rarely been studied empirically. The apparent social consensus about the nature of the events that are likely to produce certain emotions has induced most empirical researchers to concentrate on the nature of the emotional reaction once it has been elicited rather than on an analysis of the eliciting event. What little discussion there is on the nature of emotion-eliciting situations and antecedent events is rather qualitative and rather speculative. The number of actuarial studies that have attempted to assess the relative frequency of particular types of situations empirically is very small indeed. Consequently, rather than attempting a survey of the scarce literature available, we shall turn immediately to a description of the results of the present study. Whenever possible, we have attempted to compare the present results to relevant earlier work.

Following the detailed, qualitative description of the nature of the antecedent situations reported by our subjects presented in Chapter 4 a quantitative statistical approach is presented in this chapter. We focus on an analysis of the differences in the reported frequency of the various classes of antecedent events across the emotions as well as on a more systematic investigation of intercultural differences in the frequency of the reporting of particular emotion-producing situations. Consequently, in this chapter we are exclusively concerned with the more gross, combined categories of antecedent events that are described in Chapters 3 and 4. While we lose some information in this way, for example by looking at gross category 'relationships' rather than by providing a more detailed account of the nature of the personal bonds and interactions with different kinds of people, this procedure allows us to compare the relative importance of particular types of abstract features of ego-involving events across the emotions. While most of these features seem relevant for all of the emotions studied here, there are some, as we shall see, that are exclusive to particular emotional states.

In describing the results we have proceeded in the following manner. We first concentrate on the individual features or superordinate categories of antecedents and look for differences across the emotions in terms of their frequency of occurrence. We then investigate differences for the different emotions in the additional situational variables which were assessed in the questionnaire. We finally turn to individual emotions and evaluate the relative importance of the various antecedent categories as well as inter-cultural differences in this respect. Given the large number of statistical comparisons computed, only differences significant at the $p < 0.001$ level are commented upon. An exception has been made for those cases where results at a lower significance level replicate findings in the literature, particularly in our own earlier study (Scherer, Summerfield & Wallbott, 1983) in which a very similar procedure was used. Whenever possible we have attempted to check whether the results are replicated across these two studies. This attempt was not always possible, since, even though the general procedures used for the two studies were very similar, a number of modifications were introduced in the second study.

5.1 Relative incidence of the different antecedents of emotion

Figure 5.1 shows the mean percentage of cases for each of the four emotions (and the total) in which the respective antecedent category was mentioned as the source of an emotional experience. It should be noted that the percentages do not add up to 100 since double coding was allowed (see Chapter 3). The most surprising pattern that jumps to the eye immediately on looking at the figure is the high specificity in terms of the relative incidence of particular antecedents for the different emotions. Given the fairly high degree of abstractness of these rather gross categories, one might have thought that there would be fewer differences, particularly since the direction of the events, for example positive or negative relationship experiences, was not differentiated within categories.

There were only two antecedents for which there was no significant difference in relative incidence across the emotions: 'achievement' and 'social institutions'. In the case of achievement, this implies that achievement-related issues relevant to self-esteem and future well-being can evoke all of the emotions, possibly owing to the high motivational relevance of this antecedent feature. Similarly, our contact with institutions seems to be general enough to have the potential for evoking all of the emotions. It should be noted, though, that the general relative incidence was very low for this category, implying that institutions are generally rather unlikely to evoke emotional experiences. Fairly weak differences across the emotions were also apparent for 'news' and body-related factors. These data very clearly replicate the pattern of results from our earlier study (Table 2 and Figure 1 in Scherer *et al.*, 1983). In that study all of the differences between

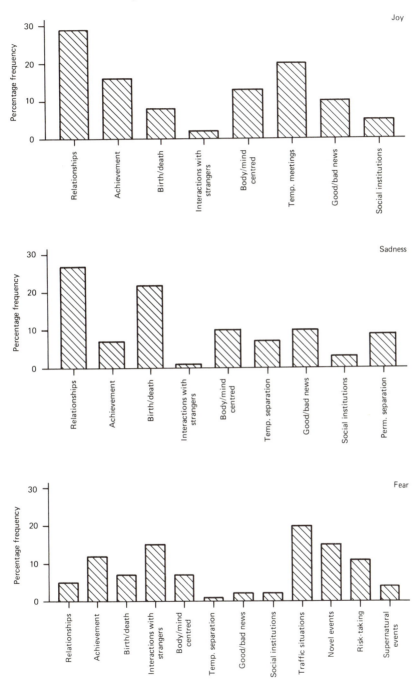

Figure 5.I. For caption see over.

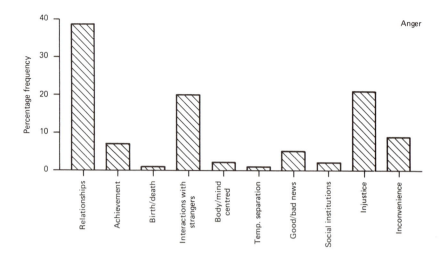

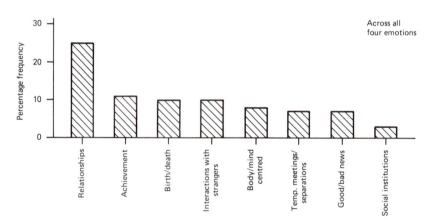

Figure 5.1   Percentage frequency of reporting of major antecedents for each emotion and across all four emotions

gross categories of emotion antecedents were significant except for 'success/self-esteem' (which is similar to the 'achievement' category in this study) and 'news'. Just as with achievement-related events, news can be of all sorts and is thus likely to evoke all of the four emotions studied here.

As in the earlier study, relationships were by far the most frequent determinants of emotional experiences, except in the case of fear. This result nicely illustrates the fact that man is a social animal. Given the important functional role of the emotions in helping man to adapt to environmental contingencies (see Scherer, 1984), it is not surprising to see that changes in the social environment, and particularly with respect to long-term bonds with others, take precedence over other kinds of emotion antecedents. One could argue that relationships are central to both the social identity and the psychological well-being of a person (see Hinde, 1979) and that any changes (or even the possibility of such changes) provoke strong emotions (both as warning signals and as adaptive responses).

None of the other antecedents was as centrally important overall as 'relationships'. Across all four emotions, achievement-related events, birth/death events, and interactions with strangers were about equally likely to produce an emotional experience (in about 10% of cases for each of these antecedents). However, whereas, as noted above, there were no differences across the emotions for achievement, such differences were highly pronounced for the other two categories of antecedents. The differences for our birth/death category, however, were due almost exclusively to the death of a loved one being the second most important elicitor of sadness. While birth did give rise to joy, the occasions seemed to be less frequent than those of death leading to sadness. The experiences of fear following this antecedent category were most likely occasioned by fear of death, presumably natural death, since in other fear categories, as we shall see, fear for life seems to be involved too.

Strangers, interestingly, seemed to be able to provoke only fear and anger, and did so fairly frequently. Given this result, it is not surprising that in most cultures strangers are regarded with some diffidence and that strangeness is a partial source for the development of stereotypes and prejudice. Strangers very rarely provoke joy or happiness, so the most we can expect is that they will leave us alone. The fact that strangers almost never induced sadness seems to indicate that this emotion is highly linked to familiarity and close relationships (see also Chapter 12). Since both the categories 'death' and 'interactions with strangers' were not used in the earlier studies, it is difficult to compare the results. However, in looking for equivalence across the different categories, the present results seem to be quite consistent with the earlier findings.

Of the antecedent categories that occurred less frequently but still across all four emotions, body-related antecedents and 'news' were important for three out of the four emotions. Anger was rarely based on body-related concerns, and in our sample at least, fear was infrequently produced by news. Apart from this, there was a fairly even distribution over the emotions. 'Temporary meetings', the next most important category, for which there were some scattered reports for fear and anger, was clearly responsible mainly for joy and to some extent sadness.

Antecedent categories that were specific for only one emotion were particularly important in evoking fear, with 'traffic' (20% incidence) being the predominant category, followed by 'novel, unknown situations' (15%), and 'risk-taking/natural forces' (11%). In addition the 'supernatural' was mentioned only in the context of fear experiences (4%). Only one category was specific to sadness: permanent separation from friends, loved ones, and relatives with an incidence of 9%. Two antecedents were specific to anger: 21% of the subjects reported that the feeling of being unjustly treated was a cause of anger, and 9% reported that unnecessary inconvenience caused anger.

From these findings we may conclude that although there were a small number of categories of antecedents that extended across the various emotions, either they were not very important in terms of the actual frequency of their occurrence, or there were sizeable differences in terms of their relative importance for specific emotions, which meant that they tended to be more specific for one of the emotions. It should be recalled, too, that the categories used here are very abstract and gross, covering a large variety of events that may show very distinct characteristics. It would seem that the abstract concept that one might see as underlying some of the comparability of antecedent events across the emotions has to do primarily with the type of motivation or concern of the person who is affected by an event, for example self-esteem in the case of achievement or relationships. This issue is discussed more extensively in Chapter 12. On the whole, the degree of correspondence between the pattern of results concerning the relative frequency and importance of particular categories of antecedents in this study and that of our earlier questionnaire study is quite remarkable. From an actuarial point of view, it seems quite possible to predict the likelihood with which a particular type of antecedent is likely to provoke a certain emotion. Furthermore, the present data would seem to provide a reasonable guide to researchers interested in designing field studies or experiments on emotion by allowing them to select antecedent situations for study or manipulation that are likely to be ecologically valid in terms of being modal antecedents.

5.2 Context variables of antecedent situations

We now turn to a discussion of some of the context variables related to the nature of the event that provoked the emotional experience reported. As mentioned in Chapter 4, it is interesting to look at the time period that had passed since the event actually happened (see Table 4.5). A statistical analysis (for details see Appendix D) of the differences in the mean amount of time passed (i.e. how long ago did it happen?) yielded a highly significant difference (*post-hoc* comparison) for the different emotions with the following order:

anger < joy < sadness = fear

In other words, sadness and fear events occurred signficantly longer ago than joy events and all of these were longer ago than anger events. Since a number of other findings relevant to this issue are presented in later chapters (especially Chapter 9), an interpretation of this finding is attempted in Chapter 12. Looking across the emotions, no significant differences between countries were found for this variable.

We also coded whether the event that caused an emotion happened to the respondents themselves or to someone else. For this variable, which we called immediacy, we found a highly significant difference between the emotions, which indicated that sadness is much more likely to be evoked by events that happened to someone else than any of the other emotions. While generally only one out of twenty emotional experiences is caused by empathy with someone else's fate, this figure is one out of five for sadness. This finding gives rise to interesting speculations. It could be that since sadness is most often produced by the end of a relationship, we are reminded of the frailty of our social embeddedness in learning about someone else's problems. It is possible that since the reactions accompanying sadness can be considered to be a very deeply rooted biological process for adjusting to a loss of significant others (see Averill, 1968), such losses are so overpowering that we are likely to share this experience empathically with others. Alternatively, it is possible that if someone else is sad because of the loss of a loved one or the end of an important relationship, this has a long-term effect on him or her which may consequently affect our own relationship with that person. It would be very interesting indeed to explore further the issue of the differential capacity for empathy in different emotions and the prominent role of sadness.

Looking at intercultural differences in the number of empathic experiences, we found a highly significant difference between the countries studied. Subjects in Great Britain, Israel, Spain, and Italy reported the largest number of empathically experienced emotions, those in West Germany reported fewer such experiences, and the lowest number of such reports came from France, Switzerland, and Belgium. These differences were particularly pronounced for joy and sadness and less so for anger. There were no significant differences for fear. It is difficult to interpret these intercultural differences in a straightforward manner. In the case of Israel, the questionnaire study was conducted during the Lebanese war, so these findings would seem to be more readily understandable than the other differences in empathic reports. Similarly, Great Britain was involved in the Falklands war when the study was carried out, and the high incidence of empathically experienced joy and sadness might be due to this factor. Italy and Spain differed most from the other countries in the case of empathically experienced anger and to some extent sadness. One wonders whether this might be related to the stereotypical 'hot-bloodedness' of the southern mentality, that is to the possibility that at least anger and sadness are more easily aroused even when an event happened to someone else.

Another aspect we coded was whether the event had actually happened or whether it had been imagined or expected but did not occur. Again, the data showed a highly significant difference between the emotions with fear being much more likely to be based on an imagined event than the other emotions. Sadness was in an intermediate position here whereas joy and anger were almost always based on actual events. This result would seem to fit rather well with our preconceptions concerning antecedent situations for the various emotions. Fear in particular is often produced by 'signal events' which seem to indicate that something adverse is likely to happen. Fairly frequently, it turns out that the fear was unfounded. It is well known that there seem to be quite a lot of individual differences in terms of 'fearfulness', that is the likelihood of regarding innocuous happenings as signs of adverse events. In terms of intercultural differences, the British were significantly more likely, almost exclusively in fear, to base their emotion on an imagined event, a finding which is all the more surprising given the reputation of English people as pragmatic and empirical.

In terms of the physical and social context of the emotional experience, we asked *where* the event had taken place and *who else* had been there. The responses to these questions provide a number of interesting insights into the ecology of emotion. As far as the physical location is concerned, we started by coding whether the event had taken place inside or outside and, in the former case, whether it was a familiar or unfamiliar place. About three-quarters of the emotion-eliciting events took place inside a building and the vast majority of these inside familiar rooms, most likely the respondent's own home or the home of friends. Only for fear was there an exception: as one might expect, about half of the fear experiences were outside, related to the finding that traffic and risk-taking, often in the outdoors, are among the most frequent antecedent conditions for the arousal of fear. Similarly, 'interactions with strangers', another important category for the occurrence of fear, are likely to occur outside in public places. Except for fear, then, which seems to be aroused in a real emergency situation, this finding supports the impression conveyed by the findings on the types of antecedent events reported in Section 5.1. Most of the emotional experiences reported were based on day-to-day events closely related to the individual's daily personal life: work experiences, relationships, and recurring activities. This impression is reinforced by reading through the detailed descriptions of the situations in the questionnaires. Only rarely do we find exotic, unusual, or startling emotion-producing events. On the contrary, the vast majority of the emotional experiences reported are linked to issues of daily concern and to central aspects of the person's life such as his or her work, family and friends, and the business of getting unharmed through the day. Emotions are fairly pedestrian affairs, then, if one looks at them from an actuarial stance. This is as one would expect, given the theoretical assumption that emotions are mechanisms that have evolved to help organisms adapt to changing environmental contingencies.

As far as intercultural differences are concerned, we had expected that climate would make a difference with respect to the location where emotions are experienced, presuming that people in southern countries might live a greater part of their lives outside, particularly with the Mediterranean culture placing emphasis on the public life in the 'plaza' or on the 'corso'. The respective results for location are not as clear-cut as one might have expected, though.

For the social ecology of emotional experience, we found very clear-cut and significant differences between the individual emotions. In terms of the number of other people around when the emotion-eliciting event occurred, *post-hoc* comparisons revealed the following order:

anger > joy > sadness > fear

The analyses showed that anger was more likely to occur in large groups, joy and sadness in somewhat smaller groups, and sadness in particular in dyads, and fear most often in solitary conditions. This seems to indicate that anger and joy are more social emotions whereas sadness and particularly fear are more individualistic. It would be interesting to pursue the question as to whether this is due to the nature of emotion-eliciting antecedent events, or to more statistical factors, that is the greater likelihood of certain types of events occurring in particular social situations. Looking back at the results on the different antecedents, it would seem that the former explanation would seem to work rather well at least for anger and fear. Whereas anger is often provoked by something that other people do, often in public settings, fear is rather often due to one's own action, as in risk-taking, or it may be caused by the very fact that one is in a solitary situation (e.g. being frightened by a noise in a dark alley).

As far as intercultural differences were concerned, there was only one major trend (which reached significance only in averaging across all the emotions (*post-hoc* comparison)): the Belgian subjects tended to experience their emotions in larger groups than the other European participants. A similar significant difference for Belgium was also found for the type of people present, that is familiar or unfamiliar others. This interesting pattern of results is discussed in greater detail in Appendix A6. As far as familiarity is concerned, the data mirror the difference for group size: joy and anger (there was no difference between these two) were usually experienced in the presence of familiar others, whereas fear was most frequently experienced in the presence of unfamiliar other people. Sadness occupied a position in the middle. This finding further supports the notion that particularly anger and joy are social emotions in which relationships play a major role and which are therefore more likely to be evoked when other people are present and relationships can be consummated (joy) or lead to problems (anger). The type of people present were less important for sadness even though 'relationships' was one of the major abstract antecedent features for this emotion since the relationship antecedents for sadness are more major instances, such as the beginning and ending of a relationship rather than everyday ups and downs in a relationship.

5.3 Emotion-eliciting situations for the individual emotions

Joy

The percentage frequencies of the various antecedent categories for joy across the different countries are shown in Table 5.1. 'Relationships' and 'temporary meetings' were by far the most frequent antecedents for joyful experiences. Again, this replicates our findings in our earlier study even though there we did not differentiate between permanent relationships and temporary meetings. In both studies, about half of the joyful or happy experiences were based on the pleasure of being with friends and relatives. There were some important intercultural differences, however. Whereas 'relationships' seemed to be the most important antecedent for the Germans and Swiss, they were of lesser importance for the Israelis and Belgians. While this pattern is difficult to interpret as a whole, some ideas can be found in Appendixes A6 and A8.

The next most frequently reported antecedents of joy were achievement-related success experiences, again replicating earlier results. Intercultural differences were not very pronounced and not very stable over the two studies. Body-related joy, such as food, drink, and sex, which we have also called basic pleasures in other contexts, were the next most frequent. Here we found a very strong replication of an interesting intercultural difference: the British subjects were the most strongly bent on such sources of pleasure. Again, an attempt at interpretation is made in Appendix A1.

There was not much interaction between the antecedent categories and the ecological variables. Achievement situations tended to have occurred

Table 5.1. *Antecedent categories for joy by country and the percentage frequency of their occurrence*

Category	Country							
	Belgium	France	Great Britain	Israel	Italy	Spain	Switzerland	West Germany
Relationships	13	25	44	18	38	18	34	53
Temporary meetings	25	19	6	13	12	30	25	24
Achievement	12	15	20	25	18	19	10	9
Body/mind centred	8	15	31	7	17	9	13	8
Good news	13	9	8	19	6	9	9	7
Birth/death	5	7	3	17	6	9	8	11
Social institutions	8	5	8	7	1	3	2	6
Interactions with strangers	—	3	—	2	6	—	1	4

Table 5.2. *Antecedent categories for sadness by country and the percentage frequency of their occurrence*

Category	Country							
	Belgium	France	Great Britain	Israel	Italy	Spain	Switzerland	West Germany
Relationships	36	26	27	8	25	24	39	40
Birth/death	13	28	30	32	18	17	17	20
Body/mind centred	10	7	6	10	14	11	10	12
Bad news	10	10	14	22	5	3	2	11
Permanent separation	16	5	11	11	4	7	14	8
Achievement	5	4	9	6	12	13	4	4
Temporary separation	4	11	7	2	5	4	4	13
Social institutions	1	3	—	8	3	2	4	1
Interactions with strangers	—	—	—	7	—	—	—	—

longer ago than other joy-producing events, and were also more unfamiliar in terms of the other people around. For the 'relationships' and 'temporary meeting' categories, as one might expect, there was a tendency for familiar others to be present.

Sadness

The relative frequencies of the various antecedent categories for sadness across the different countries are shown in Table 5.2. Only two antecedent categories elicited this emotion frequently. Problems with relationships, particularly the ending of relationships, in many cases by death, were of central importance as elicitors of sadness or grief. Body-related issues, such

Table 5.3. *Antecedent categories for fear by country and the percentage frequency of their occurrence*

Category	Country							
	Belgium	France	Great Britain	Israel	Italy	Spain	Switzerland	West Germany
Traffic	25	28	22	12	18	19	14	20
Interactions with strangers	13	16	25	21	8	17	10	11
Novel situations	9	10	16	16	29	5	13	21
Achievement	17	8	20	9	10	9	11	17
Risk-taking and external forces	14	14	14	9	5	11	14	8
Birth/death	8	8	6	8	2	9	6	4
Body/mind centred	5	2	2	14	7	9	11	9
Relationships	3	3	3	—	10	2	8	9
Supernatural events	4	5	—	3	1	12	—	2
Bad news	1	1	5	8	1	3	2	—
Social institutions	1	—	2	1	2	—	6	2
Temporary separation	—	1	2	—	3	—	1	2
Permanent separation	—	—	—	—	2	1	2	1

as illness and bad news, were secondary. In terms of intercultural differences, we again found that relationships were more important for the Germans and Swiss, but here also for the Belgians, a pattern which highlights the important role that relationships seem to play in the emotional life of individuals in these countries. On the other hand, for Israelis the importance of relationships as elicitors of sadness was rather low. In their case, it was bad news that was of relatively greater importance, although it is likely that the news often related to the fate of friends or relatives. This issue is taken up in detail in Appendix A8.

As expected, reported events related to the death of a close person tended to have occurred in the more remote past and were quite often empathic in nature even in situations in which strangers were present. Sadness due to other relationship problems, on the other hand, was of more recent origin and was only infrequently empathic in nature.

Fear

The relative frequencies of the various antecedent categories for fear across the different countries is shown in Table 5.3. We found essentially the same patterns as in our earlier study: dangerous situations in traffic were clearly the most important elicitors of fear. This illustrates not only the fact that people in modern societies, and maybe particularly students in European countries where there are no campus universities, spend an enormous amount of time going from one place to another, but also the fact that travelling on our roads is not a very peaceful activity. Given the large number of dangerous traffic situations reported in the present study, most of which had a happy ending, it is frightening to think of the potential dangers with which we are confronted daily. In the earlier study we had found a remarkably low, almost non-existent level of traffic-induced fear for the Italian respondents. This difference was not replicated in the present study – there were no significant intercultural differences for this antecedent variable this time. The next most frequent antecedent for fear was stranger impact, such as sexual assault, robbery, and hooliganism, as in our earlier study. For this type of situation, which is of course a classic fear-inducing condition, we found some weak intercultural differences which might be due to small town versus big city differences: there was a somewhat lower incidence in Giessen/West Germany, Zürich/Switzerland, and Bologna/Italy.

The next most frequent antecedents of fear were novelty situations, that is unknown persons and objects with threatening appearance, fear of failure in achievement situations, and dangers in risk-taking conditions. While the rank order of these conditions is not exactly the same as in our earlier study, there is an impressive replication of the relative incidence of these factors. In the earlier study, both the French and Italian subjects showed a greater frequency of novelty-induced fear situations than the others. This was replicated in the present study for the Italian but not the French subjects.

While fear situations arising from other antecedent categories were reported, their frequency was relatively low. It is interesting to note that while in our earlier study British subjects had reported an above-average frequency of supernatural situations, in this study it was the Spanish respondents who were frightened by witchcraft more frequently than the others.

Looking at the conditions in which these fear situations occurred, we found very strong differences between the individual antecedents. Risk-taking and stranger-impact situations tended to have happened more frequently in the remote past, whereas traffic and achievement situations had occurred more recently. This issue is taken up again in a discussion on memory effects in Chapter 12. The fairly high incidence of imagined dangers was almost exclusively due to the novelty category in which unknown persons or objects that at first appeared threatening turned out not to be dangerous. As far as the physical ecology of the events is concerned, almost all of the traffic situations and the interactions with strangers as well as the risk-taking situations occurred outside whereas achievement and novel situations tended to occur inside. In terms of social ecology, respondents were mostly alone in novel situations. For stranger impact, however, contrary to what one might have expected, there were fairly frequent incidents where fairly

Table 5.4. *Antecedent categories for anger by country and the percentage*
frequency of their occurrence

Category	Country							
	Belgium	France	Great Britain	Israel	Italy	Spain	Switzerland	West Germany
Relationships	51	42	23	18	43	40	42	48
Injustice	20	14	25	31	18	19	19	27
Interactions with strangers	18	19	30	30	6	23	22	14
Inconvenience	7	4	13	11	15	3	8	12
Achievement	4	9	—	8	11	10	3	3
Bad news	—	5	5	8	7	6	2	3
Body/mind centred	—	1	13	3	—	1	1	2
Social institutions	—	1	3	3	2	1	3	2
Birth/death	—	—	—	2	2	1	—	1
Temporary separation	1	1	—	1	—	—	1	1
Permanent separation	—	1	—	—	1	1	—	—

large groups of unfamiliar people were around. It may be possible that this was due to a number of situations in which the subjects felt threatened by groups of strangers. Fear of traffic and risk dangers is often shared with familiar others (presumably because of joint transport and leisure activities).

Anger

The percentage frequencies of the antecedent categories for anger across the different countries are shown in Table 5. 4. For this emotion, the results are more difficult to compare to those of our earlier study because we changed the coding categories quite drastically. However, in both cases, personal relationships were by far the most important source of an anger experience. In the present study this category includes some of the instances due to negligence of others that were independently assessed in the earlier study. Interestingly, there are sizeable intercultural differences, with the British and Israeli respondents reporting a much lower incidence of such anger precursors. For the British case, this is the replication of an earlier pattern.

Second in line as an origin of anger is the feeling of being treated unjustly, a category which we had not identified in our earlier study. As noted by Averill in his extensive study of anger antecedents (Averill, 1982), we found that the violation of normative standards seemed to be at the root of most of the anger experiences reported. This was, of course, particularly true for the category of 'feeling unjustly treated', but also for the 'relationships' category, where friends or relatives often behaved in unexpected or negligent ways.

The next most frequent category was 'interactions with strangers', which in most cases translates as damage to property. Again, the relative importance of this antecedent replicates results from our earlier study as well as Averill's results. Finally, unnecessary inconvenience was a small but fairly consistent contributor to anger experiences. The general flavour one gets from these categories is that anger experiences are most likely to occur when we encounter a frustration that is unexpected and appears unjustified.

Looking at the intercultural differences, we found that Israelis and Britons were less frequently aggravated because of relationship problems, which, at least in the case of the Israelis, seems to support the notion of the somewhat lesser importance of relationships as a source for emotions. Stranger impact such as property damage was more pronounced than the mean in Great Britain and Israel and less pronounced in Italy. It could be that this was partly a big city problem in the case of London, and may be related to the ethnic difficulties in Jerusalem. Judging from the low figure for Italy, Bologna seems to have less of a share of urban vandalism and violence than other European cities.

The interactions of the antecedent categories with the ecology variables provide little of interest. As one might expect, interactions with strangers occurred more frequently with larger groups of unfamiliar people than relationship and justice situations.

5. 4 Conclusions

On the whole, we found fairly little that was unexpected or surprising. On the contrary, as mentioned above, the regularity with which a number of everyday life situations keep being reported as antecedents for a number of emotions shows to what extent emotional experience is a part of our daily lives. Similarly, while there are a number of intercultural differences, the similarities in emotion antecedents across the various European cultures are, on the whole, more pronounced than the dissimilarities. While the concrete nature of the situations concerned may differ according to cultural context, the underlying abstract features are very similar.

As mentioned in Chapter 1, the major value of the present data set would seem to be the actuarial indication of the relative frequency and importance of particular types of antecedents. This will enable future research in this area to focus more directly on the kind of situations that are most likely to evoke a particular pattern of affective response.

In the following chapters we use these abstract categories of antecedent situations in an attempt to find reaction differences within emotion types that might be traced to differences between the emotion-eliciting events.

6 The physiological patterns of reported emotional states

Bernard Rimé and Dino Giovannini

In the field of the psychology of emotion, it is a very old idea that each kind of emotion – joy, sadness, fear, anger, etc. – has its own typical pattern of physiological changes. This view originated in the peripheral theories of emotions as proposed by James (1884) and Lange (1885) at the end of the last century. However, with the exception of some pioneering work undertaken in the 1950s (Ax, 1953; Funkenstein, King, & Drolette, 1954; J. Schachter, 1957), the idea of physiological patterns in emotions had to wait for a hundred years before being considered in an experimental framework. Very recently indeed, a number of experimental studies have demonstrated that this centennial view has some empirical value (Schwartz & Weinberger, 1980; Schwartz, Weinberger, & Singer, 1981; Ekman, Levenson, & Friesen, 1983).

The European cross-cultural study of emotions which is being described in this book offered an opportunity to contribute to this search for physiological patterns associated with specific emotional states. Indeed, after the description of each of the four emotional experiences which he was asked to report, each subject in the study was asked, by means of open question, to mention the kind of sensation he remembered feeling in the course of the emotion described. The coding system used to analyse the subjects' responses involved a number of items designed to record and classify the physiological components appearing in these responses (see Chapter 3). In this way, memories of physiological changes occurring in four kinds of emotional experiences for a large number of subjects from eight European countries became available. In this chapter we describe this particular aspect of the European study. It must be emphasised at the outset that the choice of the free response format led to the result, as was to be expected, that the respondents reported many diverse symptoms, some of which occurred rather infrequently. This meant that the cell sizes in the statistical analyses were generally quite small even after some pooling. However, we feel that the unprompted nature of the reports guarantees the validity of the data even if the differences reported in this chapter are often based on a small portion of the total number of subjects.

6.1 The physiological patterns of emotions: a theoretical view

Before considering the data, it might be useful to sketch some theoretical considerations concerning the general problem of the physiological patterns of emotions. In considering the question of which physiological changes are typical of a given emotional state, we are forced to return to James (1884) and Lange (1885) themselves, since in our century no single author has attempted to trace fully the patterns which scientific observation of emotions should reveal. Considering James's writings (1884, 1890), it rapidly appears that this leading proponent of the peripheralist view fails to offer any answer to the question of the nature of the specific physiological patterns. Indeed, James viewed emotional states as eminently variable from situation to situation, as well as from individual to individual. Moreover, he suspected emotional responses of being highly flexible and adaptable in relation to individual experience and learning. As a consquence, there was no reason, according to him, to look for patterns of reactions which would be typical of a given emotion. It was not even worth considering the existence of clear-cut emotions, since the underlying structures of emotional states would vary in an unlimited way. While frequently overlooked, the father of the peripheral view of emotions clearly was not in favour of any search for physiological patterning of emotional states.

Lange (1885), on the contrary, offered a very detailed description of what he expected to be the typical changes associated with the major emotions. Moreover, the four emotions for which he described such changes precisely were happiness, sadness, fear and anger, the ones which were the subject of the present study. Thus we shall briefly summarise Lange's view.

According to Lange, two kinds of phenomena are characteristic of all distinguishable emotional states: muscular innervation and vaso-motor phenomena. In sadness for instance, there is on the one hand a paralysis of muscles under voluntary control which induces a general state of muscular weakness accompanied by feelings of heaviness and tiredness. There is on the other hand a spasmodic state of the vaso-motor system: tissues become bloodless, with feelings of coldness, and the bronchioles lose their blood supply, with concomitant feelings of lack of air and oppression. The opposite manifestations would characterise joy. Voluntary muscles are increasingly stimulated, and this provokes feelings of lightness and the need to move, gesticulate, jump, and scream. By contrast, vaso-motor stimulation is reduced, and this induces a marked, generalised, vaso-dilatory response: the skin, receiving more blood, warms up and blushes, while blood circulation, being accelerated, facilitates the nutritional processes of the tissues.

For Lange fear was similar to sadness. Both are characterised by the same

Table 6.1. *Predicted physiological patterns by emotion, according to Lange*
(1885)

Physiological variables in the coding system	Predicted patterns			
	Joy	Sadness	Fear	Anger
General sensations				
Pleasant rest	—	—	—	—
Pleasant arousal	×	—	—	—
Unpleasant rest	—	×	—	—
Unpleasant arousal	—	—	×	×
Specific symptoms				
Cold temperature	—	×	×	—
Warm temperature	×	—	—	×
Perspiration	—	—	—	—
Increase in blood pressure	×	—	×	×
Chest and breathing problems	—	×	—	—
Stomach sensations	—	—	×	—
Muscular symptoms	×	×	×	×

paralysis of the motor apparatus and the same spasmodic constriction of the vaso-motor system. However, in fear situations the physiological changes are aroused suddenly and intensely, and this induces a state of freezing and extreme feelings of coldness. Moreover, contrary to what happens in sadness, every voluntary muscle participates in the spasmodic state of the vaso-motor system. As a consequence, the eyes spring up out of their orbits, the size of the pupils increases, the cardiac pulse accelerates, the stomach goes into spasmodic contractions, and so do the small hair-muscles under the skin, which induces the chill.

Anger was analogous to joy for Lange since dilation of the blood vessels and increased stimulation of the voluntary muscles characterises both. But the changes are much more marked in anger and much less coordinated than in joy. Thus, for instance, vaso-dilation, which is restricted to small vessels in joy, extends to large ones in anger, as can be seen in the forehead, neck and hands. The powerful arousal of voluntary musculature induces a drive to perform quick and strong uncoordinated movements.

Lange's proposals about the physiological changes that would be charac-teristic of the four emotions he described are summarised in Table 6.1 with respect to the categories of physiological changes which have been included in our coding system of the European study. In the next section, we examine our findings in an attempt to test Lange's patterns.

6.2 Physiological patterns of emotions in the questionnaire data

As was mentioned in Chapter 3 the data concerning physiological changes accompanying emotions were collected in this study by means of open questions, and not through systematic items or checklists. Thus, only the changes which spontaneously occurred to the subjects as they responded are considered. This made the testing of Lange's view a demanding one, since it might be postulated that subjects experienced more physiological changes during their actual emotional experiences than the ones they mentioned. Necessarily, the technique used for collecting the data led to considerable under-representation of those changes in relation to what was actually felt by the subjects. Nevertheless, we considered that if some patterning of emotional, physiological changes effectively existed, then the data should reveal it, even if in an attenuated form. The positive aspect of the adopted method of data collection was that it left the subject completely free and spontaneous in his/her answers, since no suggestion was offered to him/her in the questions.

The data revealed that 53% of the subjects in the European sample reported, for at least one of the four emotions, some general physiological sensation, that is pleasant rest or arousal, or unpleasant rest or arousal. Similarly, 59% of them reported at least once experiencing vegetative symptom, that is a change in temperature, perspiration, an increase in their blood pressure, chest or breathing symptoms, or stomach troubles. Finally, 59% reported at least once some muscular symptom. It thus appears that undifferentiated sensations, specific autonomic symptoms and specific muscular sensations came to mind to an equal extent in the subjects' memories of their emotional states. Clearly, according to these data, physiological changes occurring with emotions can hardly be considered as being predominantly of a non-specific, or undifferentiated kind, as was proposed by cognitive-physiological theories of emotions (e.g. Schachter & Singer, 1962).

More detailed results of our analysis of the reported physiological changes across the emotional states are described in Table 6.2. It is apparent from these results that raised blood pressure and muscular symptoms were among the most frequently reported symptoms; according to Lange's view, these are the two major axes around which other physiological changes are organised. However, stomach troubles and unpleasant arousal were also mentioned frequently. By contrast, perspiration, chest and breathing problems, and pleasant arousal occurred rather infrequently, even though about 10% of the subjects in the sample reported them. The most striking finding from these data is the dominant position occupied by muscular symptoms which, in this chapter, are treated as a whole. While the study

Table 6.2. *Percentage of subjects who reported a given symptom for the four emotions and the percentage who reported a symptom for at least one of the four emotions*

Symptom	Emotion				Reported for at least one of the four emotions
	Joy	Sadness	Fear	Anger	
General classes					
General sensations	30	17	14	14	53
Autonomic symptoms	23	27	58	29	59
Muscular symptoms	9	17	35	18	59
Discrete symptoms					
Pleasant rest	17	—	—	—	19
Pleasant arousal	11	—	—	—	13
Unpleasant rest	1	13	2	2	18
Unpleasant arousal	1	4	12	12	29
Cold temperature	1	3	9	2	15
Warm temperature	7	2	4	9	19
Perspiration	1	1	6	1	11
Increase in blood pressure	9	4	18	6	28
Chest/breathing problems	1	4	4	2	11
Stomach sensations	4	12	17	9	37
Muscular symptoms	9	17	35	18	59

of emotions generally has concentrated on facial changes on the one hand and on automatic modifications on the other, the present data suggest that motor changes in emotional states could well have been underestimated by investigators.

After this overview of the physiological changes occurring across the emotional states, the next step of this analysis concentrates on the corresponding data for each of the four specific emotions included in the study. As a first step, in order to check on the universality of the patterns found (and the possible biological basis), the results of the whole European sample have been divided into two major groups, according to the geographical location of each of the sub-samples along the north–south axis. Given the small cell sizes in this particular data set, this procedure ensured a reasonably sized data base for the comparison. Thus, northern data included subjects from the samples collected in London, Paris, Giessen, Zürich, and Louvain-la-Neuve, with a total of 386 subjects. Southern data comprised the samples from Lyon, Bologna, and Madrid, with a total of 291 subjects. While Jerusalem lies to the south, the cultural background of the Israeli respondents can be thought to differ considerably from that of the subjects in these 'Latin' cities. Therefore, the data from the Israeli sample were not included in this analysis.

Figure 6.1 depicts, for the northern and the southern groups of data, the

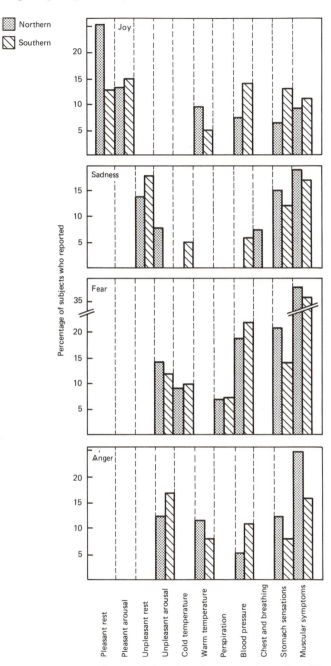

Figure 6.1   Patterns of reported physiological symptoms in northern ($N = 386$) and southern ($N = 291$) European samples. For clarity, all values of less than 5% are not shown

observed frequency of report of each physiological symptom in the coding list. Two facts immediately emerge from this figure. First, there is clear evidence of specific patterns of physiological changes associated with the different emotions. Second, these patterns appear to be reliable, since in nearly every case any elevation in the frequency for one of the two geographical groups is paralleled for the other one. A closer look at each profile reveals that in the case of joy, the pattern of physiological changes predicted by Lange and involving pleasant arousal, warm temperature, an increase in blood pressure, and muscular symptoms, is completely verified by the data. There was one supplementary finding in both geographical groups. Pleasant rest sensations were very frequently mentioned as being associated with joyful experiences. As sensations of rest and of arousal are probably mutually exclusive, it is possible that two different kinds of joy should be distinguished. An alternative possibility would be that arousal and rest constitute two successive feelings in the temporal development of the joyful experience. It should also be mentioned that pleasant rest and warm temperature were significantly more often mentioned for joyful experiences by people from northern countries, whereas southerners mentioned blood pressure increases and stomach sensations more frequently. It is possible, then, that southern joy is more active and aroused than northern joy (or happiness).

For sadness, Lange's predictions were less well-supported by the data. While these predictions included unpleasant rest, muscular symptoms, cold temperature, and chest/breathing problems, only the first two of these predicted sensations were unequivocally present in both geographical groups. Only southerners mentioned blood pressure changes, whereas only northerners reported chest/breathing problems (significant differences). There was an unpredicted finding for stomach sensations, which appeared relatively frequently in association with sadness among northern as well as among southern subjects.

For fear and anger, both the northern and the southern data supported Lange's predicted patterns. Unpleasant arousal, cold temperature, an increase in blood pressure, stomach sensations, and muscular symptoms were, as predicted, associated with fear in both sets of data. One additional finding occurred: perspiration appeared as a symptom with rather low frequency in fear, but present in both geographical groups. For anger, the predicted pattern included unpleasant arousal, warm temperature, an increase in blood pressure and muscular symptoms and this was also found. As was the case for fear, a supplementary symptom was associated with this pattern: stomach problems were referred to in anger by northerners as well as by southerners.

Seen across the emotions, the reputedly 'hot-blooded' southerners reported

Table 6.3. *Predicted and observed patterns of physiological changes across the four emotions[a]*

Symptom[b]	Joy			Sadness			Fear			Anger		
	p	OI	O2	p	OI	O2	p	OI	O2	p	OI	O2
General sensations												
Pleasant rest	—	—	×	—	—	—	—	—	—	—	—	—
Pleasant arousal	×	×	×	—	—	—	—	—	—	—	—	—
Unpleasant rest	—	—	—	×	×	×	—	—	—	—	—	—
Unpleasant arousal	—	—	—	—	—	—	×	×	×	×	×	×
Specific symptoms												
Cold temperature	—	—	—	×	×	—	×	×	×	—	—	—
Warm temperature	×	×	×	—	—	—	—	—	—	×	×	×
Perspiration	—	—	—	—	—	—	—	—	×	—	—	—
Increase in blood pressure	×	×	×	—	—	—	×	×	×	×	×	×
Chest/breathing problems	—	—	—	×	—	—	—	—	—	—	—	—
Stomach sensations	—	—	—	—	—	×	×	—	×	—	—	×
Muscular symptoms	×	—	×	×	—	×	×	×	×	×	×	×

[a] p = predicted; OI = observed by Scherer *et al.* (1983); O2 = observed in the present study.
[b] Only symptoms which were consistently associated with one of the emotions in both northern and southern sub-samples are mentioned.

significantly more blood pressure changes (in joy, sadness, and anger), whereas the cold northerners reported significantly more stomach sensations (for joy and fear) and muscle symptoms (for anger). As shown by the summary of the findings given in Table 6.3, the predictions in Lange's writings are generally supported by the reports of those subjects who did mention specific symptoms. Furthermore, the present results mirror almost exactly those obtained in the earlier study with 636 respondents conducted by our group (Scherer, Summerfield & Wallbott, 1983) using a similar methodology. Given the free response format, the replication of almost the same response pattern seems to indicate that the subjective reports are likely to be based on differentiated reactions. This suggests that Lange's theory of physiological changes in emotional states would deserve more consideration than it has been given in the past.

Figure 6.2 summarises the patterns of physiological changes as they were observed in the eight different countries in this European sample. As revealed by this summary, the four patterns evidenced for both the northern and the southern sub-samples still hold remarkably well when the data are examined by country. Indeed, the prediction from the patterns would have required 171 of the 396 cells in the matrix of figure 6.2 to be filled, and the remaining 225 to be empty. In fact, 85% of the former are effectively filled, while 90% of the latter are effectively empty.

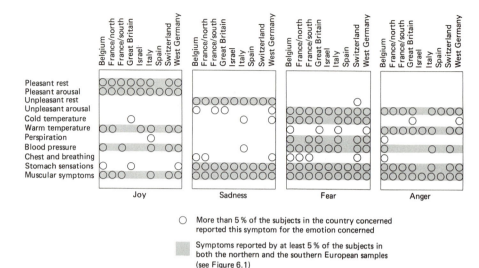

Figure 6.2   Patterns of reported physiological changes in eight European countries

Carrying this 'quick-fit' test further by considering each emotion separately shows that the patterns hold across the countries. Indeed, for joy, 76% of the cells to be filled are so, while 91% of those to be empty are as expected. For sadness, the corresponding figures are 100% and 86% while for fear they are 91% and 80% and for anger they are 78% and 94%.

6.3 Relations between physiological and expressive changes

This section considers (in a rather qualitative fashion) the relations between physiological symptoms and expressive changes. The coding system used involved a number of variables concerning perceived changes by the subjects in the quality of speech, voice, face, and body parts. While detailed data on these variables are discussed in Chapter 7, we give an overview of the relations between these expressive variables and the physiological symptoms which are considered above.

Figure 6.3 depicts the respective importance of the different aspects of the body and expressive and physiological variables for the four emotions. As can be seen, each has its own importance. Physiological changes were as frequently reported as expressive ones. Moreover, the patterning by emotion described in this chapter in relation to physiological symptoms, is considerably enriched by the introduction of non-verbal and vocal/verbal variables into the picture. Very roughly, facial changes seemed to be the dominant variable for joy and sadness, while vegetative changes appeared

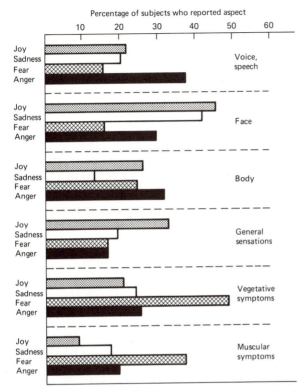

Figure 6.3   Respective importance of reported vocal/verbal, non-verbal (face and body), and physiological changes for the four emotions

to be the most typical for fear, and vocal/verbal changes were most common in relation to anger. As far as the subjects' memories of emotion reflect what actually occurred in the emotional situation, the data in Figure 6.3 totally contradict any general arousal theory of emotion.

6.4 Physiological symptoms and social variables

This section considers the possible effect of social variables on reported physiological changes. In the coding system of this study, the major variable in this respect was the kind of social context in which the emotion occurred, that is familiar versus unfamiliar. Across the emotions, 24% of all subjects in the European sample did not mention the question of social context, 65% mentioned the presence of a familiar social support, and 11% mentioned the presence of an unfamiliar social support. These two last classes were thus cross-tabulated with the presence or absence of each physiological symptom. The observed frequencies are reported in Figure 6.4, which shows that, with

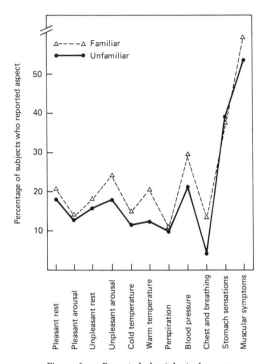

Figure 6.4   Reported physiological symptoms according to the presence of familiar or unfamiliar social support in the described emotional situation

the exception of stomach troubles and muscular symptoms, all the symptoms listed in the coding list tended to be more frequently mentioned by subjects who experienced emotion in the presence of familiar people than by those who experienced the reported emotion in an unfamiliar social environment (statistically, there were significant positive correlations between the number of symptoms mentioned and the presence of familiar others. (See Appendix D)).

Since the social context of emotional situations seemed to be important with regard to reported physiological changes, we thought it might be interesting to explore the relations between these reported changes and the subjects' socio-familial backgrounds. Thus, in the final step in our analyses, the subjects' number of brothers and sisters was taken as an independent variable, with its three levels as laid out in the coding system, that is zero versus one or two versus three or more. The number of reported physiological symptoms was then cross-tabulated in relation to these levels. As is depicted in Figure 6.5, an interesting finding emerged from these data. Each of the specific physiological symptoms (cold temperature, warm temperature, perspiration, etc.) was much more frequently reported by people with no

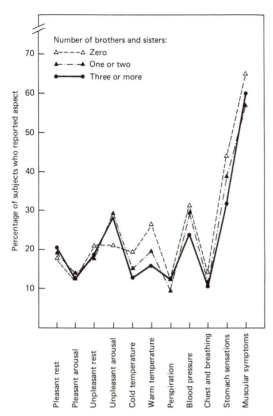

Figure 6.5   Socio-familial background in terms of the number of brothers and sisters of the subjects and reported physiological changes in emotional states

brothers or sisters than by those in the other two classes of socio-familial background. Moreover, people who shared their socio-familial background with three or more brothers and sisters generally tended to report on these symptoms least. There is a significant negative correlation between the number of brothers and sisters and the number of reported symptoms in the specific physiological classes. The fact that no comparable trend was observed for the non-specific physiological sensations considered by the coding system (i.e. pleasant rest, pleasant arousal, etc.) does not support an interpretation of these data in terms of a systematic tendency of people from smaller families to be more talkative about their emotional symptomatology. An interpretation of the results would be that people from large families were raised in an environment richer in early emotional stimulation. Such conditions could have prepared them to adapt better to emotional situations in adult life, with, as a consequence, a reduced physiological symptomatology under such circumstances. Data from animal studies on the long-term effects of enriched early environment are consistent with such an interpretation (Levine, 1960). Similarly, in his famous study on birth order, anxiety, and affiliation, Schachter (1959) found that among his subjects those from large sibships are less easily frightened than those from smaller ones.

6.5 Discussion

In the study of emotion, the last two decades have been marked by the controversy around the question of whether physiological changes experienced in the course of emotions are simply undifferentiated sensations or, on the contrary, specific automatic symptoms. The data from the present study, based on subjective report by people about these physiological changes, demonstrates that both kinds of phenomena occur. Indeed, undifferentiated sensations and specific autonomic symptoms were represented to a nearly equal extent in the subjects' memories of emotional experiences. However, symptoms of a third kind, which have been given less attention by present-day theorists and researchers on emotion, were also recorded from the European subjects' reports, as a category labelled 'muscular symptoms' was encountered in the data as often as the two former ones. Thus, if one relies on the subjective memory of emotional states, facial changes are not alone among motor manifestations of emotions, and future laboratory studies in this field could probably gain from consideration of other sites of the skeletal musculate. This could be of particular interest in relation to the study of emotional inhibition or control, as aspects of the present data suggested a link between muscular symptoms and attempts at controlling emotional states.

Our main finding was that reliable patterns of physiological changes specifically associated with the different emotions emerged from the subjects' descriptions of their emotional experiences. These patterns were fairly consistent with those predicted by Carl Lange (1885), one of the rare authors who attempted a detailed description of the specific physiological processes occurring in basic emotional states. The question of the exact status of these data thus becomes crucial. Do they represent beliefs, or culturally shared stereotypes? Or do they really describe what happens in the course of emotional situations? The fact that the observed patterns generally were reliably observed in the different European countries suggests, at the very least, that if they represent stereotypes, these are powerful ones, possibly endowed with some degree of universality, as future studies should now establish. The fact that these patterns are consistent with those described by Lange may either lead one to consider that they also represent temporally stable stereotypes, as proposed a hundred years ago, or lead one to the inference that they are not stereotypes at all, since Lange derived them from his theoretical view on the central role played by vaso-motor processes in emotional states.

At this point, it might be useful to refer to studies on implicit psycho-physiology as undertaken by Pennebaker (1981; 1982; Pennebaker & Epstein, 1983). Using a questionnaire approach with a checklist comprising physiological symptoms in one entry and emotional states in the other, Pennebaker (1982) observed, as was the case in the present study, specific constellations of symptoms covarying with specific emotions. Interestingly, in one of his studies, Pennebaker noted that about 60–70% of his subjects needed, before completing the checklist, to think of a previous occasion when they were in a situation that evoked the emotion in question. Only by reliving the previous scenario were they able to recreate the mood, and to remember the symptoms. Pennebaker also asked his subjects, after completion of the checklist, which symptoms they thought were associated with which emotions. All subjects reported that they had little or no idea, and further, that it was an impossible task, given the large number of symptoms on the checklist. Taken together, these debriefing data strongly suggest that the recorded patterns are not entirely due to experimental demand and common stereotypes, and result, at least in part, from aspects of the subjects' experience. However, it remains the case that laboratory studies have failed to find marked correlations between perceived physiological activity and corresponding polygraphic measurements (Pennebaker, 1981; 1982). This raises the difficult question of the degree of overlap between the subject's description of his/her own subjective physiological experience, and what the polygraph measures. In spite of these difficulties, one is forced to conclude here that the patterns which have been observed in the present study probably could serve as a guide in the selection of the dependent variables in future laboratory work.

A final aspect of our results concerned the relation between social context and socio-familial background on the one hand, and reported physiological symptoms on the other. The data strongly suggest that when familiar others were present during the emotional situation, symptoms were more often experienced by the subject than is the case in the presence of unfamiliar others. For social background, a negative relation emerged between the number of brothers and sisters and the presence of emotional symptomat-ology. Both of these results stress the importance of the social environment in emotional responses. They could easily form the basis of attempts at replication in the laboratory situation. If such attempts were positive, future research would benefit from the knowledge of easily accessible personal and situational factors which maximise the emotional responses to be recorded. Such results would underline the heuristic value of the questionnaire approach to the study of emotions as attempted in the present study.

7 Non-verbal reactions to emotional experiences

Harald G. Wallbott, Pio Ricci-Bitti and Eva Bänninger-Huber

7.1 Introduction: the non-verbal expression of emotion

Irrespective of different theoretical orientations, all theories of emotion agree that non-verbal behaviour such as facial expression or vocal behaviour is an important component of emotional reaction. Emotions are expressed non-verbally, and the perception of emotions is largely dependent on the observation of non-verbal reactions. In contrast to physiological symptoms (see Chapter 6), which are rarely visible to other observers, non-verbal reactions are often the focus of attention when judging other people's emotions or emotional states.

Some theories of differential emotions (see especially Tomkins, 1962/63; Izard, 1971) even claim that non-verbal reactions, especially facial expression, define differential emotions. Thus, one important question is whether different emotions are indeed accompanied by differential patterns of non-verbal behaviour. Research so far has mainly focussed on the expression of emotions in facial behaviour. The face has long been considered the most important site for expressing emotions. The study of specialised facial expression patterns specific to discrete emotions has a long tradition.

In order to answer this global question, a large number of decoding studies were conducted to clarify how many and which emotions are detectable from the face (e.g. Woodworth, 1938; Plutchik, 1962; Osgood, 1966; Izard, 1971; Ekman, 1972). Various judges were shown photographs on which actors posed different facial expressions. Ekman (1972) concluded from his studies that the following emotions can be distinguished: happiness, surprise, fear, anger, sadness, disgust/contempt, and interest. Furthermore, the cross-cultural investigations carried out by Ekman & Friesen suggest that, at least for those basic emotions, discrete, universal expression patterns exist (Ekman, 1972, 1973; Ekman, Sorensen, & Friesen, 1969; Ekman & Friesen, 1971). Photographs of such facial expressions were correctly recognised when the actors and observers came from different cultures. Likewise, members of different cultures encoded these emotions in the same way.

Ekman & Friesen (1978) constructed a table of emotion predictions on the basis of these studies as well as work on the ontogenesis of facial expression (Oster, 1978), and also as a result of theoretical considerations as contributed by Darwin (1872), Plutchik (1962), and Tomkins (1962/63). Using their Facial Action Coding System (FACS) (a coding system for the objective analysis of facial expression based on observable muscular activity), Ekman & Friesen attempted to match typical facial patterns with certain basic emotions. They described prototypical facial expressions of emotion (Ekman & Friesen, 1975). For example, for anger they claim that: 'The eyebrows are lowered and drawn together, the eyelids are tensed and the eye appears to stare in a hard fashion. The lips are either tightly pressed together or parted in a square shape'. Fear is also described: 'The eyebrows are raised and drawn together... the eyes are open and the lower lid is tensed... and the lips are stretched back'. For sadness they claim: 'The inner corners of the eyebrows are drawn up... the skin below the eyebrow is triangulated, with inner corners up, the upper eyelid inner corner is raised, the corners of the lips are down or the lip is trembling'. Finally, happiness is characterised by: 'Corners of the lips are drawn back and up, a wrinkle runs down from the nose to the outer edge beyond the lip corners, the cheeks are raised, crow's-feet wrinkles go outward from the outer corners of the eyes'.

As Ekman & Friesen themselves (1978) stress, so far no complete evidence exists for any of these facial patterns being a valid sign of emotion (with the possible exception of the study by Ekman, Friesen, & Ancoli, 1980). There is definitely a problem in that in natural interactions, emotions are seldom found in such a marked form, as a result of personal and cultural display rules (Ekman, 1972). However, the present study allows the examination of the question of whether subjects in fact report typical patterns of facial expression for the emotions studied. Discrete emotions have yet to be explained.

Compared with research on facial expressions, studies on the relations between emotional states and body movement behaviour, such as head movements and trunk movements or postures, are relatively rare. But emotions may also be signalled by means of gestures, posture, and trunk movements. Although gestures cannot usually be used on their own to identify a particular emotion, they nonetheless have a role to play in expressing emotional states; indeed, they are closely correlated with the degree of emotional arousal (Ricci-Bitti, Argyle, & Giovannini, 1978). There is a particular set of gestures, those defined by Ekman & Friesen (1969*b*) as 'adaptors', which are produced not for the purpose of communicating, but rather in order to 'regulate' the emotional state experienced. These gestures are involuntary gestures which people employ systematically in various situations in everyday life for the purpose of self-control. They represent a means of satisfying and controlling needs, motivations, and emotions related to the particular situations in which the individual finds him- or herself. These gestures in the adult are habitual, generally unconscious signals that are not intended to communicate any specific message. They are generally learnt during infancy as adaptive behaviours (Ekman & Friesen, 1969b).

There are also, however, gestures that are capable of expressing specific emotional states: for examples, clenching one's fist and stamping one or both feet on the ground as a sign of anger, or covering one's face with a hand as a sign of shame. In this regard, Hinde (1974) has identified a series of gestures that may be encountered in a variety of cultures; they consist of raising a hand to cover one's face, mouth, or eyes. These gestures, which appear to be related to shyness or embarrassment, seem to be derived in some way or another from the act of hiding.

Ekman & Friesen (1969b), though, make a point of clearly distinguishing between emotional expression and symbolic gestures and emblems. The expression of an emotion is not primarily aimed at communicating something to others (indeed, expression may be expressed even when a person is alone), whereas symbolic gestures only occur when the individual is involved in interaction, since this kind of gesture is produced with the purpose of sending a message.

Posture, that is the way in which the body as a whole is deployed in space, even if it is not capable on its own of expressing a specific emotion, nevertheless may contribute to emotional expression in combination with other emotionally expressive clues. Indeed, by alterations along the tension–relaxation continuum, posture signals the degree of intensity of emotional arousal (Graham, Ricci-Bitti, & Argyle, 1975). However, certain correlations between kinds of posture and particular moods have been demonstrated: the 'downcast' bowed shouldered posture, the 'crushed' posture of sadness and depression, or the 'upright' and wide-awake posture of euphoria (Sarbin & Hardyck, 1955; Riskind, 1983).

Finally, the relation between emotions and speech and voice behaviour has to be discussed. As one area of non-verbal behaviour, the voice is very often almost forgotten, even though it is obviously one aspect of non-verbal behaviour, if one considers not the verbal content but the way in which this content is uttered. However, there are a number of studies which indicate that in fact emotions are associated with voice and speech behaviours and that emotions may be recognised quite accurately from voice and speech samples, Scherer (1981a) has reviewed most of these studies.

The link between emotions and voice is highlighted by the fact that there seem to be 'primary affect sounds' or affect vocalisations associated with distinctive states in the animal kingdom, and probably also in human beings (Green, 1975; Tembrock, 1977). Studies of the recognition of emotions from voice samples furthermore indicate that emotions are identified correctly from voice samples above the level of chance with an average accuracy of about 60% (Scherer, 1981*a*). It seems that negative emotions are generally more easily recognised than positive emotions. Some studies indicate that the emotion recognised best from voice seems to be anger (Scherer, 1981*a*).

Although emotions may be recognised quite accurately from vocal behaviour, systematic studies indicating *which* aspects of the voice transmit emotional meaning are still relatively rare. In the review mentioned above, Scherer (1981*a*) attempted to summarise the findings to date. Although general high arousal compared to low arousal seems to be characterised by quite distinctive voice features such as high pitch level, wide pitch range, loud voice, and fast tempo, distinctive patterns for specific emotions have not been identified. It seems that 'active' emotions like happiness/joy or anger can be distinguished from more 'passive' emotions such as grief/ sadness in particular in terms of pitch level (high vs. low), pitch range (wide vs. narrow), loudness (loud vs. soft), or tempo (fast vs. slow) (Scherer, 1981*a*).

7.2 Questions asked of the questionnaire data

The short overview given in Section 7.1 indicates that distinctive patterns of non-verbal reactions may be expected, especially in facial expression and to a lesser degree in body movement, posture, and voice. Thus we would expect subjects to mention quite distinctive facial reactions in relation to the four emotions studied, but probably less distinctive reactions for the other areas of non-verbal behaviour. Furthermore, as it is the predominant indicator of emotions, facial expression might be mentioned more often than the other behavioural modalities. In terms of vocal behaviour, it might be expected that more vocal reactions will be mentioned in connection with anger compared to the other three emotions, because anger is often expressed vocally (see Section 7.1).

When studying subjective recall of non-verbal reactions and physiological symptoms, it is important to bear in mind the fact that one is not studying objective observations of reactions and symptoms but instead 'self-perceived' reactions and symptoms. Unfortunately, the relation between actual non-verbal expression and the perception and reporting of one's own non-verbal behaviour has rarely been examined.

Although some theories of facial expression involve the claim that proprioceptive feedback is very important in the experiencing of emotion (Tomkins, 1962/63), and although auditory feedback plays an important part in vocal behaviour, we do not know whether subjective reports of reactions and symptoms validly indicate how the people concerned reacted.

Some studies do indicate that, at least to a certain degree, one can trust such subjective reports. In a series of studies Pennebaker (1982) has demonstrated that this self-perception and the experience of physiological symptoms is not totally inaccurate (see Chapter 6).

Awareness of non-verbal emotional expressions may also depend to a large extent on the intensity of the emotion expressed. The greater the intensity of an emotion, the greater is the likelihood of a more pronounced expression and thus the awareness of the non-verbal expressions. Moreover, it should not be forgotten that the recall of emotional experiences and expressions involves other cognitive processes. For example, it may be presumed that when subjects have clear and specific verbal labels or concepts at their disposal (such as smiling or crying) to express their experience, the memorisation of non-verbal expressions and therefore their recall may be easier than in those situations where subjects do not have an exactly corresponding and well-defined verbal label or concept to call on.

Using the findings of our questionnaire study, we hoped to answer some of the following questions: Do specific patterns of non-verbal reactions for different emotions exist? Are there cultural differences in self-experienced non-verbal reactions? Are there differences in the amount of control that subjects report using for different non-verbal reactions? How do the empirical findings reported in this chapter relate to theories of differential emotions and to cultural stereotypes of emotional expressions?

7.3 Emotion-specific non-verbal reactions

The main problem encountered when studying emotion-specific non-verbal reactions in this survey was that nearly all of the categorised non-verbal reactions were mentioned quite infrequently by the subjects. Although just over one (1.3) reaction was coded on average across subjects and emotions, only three of the large number of possible reaction codes reached a frequency of occurrence of more than 10%. These three reactions were 'smiling' (29% for joy), 'laughing' (12% for joy), and 'crying' (27% for sadness). These data clearly replicate the findings of our earlier study (Scherer, Summerfield, & Wallbott, 1983). Thus, the variability in reported reactions was very large and answers were distributed across many categories. In order to be able to work with the data in a manageable way the primary reactions were combined into reaction groups (see Appendix C) within the non-verbal modalities of speech, voice, face (including gaze), body-part movements, and whole body movements, Within each of these modalities, further distinctions were made between the general quality of the experienced reactions, which could be classified as 'normal' or 'changed', and between more specified reactions. Most of the results that are presented here are based on these combined reaction groups (see also Chapter 3).

We have already mentioned that laughing, smiling and crying were the most prominent of all the non-verbal reactions reported, and they were almost exclusively characteristics of joy and sadness. All the reactions mentioned by at least 5 % of the respondents in at least four of the country samples are listed in Table 7.1. Other reported reactions indicating joy were: 'a happy facial expression', 'positive touching behaviour', 'to jump/dance around', and (though mentioned quite rarely) 'crying'. The specific reaction for sadness that was mentioned most often was 'crying', and the only other important non-verbal reaction mentioned was 'sad facial expression'. No specific non-verbal reactions could be identified for fear; the only reaction mentioned in some of the country samples was again 'crying'. Anger was characterised by a relatively large number of non-verbal reactions. Here, characteristics of the voice like 'increase in loudness', 'trembling voice', and 'general increase in voice' were frequently mentioned, as were 'angry facial expression' and 'face described as negatively aroused'. Furthermore, 'hand emblems' (like clenching one's fist) and, again, 'crying' were mentioned in the context of anger situations. The data in Table 7.1 indicate that the most important reactions mentioned are very comparable across country samples. Thus, it seems probable that the reactions found to be specific to certain emotions are in fact 'universal' concomitants of emotional reactions, distinguishing between the emotions studied irrespective of cultural differences.

Looking at the combined reaction groups (see Appendix C and Chapter 3), here again some groups were characteristic of certain emotions (criterion used: percentage frequency of 5 % or more for one emotion; see Table 7.2). Joy was characterised by 'laughing and smiling', 'movements toward another person', and 'expansive movements'. Sadness was exclusively indicated by 'crying', and fear by 'freezing'. Anger was characterised by reported 'changes in movement quality' and 'changes in speech quality'.

'Facial reactions' were predominant in anger and sadness, but not in joy or fear, while the lack of 'hand movement reactions' distinguished sadness, where they were not often mentioned, from the other three emotions. Finally, three reaction groups were mentioned for all emotions with a frequency of more than 5%. These were 'changes in voice quality', 'changes in facial expression', and 'specific voice reactions'. These results closely parallel the data of our first study (see Scherer *et al.*, 1983).

If we look at the different non-verbal modalities, in general facial reactions were mentioned most often, voice and body part reactions with intermediate frequency, and speech and whole body reactions least often (see Figure 7.1*b*).

Table 7.1. *Overview of the most important emotion-specific non-verbal reactions*[a,b]

	Country							
Reaction	Belgium	France	Great Britain	Israel	Italy	Spain	Switzerland	West Germany
Joy								
Smiling	36	28	47	40	19	23	14	22
Laughing	10	16	11	10	—	15	17	18
Happy facial expression	5	—	—	13	7	19	7	—
Touching another person	5	5	14	9	8	9	8	10
To jump/dance around	5	5	8	12	—	13	—	—
Crying	5	5	—	—	7	—	—	8
Sadness								
Crying	46	35	31	28	21	12	22	21
Sad facial expression	14	5	8	12	5	11	—	10
Fear								
Crying	5	5	5	—	—	—	5	—
Anger								
Angry facial expression	8	—	8	12	5	24	7	9
Negatively aroused facial expression	—	7	8	12	—	9	—	—
Increased loudness of voice	—	—	14	5	5	—	21	12
General increase of voice	21	9	—	6	—	13	—	—
Trembling voice	6	5	5	—	—	—	—	6
Crying	9	5	5	10	—	—	5	—
Hand emblems (like clenched fist)	—	5	5	—	—	—	12	6

[a] Data presented as percentage of subjects reporting that reaction.
[b] Only those reactions which were mentioned by at least 5% of the subjects in at least four countries are listed.

Table 7.2. *Emotion-specific reaction groups (across samples)*[a,b]

| | Emotion | | | |
	Joy	Sadness	Fear	Anger
Specific to one emotion	Laughing/smiling (37) Movements toward other persons (9) Expansive movements (6)	Crying (28)	Freezing (6)	Changed movement quality (9) Changed speech quality (6)
Specific to two emotions	—	Facial reactions (6)	—	Facial reactions (11)
Specific to three emotions	Hand movement reactions (7)	—	Hand movement reactions (6)	Hand movement reactions (9)
Non-specific, but often mentioned	Changed voice quality (11) Voice reactions (6) Changed facial quality (5)	Changed voice quality (11) Voice reactions (7) Changed facial quality (8)	Changed voice quality (11) Voice reactions (6) Changed facial quality (5)	Changed voice quality (25) Voice reactions (7) Changed facial quality (11)

[a] The numbers in parentheses give the percentage occurrence across the samples.
[b] Only those reactions which were mentioned by at least 5 % of the subjects in at least four countries are listed.

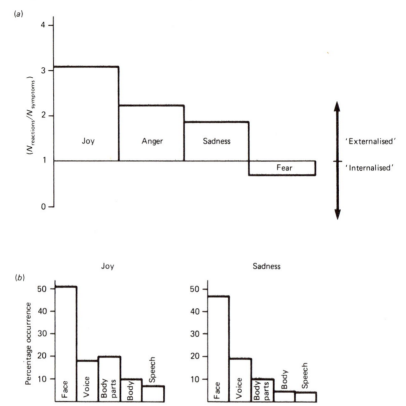

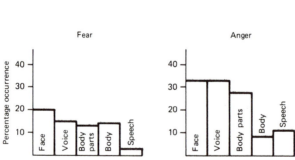

Figure 7.1   Non-verbal reaction modalities. (*a*) Index of non-verbal dominance over physiological symptoms; (*b*) relative reported frequencies of non-verbal reaction modalities. N, number

The dominance of facial expression results from the previously mentioned fact that laughing/smiling and crying were the most frequently reported reactions, thus the highest amount of facial expression was attributed to joy and sadness. Speech and voice reactions (i.e. vocal behaviour) were most important for anger. Here their frequency was about twice as high as for the other emotions. Also body part movements were more often mentioned in the context of anger. Whole body movements, although relatively rare, were most often described in connection with fear. In general, most non-verbal reactions were mentioned in connection with anger and joy, which can therefore be described as 'active' emotions; sadness was intermediate in this respect, and the fewest non-verbal reactions were described for fear. The latter two emotions may therefore be characterised as 'passive' emotions.

Apart from these differences in reactions and reaction groups, there was generally a difference across the emotions in terms of the importance of non-verbal behaviour compared with physiological symptoms. An index of 'non-verbal dominance over physiological symptoms' (number of non-verbal reactions/number of physiological symptoms) indicated that joy is the most 'non-verbal' emotion, followed by anger and sadness, with fear being the most 'physiological' emotion (see Figure 7.1a). Thus joy, anger, and sadness were experienced as being more externalised and were expressed in non-verbal behaviour, while fear was described as being more internalised and was expressed in physiological symptoms.

Thus, emotions seem to be characterised by relatively distinct patterns of non-verbal reactions, at least on the basis of the grouped reactions and the non-verbal modalities rather than the original codings. Furthermore, these patterns seem to be to a large degree independent of country differences, providing some evidence for the notion of emotion-specific non-verbal 'universals'.

7.4 Relations between the reported reactions and the country and sex of the respondent

Apart from the result that reaction patterns were to a large extent independent of country differences, it was also found that they were more or less independent of the characteristics of the antecedent situation (for details see Chapter 9). However, although in general the patterns found were largely independent of country differences, there were differences between countries in terms of the quantity of non-verbal reactions reported. The relevant data are shown in Table 7.3. While at one extreme Belgian and French subjects reported most reactions per emotion, Israeli, Italian, and Spanish subjects reported the fewest amount of non-verbal reactions.

Belgian, Swiss and German subjects reported the most vocal reactions, and Spanish, Israeli, and British subjects the least. British, Israeli, French, and Belgian subjects reported the most facial reactions, while Italian and Spanish subjects reported the least. Finally, bodily reactions (movements of body parts and of the whole body) were reported most often by English and French

Table 7.3. *Non-verbal reaction modalities by country*[a]

Reaction modality	Belgium	France	Great Britain	Israel	Italy	Spain	Switzerland	West Germany
				Country				
Joy								
Speech	9	9	3	7	4	10	7	6
Voice	26	16	11	13	31	14	13	20
Face	57	60	53	58	44	43	36	56
Body parts	23	20	28	12	27	17	13	20
Whole body	5	9	14	11	3	18	11	6
Sadness								
Speech	3	5	2	3	1	1	12	6
Voice	22	14	14	9	23	15	33	21
Face	66	54	48	55	40	26	48	37
Body parts	9	9	19	2	12	11	9	9
Whole body	5	7	2	3	3	3	6	7
Fear								
Speech	1	7	—	4	3	4	3	3
Voice	13	12	16	11	20	14	15	23
Face	17	20	33	20	16	15	22	22
Body parts	12	16	19	5	17	7	16	15
Whole body	18	17	11	20	7	13	12	13
Anger								
Speech	19	9	9	21	3	7	9	11
Voice	35	41	23	25	31	29	42	34
Face	27	36	42	57	22	29	34	37
Body parts	47	35	33	12	23	18	34	24
Whole body	9	9	9	3	3	13	9	6
Averaged across all four emotions								
Speech	8	8	4	9	3	5	8	7
Voice	24	21	16	15	26	18	26	25
Face	42	43	44	43	31	28	35	38
Body parts	18	20	25	8	20	13	18	17
Whole body	9	11	9	9	4	12	10	8
Vocal (Speech + Voice)	32	28	20	21	29	24	34	32
Non-vocal (Face + Body parts + Whole body)	74	73	78	60	54	53	63	63
Total	106	101	98	81	83	77	97	95

[a] The numbers give the percentage of respondents mentioning the respective reaction in that country.

subjects, and least often by Israeli subjects. Thus, Israeli and Spanish subjects in particular were least responsive in terms of non-verbal behaviour in all modalities, while Belgian and French subjects were most responsive. The only exception to this pattern was that German-speaking subjects (German and Swiss) reported more vocal reactions than the average (see Table 7.3).

In order to determine the relative importance of non-vocal and vocal reactions in the different country samples, an index of frequency of occurrence of vocal/non-vocal reactions was computed; this showed the relative dominance of vocal behaviour over non-vocal behaviour. The following distributions were found: Italian subjects obtained the highest scores and thus were most 'vocal' in their reaction patterns (0.54 across the emotions); these were followed by the Swiss (0.51), German (0.50), Spanish (0.47), Israeli (0.42), Belgian (0.42), French (0.39), and finally British subjects (0.25). Thus, the Italian subjects showed a relative dominance of vocal behaviour over non-vocal behaviour, while on the other hand the French-speaking and British subjects showed a relative dominance of non-vocal over vocal behaviour. It might be thought that subjects who reported having talked more during emotional experiences also reported having shown more vocal reactions. Unfortunately, Italian subjects were among those who reported having shown relatively little verbal behaviour, while British subjects generally talked more during emotional experiences (see Chapter 8)! Thus, these country differences are difficult to explain.

We also looked at country differences in terms of the relative dominance of non-verbal reactions over physiological symptoms and characterised samples with a high value on that index as relative 'externalisers' and samples with a low value as relative 'internalisers' (see also Chapter 10). Subjects from Israel and Spain constituted the most 'externalising' samples, with values of 2.8 and 2.5 respectively, followed by one other 'externaliser' sample, from France (1.8). British (1.6), Belgian (1.4), Swiss (1.4) and German subjects (1.3) were intermediate in this respect, while, contrary to all common stereotypes, Italian subjects were 'internalisers' (0.9), that is they reported relatively more physiological symptoms than non-verbal reactions. As these coefficients were not computed for each subject, but only for the total samples, statistical comparisons were not possible. Thus, these results will not be interpreted further, either in terms of magnitude or content.

Sex differences in non-verbal behaviour were also studied. The sex differences we found in non-verbal reaction modalities are reported in Table 7.4 (for comparison purposes the data on physiological symptoms are also included). Female subjects reported more non-verbal reactions than male subjects. This was especially true for facial reactions, but also for vocal reactions and body movement reactions, while smaller differences existed for speech and body part movement reactions. Interestingly enough there were no comparable differences between the sexes in terms of physiological symptoms. Although females generally reported more symptoms, the differences in terms of circulation symptoms, visceral symptoms, and muscle symptoms were relatively small (see Table 7.4). In terms of general sensations, males, on the other hand, reported more such sensations than

Table 7.4. *Sex differences in non-verbal reaction modalites across samples*[a]

	Emotion							
	Joy		Sadness		Fear		Anger	
Reaction modality	Male	Female	Male	Female	Male	Female	Male	Female
Speech	7	8	4	4	3	4	10	11
Voice	18	18	14	22	14	16	30	36
Face	42	58	39	53	15	24	27	36
Body parts	15	24	8	11	14	13	30	26
Whole body	6	12	5	5	11	16	7	8
Total non-verbal reactions	90	120	69	95	56	73	104	118
General sensations	39	32	25	17	18	17	16	18
Circulation symptoms	19	21	10	11	38	41	21	20
Visceral symptoms	5	6	15	20	23	27	11	12
Muscle symptoms	7	10	15	20	35	40	20	19
Total physiological symptoms[b]	31	38	40	51	95	107	50	52
Grand total (reactions + sensations + symptoms reported)	160	190	135	163	169	197	170	187

[a] The numbers give the percentage of male and female respondents.
[b] Data for physiological symptoms and general sensations are included here for comparison purposes: N(males) = 325; N(females) = 451.

did females. Thus, females reacted more non-verbally than physiologically compared to males, which was true for all four emotions (for illustrative purposes the coefficient 'non-verbal reactions/physiological symptoms' across emotions was 2.0 for females and 1.8 for males). Thus, females were more externalising than males. The larger proportion of general sensations reported by males than by females may indicate that males are less introspective in terms of experienced reactions and symptoms, and thus reported more general unspecified sensations. Other explanations might be that males are less accurate in terms of self-perception than females, or that display rules (Ekman, 1972) may not allow males to describe their reactions in as detailed a way as females do.

Some sex differences were found for the most frequently reported coded reaction groups. These results are shown in Table 7.5. Again, the most important sex differences were found for general sensations. For joy, male subjects reported more 'pleasant rest' sensations and for sadness more 'unpleasant rest' sensations. In terms of specified non-verbal reactions, major differences between the sexes were observed for 'laughing/smiling' and 'movements toward other persons' in joy and for 'crying' in all three

Table 7.5. *Sex differences in non-verbal reaction groups across all the samples for the individual emotions*[a]

Reaction group	Male subjects (N = 325)	Female subjects (N = 451)
Joy		
Laughing/smiling	36	46
Crying	2	6
Movements toward other persons	6	12
Hand movement reactions	6	9
Expansive movements	4	9
Pleasant rest sensations	30	17
Sadness		
Changed voice quality	12	15
Voice reactions	7	11
Crying	26	41
Unpleasant rest sensations	27	12
Fear		
Crying	2	7
Freezing	5	8
Anger		
Voice reactions	5	10
Crying	2	8
Changed movement quality	12	9
Hand movement reactions	14	10

[a] The numbers give the percentage of subjects of each sex.

negative emotions, where a larger proportion of female subjects reported the reactions in question. Otherwise differences between the sexes in terms of the reporting of the different reaction groups were negligible.

Female subjects thus mentioned the most distinctive reactions characterising the emotions more often than did males. This may imply that females are more accurate and more precise in terms of self-perception, or that they react in a more socially desirable way, reporting those reactions that one would expect, for instance, for joy and sadness. We return to these sex differences in the discussion section.

7.5 Control of non-verbal reactions

A final aspect to be considered in the context of non-verbal reactions is the amount of control reported by subjects. Does this amount of control differ for the different emotions, across the different countries and for the different sexes? There was first of all a highly significant difference for the emotions (*post-hoc* comparison). While the non-verbal reactions during joy were controlled very little (1.6), reactions during the negative emotions were controlled very strongly, though there were no significant differences between the three negative emotions (sadness: 3.5; fear: 3.8; anger: 3.5). In general, then, reactions were controlled more when negative emotions were experienced. The type of emotion experienced thus seems to be the main factor determining the amount of control, because other factors such as the number of persons involved in a situation or whether these persons were familiar or unfamiliar did not correlate significantly with the amount of control exercised over reactions and symptoms for all four emotions (for details see Chapter 11).

There were also important differences in terms of the subject's nationality. Here significant main effects for country were found for joy, sadness, and anger, but not for fear. Control patterns for the fear reaction seem to be more universal than for the other emotions. A high amount of control was reported for joy, sadness, and anger by Belgian and French subjects. British subjects also reported a high amount of control for sadness and anger but diverged from the first two groups in that they reported very low control of joy. Thus, French-speaking and British subjects in general reported the highest amount of control (thereby reminding one of common stereotypes; see Chapter 11). Low amounts of control were reported by German subjects for joy and sadness, and by Italian subjects for sadness and anger (another stereotype confirmed!). Swiss subjects were also very low in their control of anger reactions, although they were intermediate for the other emotions. These differences suggest that stereotypes about control of emotional reactions in different countries may indeed reflect existing differences between countries.

The only significant sex differences were found for control of fear. Women did not in general control their emotional reactions less than men, as another common stereotype suggests. They only reported less control of fear than men. This suggests that males try to maintain the socially desirable image of the 'fearless' male! Finally, there was only one significant interaction, for sadness, between the country and the sex of the respondents. This interaction indicated that control of sadness reactions was especially high in Israeli and Italian males compared to females, whereas in the British, the Spanish, the Swiss, and the German samples, female subjects reported more control than did their male counterparts. These results for Israeli and Italian subjects again conform to perceived stereotypes and probably also to reality (Italian funerals!), but the fact that British, Spanish, Swiss, and German females reported more control of sadness seems less easy to explain.

Finally, we examined whether the amount of reported control was different for the different reaction groups. For instance, was facial behaviour more controlled than body movement behaviour, as Ekman & Friesen's (1969a) hypothesis suggests? Each non-verbal reaction (and each physiological symptom) reported by subjects was cross-tabulated with the reported

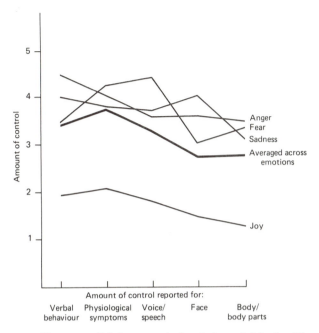

Figure 7.2   Relative amount of control reported for the different reaction modalities (for the total sample)

amount of control of the reactions, and weighted averages (weighted by the number of subjects reporting the respective reactions) for the different reaction modalities (i.e. speech/voice, face, and body) were computed for each emotion separately and across the emotions.

The results, which are shown in Figure 7.2, indicate that Ekman & Friesen's hypothesis concerning the controllability of different non-verbal modalities does not seem to hold for the control of 'normal' emotions. Indeed, for joy, anger, and especially sadness, body movement reactions were reported to be controlled slightly less than facial reactions and vocal reactions, but this trend was not apparent for fear. Thus, on average, body movements were reported as being controlled to about the same extent as facial reactions (see Figure 7.2), but both were controlled less than vocal reactions. One interesting result was that physiological symptoms and verbal behaviour were reported as having been controlled to a greater extent than non-verbal reactions. This finding is especially interesting in relation to the physiological symptoms, where one would have expected fewer control attempts, because in fact physiological symptoms are less easy to control than non-verbal reactions. Furthermore, one would expect fewer control attempts because physiological symptoms are not usually in the focus of attention of an interaction partner. Nevertheless, subjects reported more control attempts for physiological symptoms. This is difficult to explain, but it may indicate that physiological symptoms are more a focus of one's own attention than non-verbal reactions, which on the other hand, are more closely monitored by interaction partners. It may be that physiological symptoms are usually monitored to a lesser degree than non-verbal reactions because they are not noticed by other people. If physiological symptoms are very intense, however, they might very well be observed by another person (e.g. intense sweating or a face turning red) and they may therefore give rise to more control attempts, especially during intense emotional experiences. Another possible explanation is that self-perception of physiological symptoms is more accurate than self-perception of non-verbal reactions because internal feedback is more pronounced, thus resulting in greater salience of symptoms in a subject's self-perception, which then gives rise to stronger control attempts.

7.6 Discussion

The results given above indicate that the four emotions studied, that is joy, sadness, fear, and anger are characterised by specific non-verbal reaction patterns and, furthermore, by different amounts of control of these reaction patterns. It is important to note the more substantial control attempts accompanying the experience of negative emotions reported by subjects. These results indicate that there seem to be general display rules which imply that positive emotions have to be controlled to a lesser degree than negative emotions, though from the data gathered in this study we cannot decide whether the reported amount of control reflects general regulation attempts by subjects independent of the social situation, or social display rules that specifically guide the expression or repression of non-verbal emotional reactions.

Sex differences are of some importance in the experiencing of emotional situations and the reactions that follow, but they are less pronounced than expected. The reaction patterns accompanying the different emotions were almost identical for male and female subjects. Of specific interest, however, is the result that females reported more non-verbal reactions than did males, especially for joy and anger. Males, on the other hand, reported more non-specific reactions, that is general sensations. One way of interpreting this result is that males are less 'introspective' in terms of non-verbal behaviour than are females, and thus report more non-specific sensations. However, it is possible that this result is due to sex-specific display rules, allowing females to show non-verbal reactions such as facial reactions, vocal reactions, or body movements to a larger degree than males. Perhaps for males the display rule 'show no (or at least not such intense) emotions' operates so that they do not report specific reactions characterising the emotion experienced but only reactions on a very general level (i.e. general sensations).

Differences in non-verbal reactions also exist between countries, but these are quite small. This implies that non-verbal reactions to emotions are to a large degree 'universals', that is distinct components of the emotional reaction, largely uninfluenced by cultural differences and by the type of situation triggering the emotion. This is important in terms of discrete emotion theories. If certain stimuli evoke predetermined affective programmes with associated symptoms and reactions such as specific facial expressions (see Ekman, 1972), this result would be expected. Situations affect the type of emotion elicited, but not the specific non-verbal reactions expressing the emotion.

A major problem with this study was the fact that subjects generally reported very few non-verbal reactions and that only three of the large number of possible categories were reported with a frequency of more than 10%. These results in a way contradicted our expectations. Given the central importance of non-verbal reactions in the experiencing of emotions, reports of non-verbal reactions should have been much more predominant. We suspect that this discrepancy may be accounted for if we consider that the data are based on self-reports. The problem of how accurately subjects describe their own non-verbal reactions has been studied empirically only rarely and results so far do not allow a clear-cut conclusion. However, studies such as those of Pennebaker (1982) and Schwartz (1982) indicate that subjects are able to describe their own reactions, especially physiological symptoms, with some accuracy, but this accuracy is lower than the accuracy of observers.

As the results obtained so far do not allow any conclusive interpretations, we wish to conclude by outlining some suggestions to explain the relatively low level of reporting of non-verbal reactions. In order to describe emotional reactions, subjects have to experience these reactions 'consciously'. With respect to non-verbal reactions this seems to occur only to a moderate degree. Non-verbal reactions are, in general, more or less automatic, 'unconscious' processes accompanying emotions. They are guided by display rules (Ekman & Friesen, 1969*a*) which are internalised, that is subjects are unaware or 'unconscious' of them. These display rules imply that non-verbal reactions are usually modified in such a way as to account for the situational constraints. When this 'non-verbal management' is subjectively successful, this process is usually not in the conscious mind of subjects. However, there may be situations where these control attempts are not successful. If the intensity of an emotional reaction is very high, non-verbal cues may leak affective information even though the sender does not intend it. In such situations it is possible that the sender will focus his or her attention on his or her non-verbal reactions, which may thereby enter the awareness. But very often there may be instances where such unintended non-verbal cues might leak the affective information (Ekman & Friesen, 1969a) while still remaining outside the awareness of the sender.

Given these restrictions, one can argue that only a small proportion of all emitted non-verbal reactions will enter subject's awareness. This implies that in this questionnaire study we have collected information not on all the observable non-verbal behaviour, but only on that subset of non-verbal reactions of which subjects were conscious. We can further argue that these reactions appeared mostly in emotional situations which were very intense. But we cannot decide whether strategies of self-presentation or unconscious processes interfered with the awareness and memorising of emotional reactions.

Another explanation for the relatively low level of reporting of non-verbal reactions might be the fact that subjects are not usually trained in the perception of their own non-verbal reactions. For an interaction partner the decoding of the emotional states of the partner may often be more important in coping with an interaction situation than the perception of his or her own non-verbal behaviour.

Finally, a possible explanation might be that for many non-verbal reactions we do not have explicit verbal labels. The finding that reaction categories with unambiguous verbal labels like 'laughing/smiling' or 'crying' were mentioned most often is consistent with this interpretation. For facial expressions, for instance, where studies indicate that distinctive patterns related to specific emotions seem to exist, subjects reported predominantly 'sad facial expression' or 'angry facial expression' as non-verbal facial reactions, but not specific descriptions of their expressions. Again, this may be due to the fact that aside from some verbal labels like 'smiling' or 'frowning', facial expressions cannot be described verbally to a high level of accuracy because distinct verbal labels do not exist.

The most important result from this study seems to be that despite the fact that relatively few non-verbal reactions were mentioned, the reactions reported for the four emotions joy, sadness, fear, and anger were quite distinctive, replicating most of the results of Scherer *et al.* (1983), and largely independent of cultural differences or person characteristics such as the sex of the subjects. The theoretical notion that discrete emotions are characterised by differential non-verbal reaction patterns seems to be supported by the findings of this questionnaire study.

8 The verbalisation of emotional experiences

Jacques Cosnier, José M. F. Dols and Alfonso J. Fernandez

8.1 Introduction: definition and general problems

Emotion is a term that, although in common use, is difficult to define. This lack of an accurate and operational definition is, no doubt, partly the cause of numerous contradictory opinions about its 'nature' and functions. In a pragmatic way, it may be characterised by several facets (Scherer, 1984) and, in general, the different authors agree on the existence of three components:

> *a subjective sensation* (*vécu*, sentiment, feeling, affect), which allows
> one to distinguish many kinds of emotion: joy, fear, anger, etc.
> *vegetative bodily manifestations*
> *observable behavioural manifestations* (gestures, postures, actions)

It must be noted that among the latter, motor reactions to emotion are mentioned, but verbal manifestations of emotion are rarely referred to. This chapter is concerned with verbal manifestations of emotion. Speech 'parole' or 'verbalisation' seems to have many important relations with emotions, and the omission of verbal reactions in definitions of, and research on emotion seems striking. It is perhaps linked to the frequent contrast which authors have made between 'cognition' and 'affect', with verbalisation generally being placed on the cognitive side and emotion on the affective side. In recent discussions on the functions of the hemispheres of the brain, right and left, these old ideas have returned in a more modern form.

However, despite this lack of general concern with verbalisation, emotion and speech (parole) have been linked and placed at the centre of clinical psychologists' concerns since the end of the last century. The ideas of Breuer & Freud in 1895, when psychoanalysis was originated, may be remembered here. These authors had noticed, when treating hysterical patients subjected to a prehypnotic state, that the accurate verbalisation of their feelings and memories had the power of making the symptoms and the anxiety disappear. This procedure, significantly named 'talking cure' by their famous patient Anna O., was used, as is known, in the early days of psychoanalysis. Since then it has taken the form of an exclusively verbal therapy but psychoanalysts continue to claim that the relinkage of disorganised memories to produce a 'presentation of words' allows regulation of affect and frees the patient from his or her unconscious handicaps. We also know that some successors of Freud, such as Reich (1942), stressed particularly the non-verbal catharsis of emotional experiences, giving speech (parole) a more secondary role than in classical psychoanalysis.

'Body' or 'emotional' therapies are again of current interest today, and in two of their more elaborate forms, 'Gestalt' therapy and 'bioenergetics', the instances of linkage between emotions and speech (parole) are common. In fact, it now seems evident to clinicians that speech and emotion have many complex and almost permanent relations, in the releasing, in the discharge, or in the control of the so-called 'emotional' states. Placed in a new situation, each individual will behave on three levels: verbal, motor, and visceral. The reactions interact with one another and, depending on the individual, speech will play a more or less effective homeostatic role in such processes. These aspects have been particularly underlined by the psychosomaticians ('Pensée opératoire' of the 'Ecole de Paris', and 'alexithymy' of the American authors).

In addition to this role for speech in intrapersonal emotional regulation, work carried out in microsociology and contemporary ethnomethodology allows us to visualise another role for speech, in interpersonal emotion regulation. Ritualisations and social codifications of life provide behavioural models (stereotypes) that encourage control of the emotions in the presence of others and help a person to keep his or her emotions within the limits acknowledged as culturally suitable (see Chapter 1). Aristotle underlined this relation between emotional control and social organisation, and Elias (1977) has been able to maintain that the history of human civilisation is mingled with the history of the control of affect. The relations between speech and emotion are thus manifold and we have tried to treat them systematically in this chapter.

The present study is based on data from written questionnaires rather than on direct observations. Two levels of verbal activity may therefore be considered: the writer's activity, which produces a written discourse, and the verbal activities reported in the contents of the written discourse. We may say that the written text is a 'metaverbalisation' about 'verbalisations' which have taken place at another time and in another place. It is true that, as far as the study of verbal activity is concerned, the purpose of the questionnaire was to allow us to study the verbalisations, but we thought it was better to consider, if only briefly, the study of metaverbalisation as well.

8.2 Verbalisation

Speech, in its different forms (written or oral) is mentioned in various parts of the questionnaire: at the antecedent level, at the reaction level, and at the control level. We shall, therefore, study it successively at these three levels.

Speech and the release of emotion

The circumstances ('antecedents') that produce emotion are numerous, variable, and dependent on the individual and his or her culture. It is commonly considered that emotion is produced most often because the subject cannot or does not know how to elaborate an adequate response to the stimulus, and three features of a situation are considered to cause emotion: the new, the unusual, and the sudden (Fraisse, 1963).

Other aspects referred to as causes of emotion have been excess of motivation and emotional contagion. However, it seems to us that the relationship with the other person in a situation is an element that is very often present, even if it is not always mentioned. The accurate coding developed by our research group to quantify the items in the antecedent situations revealed situations involving social interactions to be predominant factors in eliciting the various emotions (see Chapters 4 and 5).

Social relationships and social interactions play an important role in joy, sadness, and anger, and even fear. These findings easily permit us to foresee the intervention of language (of 'verbality') in the antecedent situation. In order to specify the form of this verbalisation, we quantified its presence in two samples, the Spanish and the French subjects.

Speech was categorised by:

the 'announcement of events': written or oral (informative speech)
the 'means of interaction' (discussion): written or oral (interactive speech)

From this general analysis we found that, in general, the importance of speech in the production of emotion was, in decreasing order, as follows: anger; joy; sadness; fear. The basis for this highly significant effect is the difference between fear and the other three emotions in that there was a lack of the presence of others in situations which gave rise to fear.

Speech and the expression of emotions

The data concerning the use of speech in the expression of emotions come mainly from responses to the question: 'What did you say?' The reading of these responses readily shows that they are of three types:

no response, 'nothing'or inner speech
exclamations
longer sentences or elements of discussion

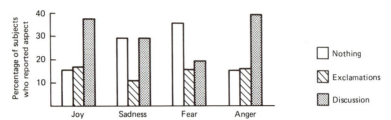

Figure 8.1   Types of verbalisation across the emotions

Table 8.1 *Percentage of verbal expression by emotion in each country*

Emotion	Country							
	Belgium	France	Great Britain	Israel	Italy	Spain	Switzerland	West Germany
Joy	71	73	82	63	77	66	79	88
Sadness	63	46	68	46	52	42	59	76
Fear	59	61	53	45	46	35	45	45
Anger	73	84	83	71	74	74	83	76
Total	67	66	72	56	62	54	67	71

This categorisation allowed us to establish the type of speech used for each emotion (see Figure 8.1). As can be seen from the figure, two groups of emotions emerge: those where 'discussions' are numerous and the absence of speech rare ('talkative' emotions), these being joy and anger; and those in which the absence of speech is frequent and discussions are less numerous ('silent' emotions), these being first fear, and then sadness.

There were highly significant country differences among these variables, as can be seen in Table 8.1. Subjects from Spain and Israel clearly tended to be 'silent' during emotional situations, compared with those from countries such as Great Britain and West Germany, who tended toward the verbal expression of emotions.

Verbalisation is linked to the presence of others in the antecedent situation, but, in addition, a highly significant result shows that subjects reported that they spoke more in the presence of relatives or friends than in the presence of unfamiliar others, except in the case of anger, where familiarity is irrelevant. This analysis can be supplemented by a more qualitative survey of the form and content of responses.

   (a) *'Nothing' responses.* There may be two reasons for these. First, that the emotional *vécu* and the reactive pattern block verbal enunciation. This is the mechanism prevailing in both sadness and fear. The second reason is linked to the first. It is evident that 'lonely' emotions predispose little to verbal reactions. This is the case for a number of situations with respect to sadness, and numerous situations with respect to fear. In the latter case, moreover, the high number of 'no response' replies seems to correspond largely to the inadequacy of the question: 'What did you say?' with respect to the situation described, where there was no reason to say anything in the absence of an interlocutor.

(b) *Exclamations*. This category was defined as 'exclamation', 'affect', 'word', 'humming', or 'vocal-emblems' (see Scherer, 1977). Although exclamations and interjections may, by definition, be expressive of emotion, an exhaustive analysis of the responses reveals other possibilities. For example, calling another person: 'help!'; categorical commands: 'stop!', 'go!'. These exclamations of a relational value have both an 'operative' and an 'expressive' value. Added to this must be the laudatory exclamations such as 'Bravo!', or the aggressive ones such as various types of insults.

There are, therefore, 'expressive' exclamations and 'relational' exclamations. Moreover, the fact that 'word' is included in the category of exclamations and 'complete expressions' in the category of 'discussion' is also worthy of comment when, as we have just mentioned, certain 'words' have non-expressive functions and certain 'complete expressions' are, on the contrary, equivalent to expressive exclamations: 'It is impossible', 'It is wonderful', 'How stupid I am'.

Taking these different observations into account, it seems that 'expressive exclamations' are frequent, above all in joy and fear, pejorative 'relational exclamations' are frequent in anger, and operative 'relational exclamations' are frequent in fear.

(c) *Discussions* (sentences, complete expressions, discussion). These obviously include responses of several kinds. For example, speech can act as a means of 'emotional discharge', in that the subject feels the need to speak; this is typically the case in anger, where the aggressive discharge is often not controllable. But there are also other forms of discharge, for example exchanges which tend to make the other person share an emotional state. This is often the case in joy and sometimes in sadness.

8.3 The regulation and control of speech

In our questionnaire, questions were first asked about antecedents, then about reactions, and finally about control. In relation to control, two aspects were considered: (a) the intensity and method of control of verbal reactions;

and (b) the intensity and method of control of non-verbal reactions. However, this general concept of regulation and control implies a theoretical simplification containing ambiguities, since the regulation becomes apparent simultaneously at both an intra-individual and an inter-individual level (individual homeostasis and social homeostasis).

We have already seen that emotional reactions, for example those we have called 'expressive reactions of discharge', may play a role in individual homeostasis. And it appeared clearly in the responses, either to the question 'What did you say?' or more often, to questions on control, that these were clearly conditioned by social conventions and are therefore linked to inter-individual homeostasis. It seems evident that both intra-individual and inter-individual regulations are closely intertwined and that responses to the question 'What did you say?' are a consequence both of one and of the other.

In addition, in these processes, the verbal activity may be considered in two ways: *either as the object of regulation*, this being the sense of the question on the control of speech, or as an *instrument of regulation*, the subject using, for example, the speech activity to reduce bodily tension or to conceal his or her feelings. It is therefore advisable to study the control of speech and speech as an instrument of control successively.

The control of verbalisation
The level of control of verbalisation was reported by subjects on a scale from 0 to 9 in response to the question 'How did you try to control what you said?' The proportions of subjects in each sample reporting high control of verbalisation (scale values 6–9) for each emotion are shown in Table 8.2. For the responses on this scale we found highly significant differences between the emotions. The least controlled emotion was joy and the most controlled was anger, with fear and sadness in an intermediate position.

An examination of the degree of interaction shows a relationship with the social nature of the situation. There was a highly significant increase in the control of verbalisation in proportion to the number of persons involved in the situation, and, moreover, control increased very significantly with the familiarity of others present, especially in sadness and anger.

As might be expected, efforts to control verbalisation increased with the importance of the emotional verbal expression, especially in the case of anger, which proved to be both the most 'talkative' emotion and the most difficult to control. Finally, it is interesting to note that these findings also apply to the control of non-verbal manifestations and that the control of verbal expression and the control of non-verbal expression correlate positively, correlation coefficients for all subjects ($N = 779$) being as follows: 0.60 for joy, 0.51 for sadness, 0.52 for fear and 0.47 for anger.

Table 8.2. *Percentage of subjects reporting high verbal control (scale values 6–9) by emotion in each country*

Emotion	Belgium	France	Great Britain	Israel	Italy	Spain	Switzerland	West Germany
				Country				
Joy	28	28	8	27	25	17	15	16
Sadness	53	53	52	45	45	39	45	36
Fear	41	55	55	49	48	45	50	48
Anger	56	56	45	45	42	41	37	43
Total	45	48	40	42	40	35	37	36

We also cross-tabulated this variable by country, finding significant differences. It can be noted that subjects in France, Great Britain, Italy, Spain and Switzerland had a lower control of verbalisation during emotions than subjects in Belgium, Israel, and West Germany (see Table 8.2).

The study of the responses given to the question 'What did you do to control what you said?' allowed us to study the different mechanisms involved in the control of speech. In order to identify these mechanisms, a preliminary qualitative study was carried out on 50 questionnaires from the French sample, using the following categories:

(a) *Repression.* Control of speech is achieved by an attempt at control over the voice, syntax, or semantics, that is as the subjects said: 'to say as little as possible', 'to explain calmly', 'to attenuate the sound of my voice more and more', 'to say the minimum number of words', 'to try not to be rude', 'not to use words connected with nervousness', 'not to speak in too abrupt a manner'. Examples of body repression such as: 'I held back my tears', 'I grit my teeth tightly', may appear here but they were generally more often quoted for control of the non-verbal manifestations. Repression was reported in 40% of the cases of anger, 10% of the cases of sadness, 5% of the cases of joy, and 4% of the cases of fear.

(b) *Diversion.* Under this term we have grouped the mechanisms of the diversion of speech, the diversion of mental activity and the diversion of bodily activity. Examples are: 'I spoke of something else', 'I became immersed in reading', and 'I went to the cinema'. The cognitive activity seems evident to us: subjects focus their attention on what they do, or 'think about themselves'. These mechanisms were reported as follows: in 10% of the cases of sadness, in 8% of the cases of anger, and in 2% of the cases of joy.

(c) *A group of categories that were reported with a frequency of less than 5%.*
avoidance and flight: 'I left', 'I tried not to look at him';
'masking' or inversion of affect: 'I hid my feelings'; in fear and
anger: 'I smiled', 'I joked', 'I tried to adopt an indifferent attitude';
neutralisation by convention: sheltering behind trivialities of conversation, acknowledgment, congratulations, condolences;
physiological activity: drinking, holding one's breath; discharge:
intense word activity;
relationship with the other person: sharing feelings, looking for
sympathy, asking for help.

Verbalisation as an instrument of control

As seen in the previous section, the control of verbalisation is part of a more general control of emotion, but, in addition, it seems that verbalisation may also be used as an instrument of control. This appeared particularly in the responses to the question: 'What did you do to control your non-verbal reactions?'

An examination of the responses led us to two conclusions:

(a) The mechanisms of control involved were the same as those for the control of verbalisation (repression, deviation, etc.), but, obviously, with a greater bodily participation 'I shut my fists tightly', 'I contracted my muscles', 'I held back my tears', 'I thought of something else', etc.
(b) Speech was referred to in the same terms as for the control of verbalisation.

These considerations encouraged us to study the distribution of speech activity across the emotions so that we might distinguish the emotions more precisely with respect to the type of mechanisms of speech used. We did this in accordance with a simplified classification, 'Repression of speech' and 'Regulation by speech' (in the latter term we included diversion, discharge, calling the other person, etc.). For this preliminary attempt we used questionnaires from the Spanish sample only. The results are shown in Table 8.3.

We have in these results a general confirmation of all the preceding statements. Joy and anger are 'talkative' emotions, but anger is more repressed. Sadness and fear are less talkative. Subjects use repression in sadness in particular. We also see that repression via verbalisation is the most commonly used mechanism of control. The relation between the regulation of speech and physiological symptoms still remains to be discussed.

The hypothesis of 'verbo-viscero-motor' organisation suggests, in effect, that speech, like motor activity, plays a regulating role in the emotional state and, therefore, that it would be logical to find an inverse relation between the intensity of physiological symptoms and the degree of verbal activity.

Table 8.3. *Percentages for two types of speech control strategies (Spanish sample only)*

	Percentage by emotion[a]		Percentage of subjects[b]		
	Speech indicating regulation	Speech indicating repression	Speech indicating regulation	Speech indicating repression	Not codable as repression or regulation
Joy	54	46	72	10	78
Sadness	28	72	6	16	78
Fear	35	65	6	12	82
Anger	35	65	14	25	61

[a] Percentages of descriptions in Spanish sample, where verbalisations could be classified as indicating either 'regulation' or 'repression'.
[b] Percentages with additional category, 'no speech', mentioned.

But it was difficult to treat this aspect in the questionnaire used since the physiological symptoms were mentioned too irregularly, making the correlation between various control mechanisms virtually impossible. The reader is referred to Chapter 6, where some relevant findings are presented.

8.4 Metaverbalisation

Those completing the questionnaire also had to recall memories of the emotional situation through which they lived, and had to construct a verbal written report of this representation (Metaverbalisation). It is possible that they had to control the affective state evoked by these representations and that this would be reflected in the form of the written text.

We dealt with metaverbalisation in its quantitative aspect, comparing verbal production in some of the countries (France, Great Britain, Italy, Spain, and West Germany) and across the emotions using the following two questions:

(a) What happened? ('antecedents')
(b) What did you say?

Analysis of variance demonstrates differences in the number of words used in the replies. For the first question (a) we found highly significant differences of 'wordiness' among the countries. In decreasing order these were: West Germany; France and Great Britain; Italy; Spain. Differences between the emotions were not significant in this case. For the second question (b), we again found highly significant differences of 'wordiness' among the countries, in the following order: West Germany; Great Britain;

Italy; France and Spain. We also found significant differences for the emotions in the following order: anger; joy and sadness; fear.

The interpretation of these results is difficult, because several factors are involved. The country differences in the description of antecedents may result from the nature of language itself (it is known that certain languages are more concise and economical in the use of words than others), and it may also involve a greater ease of written expression in certain countries. The fact seems to be that the 'Anglo-Saxon' speaking countries are more verbose than the Latin countries which, however, have the reputation of being more talkative. As far as the differences among emotions are concerned, the fact that anger occurs in the first place may be the result of the fact that anger leads to the most verbalisation, since it is the most 'talkative' emotion.

Finally, we think it worthwhile to underline the interest, together with the quantitative and general studies, of qualitative studies of particular cases which, in our opinion, allow an exceptional understanding of the intricacy and articulation of the various factors and mechanisms described above. We shall take two examples.

Example 1 (Subject 309, French. Emotion: Fear)
- Where did the situation occur? 'In an airplane.'
- How long ago was it? '2 months ago.'
- Who was involved? 'A friend of mine and I.'
- What exactly happened? 'I am never calm when travelling by plane. That flight was in an extra plane chartered by Air-Inter. The aircraft was old and looked awful, both inside and out. I did not move from my seat throughout the whole flight.'
- How long did the feeling last? 'The duration of the flight (1 hr).'
- How did the situation end? 'After a landing during which I was terribly afraid.'
- In your opinion, what words would best describe your emotion? 'Irrational panic.'
- What did you say? 'I felt stupid at having taken the plane knowing my reactions.'
- What were your bodily reactions? 'Intense nervousness; "torture" to hold my friend's hand which I did during almost all the flight; non-stop smoking; trying to shelter behind the reading of a newspaper.'
- What did you do to control what you said? 'Very little. I tried not to show my fear to passengers around me.'
- What did you do to control non-verbal reaction? 'I wasn't able to control it, or only at the beginning.'
- What would you do differently if you found yourself in such a situation again? 'I would avoid finding myself in such a situation

again; but everytime I take a plane I promise not to do it any more. And I do it again!'

This example clearly shows the overlapping of factors:

an intellectual (cognitive) defence against fear, which is reflected not at a verbalisation level but at a metaverbalisation level – it is 'irrational' and 'stupid' to be afraid to take a plane;

reasonings of justification (which attenuate for *the reader* the claimed stupidity, since, anyway, the subject is never calm in a plane) – the plane is old and its inside and outside are in a deplorable condition;

control reactions – the utilisation of the relationship with the other person (the friend plays a counterphobic role: 'torture to hold his hand'), the distraction of attention (the reading of a newspaper), the diversion of activity (non-stop smoking), repression (disguising oneself with respect to the persons nearby);

humour at the metaverbalisation level (since it is manifestly for the reader's benefit) – 'I promise not to do it any more...and I do it again!'

Example 2 (Subject 311, French. Emotion: Anger)
- Where did the situation occur? 'At the University.'
- How long ago was it? 'A week ago.'
- Who was involved? 'The professor and I.'
- What exactly happened? 'I passed my written exam. It turned out that I had already done that exercise when going over the different subjects. Well, I found the correct result doing the intermediate calculations wrong. The professor then thought I had copied. She marked it on my copy and was very unpleasant to me during the last class, and at the end she gave me the copies back.'
- How long did the feeling last? 'Until the following day.'
- How did the situation end? 'Next morning I went to see her to explain that I remembered the result (it was not cheating!) and that I had made a mistake in good faith, so to speak, in the calculations. She was very cold towards me. I hope she realises the unfairness of her reaction.'
- In your opinion, what words would best describe your emotion? 'Rage, a sense of unfairness, lack of understanding, hasty judgment.'
- What did you say? 'I explained the situation. I said it was extremely painful for me to be accused of something for which I was not to blame.'
- What were your bodily reactions? 'The moment I saw her insinuations as to my copying I understood her frankly disagreeable attitude in class. I felt like shouting, screaming at her, hitting out wildly. (I didn't do so. I was in the playground then!)'
- What did you do to control what you said? 'I spoke about it to my friend; I thought of what I would say to the professor the next morning.'

- What did you do to control your non-verbal reaction? 'I wanted to shout but I knew I was able to keep a hold on myself! Moreover, thinking of an explanation for the next morning relieved my feelings.'
- What would you do differently? 'I would do the same.'

The following points emerge from the example:

the presence of verbalisation at all levels – at the level of antecedents (conflict with the professor), and with one's friend (search for relationship and social sympathy);

defences are of a cognitive kind (reasonings, justification, anticipation of behaviour), of a relational kind (relationship with one's friend) and use discharge (speaking with my friend, relieving my feelings);

these mechanisms are also present at the level of metaverbalisation (for the reader's benefit) – repeated details and reasonings to justify himself, and using the reader as a witness: 'It is not cheating!', 'I can keep a hold on myself', etc.

8.5 Conclusions

The study of the antecedents (see Chapters 5 and 11) has shown the importance of social and interactive factors in producing an emotion and the importance of language in emotional episodes. Once the emotion has been released, speech may occur. In addition there may occur various functions which it is difficult, and in fact artefactual to separate into the categories 'expression' and 'control', but which would seem to be more adequately described in terms of mechanisms of adaptation (individual homeostatic: regulation of the emotional experience; social homeostatic: regulation of the experience and control of emotional reactions at the same time). Among these mechanisms we should consider in particular:

discharge mechanisms – speaking a lot, loudly, fast, etc;

repression mechanisms – trying to control one's voice, speech, thinking;

cognitive mechanisms – speaking with close attention and concentrating on verbal elaboration, quite often with one's attention and speech distracted and directed toward other objects;

relational mechanisms – pragmatic: looking for help; appropriate or empathic action: using a witness, being understood, receiving support, sharing one's mood.

There is no doubt, as we have seen, that these mechanisms vary with the emotion, with culture, and, within each culture, with the individual's verbo-viscero-motor organisation. Further specific research should be carried out along these lines.

9 Interrelations between antecedents, reactions, and coping responses

Pio Ricci-Bitti and Klaus R. Scherer

In this chapter we deal with the relation between the types of antecedent events that elicited particular emotions, the reaction patterns shown, and the type of coping or control responses reported by the respondents. More specifically, we try to explore the question of whether the type of reaction reported depends on the specific class of the antecedents.

It is possible that the emotion labels we used are very general category labels which mask differences between individual reaction patterns to specific types of antecedents. Thus, we have tried to explore whether, for example, the death of a relative produces a different pattern of sadness than the loss of a favourite piece of jewellery. Clearly, this depends on how much one liked and valued the relative and the particular piece of jewellery, respectively, but these are factors which we obviously could not investigate with the methodology used in this questionnaire study. However, it would seem of interest to assess potential differences between classes of antecedents in terms of the duration and intensity of the reported emotion, and the specific pattern of the behavioural and physiological reactions that accompanied it. Similarly, we were able to explore to what extent different classes of antecedents led to differences in coping responses, in this case the strength of the attempt to control verbalisation, non-verbal behaviour, and physiological symptoms. It would seem possible that an emotional reaction to specific antecedents is less valued socially (or is even negatively sanctioned), or is less consistent with self-concept demands, than other reactions, and thus more subject to control attempts.

Such differential control may not be independent of differences in the reaction patterns to specific emotions. It seems highly likely that the attempt to control and regulate emotional feeling and reaction depends on the nature and strength of the behavioural and physiological symptoms that are evoked. Clearly, this is not independent of the ability to monitor or focus attention upon specific modalities of behaviour or of physiological responses. We would expect more intensive coping attempts for those behaviours and symptoms that are likely to be monitored rather closely (see Ekman & Friesen, 1969*a*; Pennebaker, 1982).

Whenever possible, intercultural differences are discussed. However, we have not tried to analyse differences between the various countries as far as the interaction between classes of antecedent events and particular response categories is concerned. Since specific reaction patterns to specific classes of antecedents are being studied, the number of cases in each cell becomes very small rather quickly in spite of the generally large number of respondents.

9.1 The differential effects of specific antecedents on response variables

In this section, we take each of the response variables in turn and determine to what extent there were differences in the variable depending on the specific kind of situation that evoked the emotion.

Intensity

Before we begin to examine the differences in reported intensity of the specific emotions, following specific antecedents to each of the four emotions studied, it is interesting to look at differences in intensity between the emotions, independent of the specific antecedents. The data analysis yielded a highly significant effect, the difference being exclusively due to anger being reported as occurring with lower intensity than the other three emotions. Exactly the same significant difference was found in our earlier study (Scherer, Summerfield, & Wallbott 1983). Since the scale values were different in that study, owing to the fact that a five-point scale rather than a ten-point scale was used, this finding is illustrated in Figure 9.1 in terms of the deviation from the mean intensity across all the emotions, corrected for the number of scale points.

The finding that anger occurs with lower intensity is interesting and possibly somewhat counter-intuitive, given experiences with extreme rage which one has experienced oneself or observed in others. There could be a number of possible explanations for this finding. One possibility is that anger is a much more ubiquitous emotion than the others, occurring with sufficient intensity to be memorised. This would mean that more frequent (and therefore recent) but somewhat lower intensity anger situations were more easily recalled and reported in the questionnaire, whereas for the other emotions more infrequent and higher intensity episodes that occurred longer ago were recalled.

This hypothesis is to some extent supported by the data (see Chapters 4 and 5). The anger (and joy) incidents reported had mostly happened a shorter period of time ago than the sadness or fear incidents. Another possibility is that anger is a socially undesirable emotion and there is a tendency to suppress or control it. Later on in this chapter we present some

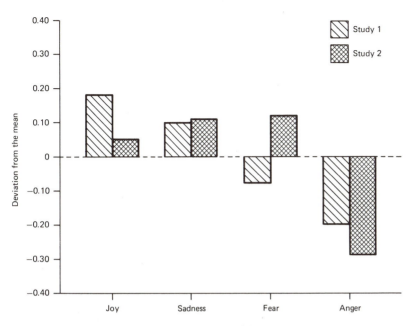

Figure 9.1   Differences in the intensity of the emotions

evidence that this also seems to be the case. This tendency toward suppression might also manifest itself in a tendency when responding to the questionnaire to devalue the intensity of the anger experience.

In order to check whether the relative intensity reported for the different emotions interacted with the nature of the situation, particularly in terms of the other people in the situation and their relationship to the respondent, we examined two-way interactions between type of emotion and group size and familiarity of others present. However, none of the interactions reached significance (see also Chapter 11).

Are there intensity differences across the four emotions for different types of antecedent events? While there were tendencies toward differences for the most important classes of antecedents for all four emotions, there was no significant effect. The trends were quite consistent, however. Joy, sadness, and fear situations that were categorised as relevant to the beginning and end of life (birth and death), were consistently rated with the highest intensity, whereas situations describing achievement-related events for those emotions tended to be in the lower intensity range. Within anger, however, achievement-related situations provoked the relatively highest intensity, situations merely involving inconvenience provoking the lowest intensity.

The social context of the situation may also affect the intensity of some emotions. Thus, sadness was reported as significantly more intense in the presence of small groups of familiar others (see Chapter 11).

In this study we did not find any significant intercultural differences for the intensity with which the emotional experiences were felt. We were not able to replicate the finding in our earlier study that the British subjects reported a significantly lower intensity of emotion compared to the other nationalities across all the emotions. In the present study neither an overall effect for nationality differences, nor differences for individual emotions have been found. The fact that the degree of reported intensity is very consistent across cultures, and across studies, provides some reassurance that the emotional situations studied are indeed comparable in terms of the degree of emotionality.

Duration

There were very stable and highly significant differences across the emotions in terms of their reported duration. A *post-hoc* comparison of the means showed them to be significantly different from each other, yielding four clearly distinct duration patterns. The shortest experience of the emotional reaction occurred in fear; fear seems rarely to last longer than an hour with a large number of cases lasting for less than five minutes. In more than 82% of the cases the feeling lasted for not more than a few hours. The experience of anger seems to last somewhat longer. About 75% of the incidences lasted for not more than a few hours, but in the majority of cases the emotion lasted for longer than a few minutes. Joy generally lasted longer. Here only about 22% of the cases were of less than an hour's duration and a large percentage lasted for several hours to a day with quite a few (29%) lasting for several days. The longest-term emotion seems to be sadness, with only very few cases (19%) lasting for less than an hour and a large percentage (55%) lasting for several days or longer.

Again, as for intensity these findings directly replicate the results from our earlier study (Scherer *et al.*, 1983) (see Figure 9. 2). Not only is the rank order of the individual emotions exactly the same, but even the mean values for the duration are very similar indeed. Since the same coding scale was used in the two studies, this means that the relative duration of the various emotions is a highly consistent feature of the emotional experience. While in the earlier study we found some significant differences between countries, in particular the respondents in France and West Germany reporting shorter durations for all of the emotions, this pattern of results was not replicated in the present study. There were no significant intercultural differences across the emotions or for any of the individual emotions. This absence of

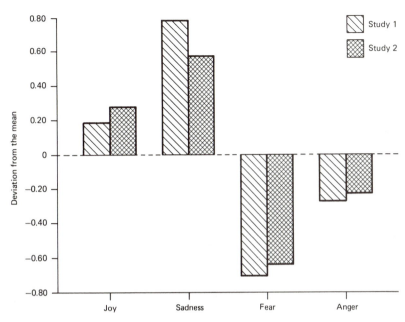

Figure 9.2   Differences in the duration of the emotions

cultural differences also supports the notion that the four basic emotions have very characteristic, consistent time courses.

The results for duration are very consistent and clear-cut, then, and it seems fairly easy to interpret them. Fear is an emergency response and likely to be short-lived, otherwise it might often become unbearable. Anger also often occurs in a short-range period of time, given that it is often connected to everyday events. It may be that joy, at least in terms of the intensely joyful emotions reported here, lasts somewhat longer since the events that cause joy may be rather important for the person and affect his or her behaviour for a longer period of time. Sadness almost always seems to be produced by events that are of lasting significance for a person and that affect his or her future life in a fairly substantial manner resulting in extended duration.

We now examine to what extent there were differences in duration within the emotions following the various classes of antecedents. For each of the emotions, except for anger, there were highly significant differences between the different antecedents. Again, for joy, sadness, and fear, situations involving life (either birth or death) resulted in the longest duration, just as for intensity. Clearly, this can be interpreted in terms of the importance of the event for the organism, with life-and-death issues resulting in more powerful emotional feeling states. Interestingly, fear related to the integrity of one's body was also of a rather long duration, presumably being related to the life-and-death issue in many instances of fear of illness. Otherwise, for joy and sadness, body situations ranked at the lower end of the duration continuum. Sadness about bad news also seemed to be fairly shortlived. As one might expect, traffic and risk situations led to fairly short durations of feeling, being prototypes of emergency reactions.

For anger, as was the case for intensity, there was a tendency for achievement-related anger feelings to last somewhat longer than in other situations. This may imply that situations in which lack of achievement is the source of self-anger are caused by events of major importance for the self-concept, and, therefore, lead to a longer duration of the anger feeling.

The duration of the emotion seems also to depend on the other people that are present in the situation (see chapter 11 for details). Generally, emotional feelings seemed to last significantly longer if familiar others were present. This effect was particularly pronounced for sadness. Furthermore, the duration of sadness was significantly longer if the situation took place inside familiar places, especially for the potentially family-related types of antecedents. It is difficult to decide whether these effects are due to important sadness events generally occurring in familiar social contexts or whether the sheer presence of familiar others enhances the emotional experience.

The duration of fear was also significantly longer if it was experienced inside familiar places. It may be that one generally does not expect fear-provoking events to happen in safe, familiar places, with the result that when they do occur, they elicit a more lasting fear experience.

Verbalisation

Again, there were highly significant differences for verbalisation across the different emotions (see Chapter 8). *Post-hoc* comparison again showed four significantly different means, suggesting that the differences between the emotions were not due to chance. The lowest amount of verbalisation occurred in fear, followed by sadness, joy, and anger. As for intensity and duration, these results very clearly replicate our findings in the earlier study (Scherer *et al.*, 1983) (see Figure 9. 3). While the mean values for the two studies were slightly different because of a change in the number of scale points, the pattern and the rank order of the means were exactly the same. As one might expect, anger seems to be a very 'social' emotion, requiring more communication of the feeling state than sadness or fear.

This impression is strongly confirmed by analyses of the effects of group size and familiarity of others present (see Chapter 11 for further details). As one might expect, there was significantly more verbalisation when the person was with others rather than alone, and respondents talked significantly more when they were with familiar others rather than unfamiliar others.

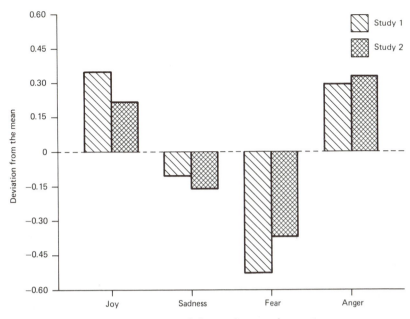

Figure 9.3   Differences in verbalisation between the emotions

However, there was also an interesting interaction effect due to the fact that there is more verbalisation for joy and sadness in the presence of familiar others, whereas people seem to talk more in the presence mainly of unfamiliar others in the case of anger. One apparently does not need the encouragement of familiar others to verbalise about this emotion. It may well be that this is because it is often anger about other people that tends to make us express our anger verbally toward them.

We now turn toward an examination of possible differences in verbalisation following different antecedents. We found highly significant differences between different types of antecedents for all the emotions except fear, where there was a single tendency. The *post-hoc* comparisons showed quite consistent patterns for joy, sadness, and anger, In each of these cases, achievement-related situations gave rise to the lowest amount of verbalisation, and situations related to relationships gave rise to the highest means for verbalisation. Other categories giving high means were temporary meeting situations for joy and injustice situations for anger. Just as in the 'relationships' category, the latter two refer to interactive situations in which the emotion occurs and in which it may often be based on the kind of relationship with another person. Interestingly, the achievement situations which provoked very little verbalisation for the other three emotions, provoked among the highest amount of verbalisation for fear. The other category producing much verbalisation was body-related fear. This is reminiscent of Schachter's (1959) early finding that some people like to affiliate with others and talk about the objects of their fear or anxiety.

Physiological symptoms and non-verbal behaviour
Since the general patterns of results concerning the types of symptoms and non-verbal behaviours that have been reported by the respondents are treated in Chapters 6, 7, and 10, we concentrate here on the question of whether there were differential reactions to the specific antecedent classes within each emotion. For this purpose a cross-tabulation listing the coincidence of particular symptoms or non-verbal behaviours and of a particular type of antecedent situation was compiled. Clearly, the criterion for ascertaining interesting and important differences in response to different antecedent categories is whether there are more reports of a specific symptom for a specific antecedent category than one would expect for this category on the basis of the percentage of all respondents who reported experiences based on that antecedent situation. Consequently, we tested whether the distribution of responses for these reaction parameters over the antecedent classes differed significantly from the expected values based on the general distribution of the respondents over the antecedent classes.

The findings were quite different for the different emotions. For anger there was only one significant difference for any of the symptoms or behaviours that occurred with any frequency. Changes in voice quality were mentioned more frequently as being provoked in relationship situations than by other anger antecedents. While there were some other tendencies, these differences were too weak and based on too few cases to be interpretable. Similarly, for sadness there were no significant differences except for a strong difference for crying. Many more respondents than expected on the basis of the overall distribution reported crying in situations related to life changes (the birth/death category).

For fear there were significant differences for three of the non-verbal behaviour categories: voice reactions, hand movements, and 'freezing'. For voice reactions and hand movements the differences resulted from a larger than expected number of reports for achievement-related situations. Freezing occurred most often in fearful encounters with strangers and in risky, novel situations. Furthermore, two physiological symptom groups were differentially related to fear antecedents. Muscle symptoms (like muscle cramps or tense muscles) were reported most often for dangerous traffic situations, and perspiration (a statistical trend) was a fear symptom mentioned frequently in the context of achievement situations.

The largest number of antecedent-specific differences occurred for joy. Most of these concerned non-verbal behaviour. Temporary meetings accounted for a larger than expected number of reports of body movement toward a person and of hand movements. This can probably be explained by the nature of the responses demanded in a situation where one suddenly meets a friend one hasn't seen for a long time (which seemed to constitute the majority of the situations in this category). More hand movements than expected were also reported for body-related joy. It was interesting to find that for the non-verbal behaviour category 'expansive movement' or 'expansion of the body' there were much higher reports for achievement-related situations than for other situations. This finding seems to correspond well to reports in the ethological literature that posture is more erect in successful and dominant individuals (Weisfeld & Beresford, 1982). Another significant finding for joy, this time for the physiological symptoms, concerned blood pressure. Here joy associated with relationships and temporary meetings accounted for more than the expected number of reports. Also, in terms of a more general indicator, there was a significant difference for pleasant rest feelings, which were more frequent than expected in the body and relationship-related antecedent categories.

On the whole, this analysis demonstrates more similarities in response than differences for the different antecedent categories. The patterns of differences reported above were in part due to specific reaction tendencies that seemed to be demanded by the nature of the situation. There is little to suggest that there were major differences in the response patterns for specific antecedent events. This is as one might have expected given the fact that we have used general emotion labels to refer to uniform response tendencies for different classes of eliciting events. On the other hand, it should not be overlooked that the free response reports which we used for such symptoms in the study may not be sensitive enough to reveal subtle differences in the response to specific situations. Furthermore, it is possible that much of the uniformity in the symptom reports is due to preconceived notions as to what the 'proper' symptoms for specific emotional states are (see Chapter 12).

9. 2 The differential effects of specific antecedents on control attempts

Control of verbalisation
There were highly significant differences between the emotions. The *post-hoc* comparison showed that the means were significantly different from each other, constituting four independent subsets. The lowest amount of control of verbalisation occurred in joy. After a fairly sizeable jump, more control was exercised in fear, then in sadness, and the greatest amount of control was exercised in anger (see also Chapter 8). These results again point to the possibility that anger is the most negatively sanctioned emotion requiring

a high degree of control. However, sadness also seems to require a fairly high amount of verbalisation control. The fact that the amount of control exercised in fear was relatively low may be a result of the spontaneity with which fearful expressions occur in emergency situations.

The tendencies outlined above were complemented by interesting and highly significant interaction effects with the indicators of the social nature of the situation (see Chapter 11 for details). The size of the group in which the emotion occurred played a major role: the amount of control of verbalisation increased with the number of people present in the situation. There was also an interaction effect indicating highly elevated levels of verbalisation control in sadness and anger situations where the subject was not alone, particularly when familiar others were present. This invites interesting speculations about the perceived consequences of uncontrolled anger and sadness verbalisation on the nature of close relationships (see Chapter 11).

There were highly significant differences for the amount of control of verbalisation following specific antecedents for all the emotions. For both joy and sadness, body-related antecedents produced the lowest amount of control of verbalisation. Apart from this, there were few communalities in the findings for the different emotions. For joy, control of verbalisation was highest for life-relevant situations, that is probably birth, and for achievement situations. The latter may well be due to attempts to avoid self-praise or to discourage envy from others. For sadness, control of verbalisation was highest for relationship-related antecedents, maybe to avoid the danger of increasing the sadness of the other(s). For fear, the lowest amount of control of verbalisation was reported for situations involving risk or external forces, and the highest amount for situations with body-related and achievement-related antecedents. We can interpret these results as follows: here we have two different forms of fear. The situations involving risk and external forces are unexpected and sudden and therefore provoke a ceasing of reactions (emergency situation) and control of verbalisation is not required. The achievement-related situations, on the other hand often imply an expected, foreseen event and therefore provoke increasing arousal (sometimes called fear, but also anxiety) which produces verbalisation and other expressive reactions. In this case control of verbalisation may seem necessary, particularly in order to protect one's public self, especially as far as competence attributions in achievement situations are concerned.

For anger, the lowest amount of control of verbalisation occurred in inconvenience situations, and the highest amount in situations involving injustice and stranger impact. It is possible that there is less blame of others in inconvenience situations, and this would render copious anger verbalisations less aggressive. The opposite is the case, of course, for perceived

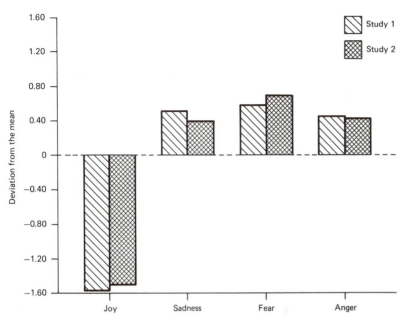

Figure 9.4   Differences in the control of physiological symptoms and non-verbal behaviour

injustice or feeling bothered by strangers. Here, verbalisations may be perceived as an attack and lead to serious conflict.

Control of physiological symptoms and non-verbal behaviour

There was a highly significant effect across the emotions for this variable, being mostly due, as the *post-hoc* comparisons showed to the difference between joy, where there was very little control, and the other three emotions (see also Chapter 7). As Figure 9.4 shows, this finding is again a replication of the significant difference found between joy and the other emotions in our earlier study (the differences being of almost the same magnitude) (Scherer *et al.*, 1983). In this case, the variables related to the social context of the situation had less effect than for the control of verbalisation. There was a highly significant effect for group size indicating that there was more control of physiological symptoms the more people there were around. Also, control of reactions was greater in the presence of familiar others than in the presence of unfamiliar others for sadness and anger; this partially replicates the control of verbalisation findings.

Generally, the findings concerning control attempts seem to indicate a concern with the potential consequences of verbal and non-verbal expressions of negative emotions in social situations where close relationships may be affected or conflict may result. This tendency was much less pronounced for fear, which is clearly a more personal and less social emotion than the others both in terms of potential contagion (as in sadness) and as a source of conflict (as in anger).

9.3 The effect of reaction patterns on control responses

To what extent did the nature of the control or regulation attempts depend on the intensity and the specific nature of the emotional reaction to a particular stimulus? Unfortunately, this was difficult to assess, given the free response format chosen in this study. The number of responses given in terms of physiological symptoms and non-verbal behaviours did not allow the piecing together of a specific typology of responses that could then be compared to the coping or control reaction. It would not have been very useful to do this for each individual symptom or behaviour category, given the number of respondents. However, it was possible to study to what extent the intensity and duration of the emotional reaction determined the control response. For this purpose we computed three-way analyses of variance (ANOVA) for the control of verbalisation and the control of physiological symptoms with emotion type and categorised versions of the intensity and duration variables (for details see Appendix D). For the control of physiological symptoms we obtained highly significant main effects for emotion (see above) and for the intensity level. As one would have expected, the control response was stronger the more intensely the emotion was experienced. There was apparently an intensity level effect since the difference seemed to be mainly due to the gap between the first intensity level (mean of 2.4 for level 1) and the two remaining ones (means of 3.2 and 3.0 for levels 2 and 3 respectively). There was also a significant interaction effect between emotion and intensity which was mostly due to particularly strong coping responses to high intensity level (again levels 2 and 3) in sadness and anger. The intensity by duration interaction was also significant; this seemed to be mostly based on a very low control response in the low intensity/long duration cell. It seems possible that the reactions reported here may come close to moods in terms of their duration and intensity characteristics.

For the control of verbalisation we also found significant emotion effects (see above) as well as significant intensity and duration effects. As before, there were stronger attempts to control verbalisation the higher the intensity and this was again true for levels 2 and 3 as compared to level 1. For the duration of the response the means seem to represent a linear trend with increasingly strong attempts at control of verbalisation as duration increases. It is interesting to speculate whether this may be due to a largely involuntary or spontaneous effect of verbalisation in very short term emotional reactions as compared to a more consciously controlled type of reaction in longer emotional experiences.

Does the attempt to control verbalisation increase with the amount of verbalisation? This is indeed the case. We found highly significant differences in the control of verbalisation between the emotions (see above) and between levels of verbalisation as well as a significant interaction between emotion and verbalisation. There were indeed, as one might expect, stronger control attempts where more verbalisation was reported. The interaction effect is due to the absence of this relationship in the case of joy, and, possibly, the very strong effect for fear. Apparently, the more one is tempted to talk the more one feels compelled to control the urge, a finding which again testifies to the great importance of social norms and rules in the outward expression of emotion.

In general, the differences between individual countries were very small indeed for the control variables and did not, as in the earlier study, reach significance. The only exception was the control of reactions and verbalisations in joy. In this case, it was particularly the French but also, to some extent, the Italians, Belgians, and Israelis, who showed a greater amount of control. Consequently, the French subjects reported a much lower amount of verbalisation than the subjects from the other countries. This difference did not, however, extend to any of the other emotions. It is difficult to know which factor might account for this very specific finding.

9.4 Conclusions

The pattern of results reported in this chapter suggests that the nature of the situation or event which elicits a specific emotion may have quite noticeable effects on the strength and form of the emotional reaction and the subject's attempts to control this reaction. If this finding can be replicated in further studies, including observational or experimental approaches, a number of important implications need to be considered. If reactions differ within a particular emotion as a function of the nature of the antecedent situation, it would hardly be surprising to find a lack of replicability of reaction patterns for instances of the same general emotion elicited by widely different antecedents (as is the rule in different studies). For example, the repeated failure of stress researchers to find replicable patterns of responses to negative emotions may well be due to the neglect of the specific effects of the respective antecedents, that is the type of experimental or real-life stress situation. If this is the case, new approaches are required – both in terms of theory and research design – in which specific predictions for well-defined emotion antecedents are proposed and empirically investigated.

10 Individual differences in emotional reactions

Heiner Ellgring and Bernard Rimé

10.1 Introduction

Though essential to our understanding of human adaptation, the question of individual differences in emotional responses still appears to be largely unresolved. In spite of the considerable range of individual ways of responding that we can observe in everyday life emotional situations, and in spite of the essential relevance of this question to clinical practice in psychology, the scientific attack on it is only recent and the available concepts still remain rough and tentative.

One of the older and perhaps most basic distinctions existing in this field is the one contrasting repressors and sensitisers. Repressors, who have attracted the attention of clinically oriented psychologists since the end of the last century, are people who consistently report low emotionality, though their behaviour and physiology in the presence of emotional stimuli generally appear otherwise. Byrne (1964) contrasted this class of people with another one which he called sensitisers. Sensitisers are people who employ mechanisms that enable them to deal more or less directly with the emotional situation. They may even exaggerate the threat potential in a situation or take special pains to expose themselves to it. Their reported symptomatology for such situations generally is a rich one. It was recently, however, that studies initiated by Weinberger, Schwartz, & Davidson (1979) and extended by Asendorpf & Scherer (1983) offered scientific grounds for this distinction between repressor and sensitiser styles of emotional responding. In Asendorpf & Scherer's (1983) study, when exposed to an emotion-arousing situation, repressors indeed exhibited a discrepancy between low self-reported emotionality and high indices of physiological and expressive changes. By contrast, sensitisers, or high-anxious subjects as they were called by the authors, showed consistently high values on all three variables. Nevertheless, our knowledge about these two contrasting styles of emotional responding remains limited. For instance, it is not known whether repressors act in a self-deceptive or in an other-deceptive manner. Would they, or would they not, report that they strove to control their emotional arousal? Also, nothing is known about the social variables which are associated with these styles, in spite of the many stereotypes. Indeed, naive psychology easily suggests that our educational standards lead males to be more prone to adopt a repressor style in emotional situations while females tend to adopt a sensitiser style. One would also guess that people from urban settings would repress their emotional responses more than people from rural settings. Moreover, we all share particularly strong ideas about cross-cultural differences in this domain. In Europe, one readily takes it for granted that people in northern countries – and perhaps especially the British – would adopt a repressor style, while people in southern countries – and perhaps especially the Italians – would react with a sensitiser style.

A second distinction about individual ways of responding emotionally, which was also introduced a long time ago, similarly had to wait until recently to be documented by research data. In 1935, Jones used the term externaliser to describe a person who was high in overt emotional reactions and low in physiological responses and the term internaliser to describe one who had little overt expression but experienced large physiological changes. His pioneering observations of this distinction were more recently supported by data by Buck, Savin, Miller, & Caul (1972), by Buck, Miller, & Caul (1974), and by Notarious & Levenson (1979). In this last study, internalisers or natural inhibitors, as selected on the basis of their facial responsiveness in a preliminary observational situation, were revealed as less facially expressive and more physiologically reactive than were natural expressors or externalisers in an emotion-arousing situation such as that induced by the threat of electric shocks. A recent study by Notarius *et al.* (1982) confirmed this observation using female subjects in another kind of emotional situation. However, apart from some data suggesting that male subjects would be more oriented toward internalisation and female subjects more prone to externalisation (Buck *et al.*, 1972), we know practically nothing about the correlates of this second bipolar distinction. As compared to internalisers, do externalisers experience emotional situations as more immediate or more intense? Do internalisers consciously attempt to control their emotional manifestations? Are they satisfied by their way of handling the emotional situation? Apart from sex, are there other classes of social variables which correlate with the internaliser–externaliser distinction? Such questions have not yet been documented by scientific investigations.

In the present European study of emotional reactions, it was possible to investigate some of the questions which have been raised here about the correlates of the two bipolar variables under consideration.

10. 2 The assessment of individual differences in reaction tendencies

The assessment of individual differences in our study needs specific approaches. Whereas most of the analyses discussed in the other chapters compare reactions with regard to the different emotions, the individual differences were studied as general modes of experiencing emotions and reacting to them. Thus, the individual might be characterised as, for instance, reacting with *very many* or *very few* bodily symptoms independent of the specific emotion. General reaction tendencies like these, which are defined in detail later, are to be compared with regard to the influence of cultural background, socio-economic background, sex, etc. Furthermore, do people with, for instance, a strong tendency for reporting bodily symptoms experience generally more intense and longer emotions than other people, and would they behave the same way on another, similar occasion?

There are three areas for which individual response tendencies can be defined:

> modes of experiencing emotional situations;
> reaction tendencies;
> control and coping tendencies

Reaction tendencies

In order to assess individual differences in reactions, we used the notions of sensitiser–repressor, externaliser–internaliser, vocal, and body reaction type. These were assessed by combining the specific information given about non-verbal and bodily reactions.

Our procedure for defining these variables by reactions according to their frequencies in the self-report responses followed the act-frequency approach to personality (Buss & Craik, 1983). According to this approach, personality may be defined by the frequencies of the behaviours displayed by the individual in different situations. As may be seen from Figure 10.1, we define these reaction tendencies in a hierarchical way. Here externalising an emotional experience means that another person theoretically may observe the reported bodily or verbal/vocal reactions, whereas internalising means the experiencing of physiological symptoms or inner sensations. Both taken together represent sensitising tendencies, that is a tendency to react either non-verbally or physiologically. Repression by the subject, on the other hand, would mean that very few symptoms of *any* kind would have been reported.

One problem that arises from this kind of definition is that values may be dependent on the duration and, even more, on the intensity of experienced emotions. One could argue that more symptoms are reported when people

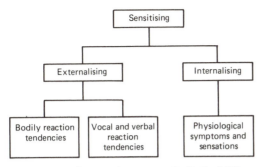

Figure 10.1   Theoretical structure of individual differences in reaction tendencies

experience the emotional situation more intensively or for longer periods. In this case, one could take into account the intensity as a moderator variable by using methods of correcting for covariation. On the other hand, it could also be the case that repressors not only report fewer symptoms but also repress the intensity of the experienced emotion. In this case, correcting by covariation would obscure a given general disposition for intensive subjective experiences and the reporting of many symptoms. Repression would then mean that at the subjective level as well as at the behavioural level there would be a lower readiness to report on experiences associated with emotions. We studied five reaction tendency variables.

Sensitising. The degree of sensitising is defined by the number of reactions across different behavioural aspects and emotions. Regardless of the kind of non-verbal or bodily reactions reported, a person who reports many symptoms and reactions will be regarded as a sensitiser in contrast to a repressor, who is supposed to name very few symptoms and reactions. Score values for sensitising ranged between 0 and 15, the median being 6. Since four emotions were combined into this score, there were on average about 1.5 named reactions for each emotion. This general score was further divided up as described now.

Internalising. Physiological reactions and bodily sensations can be seen as an internalisation of the emotional experience. Therefore, these symptoms are taken as an indicator for internalising tendencies. Score values ranged from 0 to 11, the median being 3. On average, 0.75 internalising reactions were mentioned for each emotion.

Externalising. Vocalisation and bodily reactions can both be regarded as an externalisation of the emotional experience. The two aspects were therefore taken together. This yielded score values ranging from 0 to 11, the median being 3. On average, as for internalising, 0.75 externalising reactions were mentioned for each emotion.

It should be noted that internalising and externalising are not considered as being two poles of a continuum. They are seen rather as variables on which individuals may be located, even in some cases with high values on both of these scales. In fact, internalising and externalising, as defined here, were moderately correlated in our sample ($r = 0.33$, significant).

Bodily reaction tendencies. All non-verbal visible behaviours (gaze, facial expression, body movement, etc.) are subsumed in this category. Score values ranged from 0 to 8, the median being 2. On average 0.5 reactions of this kind were mentioned for each emotion.

Vocal reaction tendencies. Codes for vocal reactions (speech and voice) were combined. Score values ranged from 0 to 5, the median being 0.8, indicating that on average 0.2 vocal reactions were mentioned for each emotion. In contrast to the other variables, which yielded a normal distribution of values, the frequency distribution of this variable was highly skewed to the left. More than one-third of the subjects (37%) reported only one vocal reaction for all four emotions. Therefore, in contrast to the situation for the other variables, no extreme groups as described below could be set up for this variable.

Comparison of extreme groups. For the statistical analyses and in order to get concise comparisons, extreme groups for the various reaction tendencies were formed. For this, 10–17% of the subjects in the whole sample for each variable were considered to be either high or low scorers. Table 10.1 gives the frequency distribution for sensitising tendencies as an example of this procedure.

In this case, from the total sample of $N = 779$, $n = 108$ subjects ($= 14\%$) were classified as high scorers, $n = 121$ subjects ($= 16\%$) as low scorers, the cutting points being 2.7 and 0.9 (average number of reactions per emotion) for low and high scorers respectively. The high and low cutting point values and the number of subjects, n, for each of the reaction variables are given in Table 10.2.

As can be seen, a rigid criterion of 10% for the highest and lowest values could not be adopted because of the peculiarities of the frequency distributions. As mentioned before, for vocal/verbal reaction tendencies, no high and low cutting points could be defined because of the extremely skewed distribution and the small range of this variable.

On average, about 110 subjects (14%) are located at each pole of the scales

Table 10.1. *Frequency distribution of score values for sensitising tendencies*

Value	Number of subjects, n	Cumulated percentage	Classification of score
5.5	1	0.1	
4.5	3	0.5	
4.0	2	0.8	
3.8	11	2.2	High
3.5	11	3.6	
3.3	14	5.4	
3.0	26	8.7	
2.8	40	13.9	
2.5	60	21.6	
2.3	74	31.1	
2.0	72	40.3	
1.8	92	52.1	
1.5	105	65.6	
1.3	79	75.7	
1.0	68	84.5	
0.8	56	91.7	
0.5	37	96.4	Low
0.3	21	99.1	
0.0	7	100.0	

Table 10.2. *High and low values for reaction tendencies. The values indicate the average number of reactions per emotion*

Variable	High values			Low values		
	Cutting point value	n	%	Cutting point value	n	%
Sensitising	2.7	108	14	0.9	121	16
Externalising	1.7	93	12	0.4	136	17
Internalising	1.7	113	15	0.4	99	13
Bodily reaction	1.2	126	16	0	81	10

in Table 10.2. Thus, on average, 28% of the subjects in each sample were taken for extreme group comparisons.

10.3 Factors determining individual reaction tendencies

Cultural background

In order to give an overview of significant effects of cultural background, we have listed the χ^2 values for the effects of various cultural factors on

Table 10.3. *Effects of external variables on reaction tendencies. The values are* χ^2 *values obtained by comparing high and low reaction scores*

Background	Degrees of freedom	Reaction type			
		Sensitising	Internalising	Externalising	Bodily reaction
Country	7	$81.9^{a,b}$	$80.6^{a,b}$	$19.3^{a,b}$	$19.5^{a,b}$
North–south countries	1	4.3^d	0.5	2.0	4.9^d
Main place of residence	2	9.8^b	$13.2^{a,b}$	0.2	0.3
Social class	1	2.1	0.1	0.3	0.7
Field of study	2	9.0^c	4.5	4.4	2.9
Sex	1	$10.6^{a,b}$	1.5	$14.0^{a,b}$	$24.8^{a,b}$
Age	2	1.2	0.8	1.0	1.0

[a] Values are those for which the corresponding effect size amounted to $d \geqslant 0.30$.
[b] $p < 0.01$.
[c] $p < 0.02$.
[d] $p < 0.05$.

reaction tendencies in Table 10.3. As can be seen from these values, the most important effects stem from country and sex, followed by the place of residence and the field of study. No significant effects were observed for social class or for age.

Comparisons relative to the sensitising reaction type were the most informative ones, with significant χ^2 values for six out of the seven variables of cultural background. These data will now be considered in a more detailed manner.

Countries. There were markedly fewer reported physiological symptoms from the Spanish and Israeli subjects compared to the others. As can be seen from Figure 10.2, there was a high proportion of low scorers for these countries with regard to internalising tendencies.

The data shown in Figure 10.2 indicate the partitioning of the low and high scorers within each country. Thus, from the 34 extreme scorers in the Israeli sample, only 3 (= 9%) were high scorers, and 31 (= 91%) were low scorers for internalising tendencies. For the British, Belgian, Italian, and German samples, there was a much higher proportion of high-scoring internalising subjects (74–85%), whereas the Swiss and French samples contained a more even proportion of high and low scorers.

For externalising tendencies, the relative proportions were not so clear. Here the Italian sample, in addition to the Spanish and Israeli samples, had a high proportion of low scorers, whereas for the other countries the proportions of high and low scorers were quite even. Taking the whole

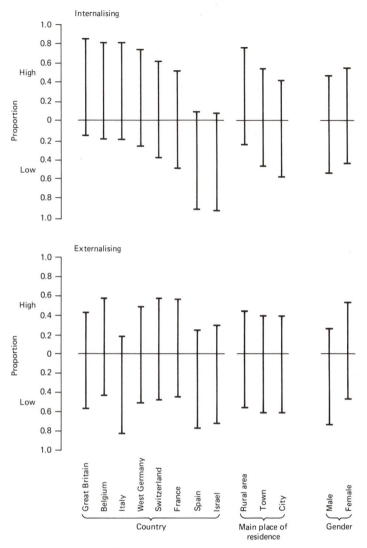

Figure 10.2 Differences in individual reaction tendencies by country, place of residence, and gender

sample into account, the analysis of variance yielded an effect of country for sensitising and internalising tendencies, but not for externalising tendencies and bodily reactions.

These differences between countries were only slightly related to the north–south division we made (see Table 10.3). Moreover, the observed relations to this respect are opposite to the currently held notions of stereotypes. Thus, for subjects from northern countries, the proportion of high sensitisers (53%) was greater than that of subjects from southern countries (38%). The data for bodily reaction were in the same direction.

Main place of residence. The more rural the place of residence, the higher was the proportion of high sensitisers. Indeed, this proportion was 38% for people living in cities, 49% for those living in towns, and 67% for those living in a rural environment. These figures should be considered together with the ones for internalising, as it is apparent that more rural areas also contain higher proportions of high-scoring internalising individuals, that is subjects reporting more physiological symptoms. As can be seen from Figure 10.2 this proportion rose from 43% for subjects living in cities to 77% for those living in rural areas. For externalising tendencies, the proportions of high and low scores were quite even.

Sex. As might be expected, there was a much lower proportion of highly externalising male subjects than of female subjects: 53% of the female subjects were high externalisers compared to only 27% of the male ones (see Figure 10.2). This considerable sex difference was also found for purely bodily symptoms, and for general sensitising tendencies. There was also a slight similar tendency for internalising: 48% of the male sub-sample and 57% of the female sub-sample were high sensitisers. However, this effect was not very strong.

Thus, in contrast to differences due to one's country of origin and main place of residence, sex had an effect mainly on externalising tendencies and not on internalising ones (see also Chapter 7).

Field of study. Compared to social and natural science students, there was a somewhat higher proportion of high sensitisers among psychology students. Whereas for natural science students this proportion was 39% and for social science students it was 35%, 57% of psychology students had high scores. However, the effect was not very strong in this case.

As with cultural and sex influences, the influence of the field of study was in accordance with the expectation that psychology students sensitise more than other students. The effect, however, was comparatively small.

Situational and coping aspects

The intensity with which one experiences an emotion as well as the ways of coping with the situation are related to sensitising and, more specifically, internalising tendencies. As can be seen from Table 10.4, high sensitisers and high internalisers experienced the situations significantly more intensely

Table 10.4. *Differences in situational and coping aspects with regard to differences in individuals.*

	Sensitising		Internalising		Externalising	
	Low	High	Low	High	Low	High
Situation						
Duration	2.8	2.7	2.9	2.8	2.9	2.8
Intensity	6.7	7.3	6.5	7.5	7.1	7.3
Control/coping						
Control of Symptoms	2.8	3.3	2.7	3.3	2.8	3.3
Control of Verbalisation	2.9	3.5	3.0	3.6	3.1	3.6
Handle situations differently	0.66	0.48	0.64	0.49	0.60	0.52

than those who scored low. They also had a greater tendency to handle situations differently on similar occasions.

We also found reportable effects for control tendencies. High sensitisers and, more specifically, internalisers tend to control their symptoms and verbal reactions more than low scorers. For externalising tendencies no clear effect was observed except that high externalisers tended to handle the situation differently on similar occasions.

It is noteworthy that the duration and intensity scores correlated moderately with one another ($r = 0.32$) and control of verbal behaviour correlated with control of reactions ($r = 0.56$). Both of these correlations were highly significant, possibly indicating a general tendency to control one's reactions and also, to a lesser extent, that the duration and intensity of the emotional experience are related to each other. With regard to internalising tendencies, however, intensity had a strong effect, as mentioned before.

The immediacy aspect of the situation, which would be of interest here, could not be evaluated because it lacks differentiation. For example, 71% of the situations were reported as being the subjects' own experience; similarly, 87% of the situations were reported as being real as opposed to imagined. The low proportion of empathic experience or imagined situations did not allow comparisons with other variables.

10.4 Conclusions

Individual differences in the reporting of physiological or non-verbal vocal or non-vocal symptoms in connection with the experience of emotion can be traced to cultural and sex differences. It has been shown that females are better at decoding non-verbal cues (Hall, 1978), but this is also dependent on age and thus socialisation (Blanck *et al.*, 1981). In our study, sex seemed to influence non-verbal bodily reactions in that there was a higher proportion of low externalisers among the males. Thus, males seemed to hold back on these reactions, at least in their reports, more than females.

Tendencies to report physiological symptoms and bodily sensations, on the other hand, that is to internalise the experience, seemed to be influenced more by the general cultural background. There were more high internalisers from rural areas than from towns or cities. Low internalisers came specifically from Israel and Spain. It might be the case that students in these countries were not as used to reporting on these kinds of symptoms. Unexpectedly, the Italian sample contained a high proportion of low externalisers. We cannot decide if this result is some evidence against a cultural stereotype of the non-verbal active, gesticulating southern people. Other explanations are also possible. People know about this stereotype and, when asked to write down these symptoms, try to put their own case against this stereotype. It is also possible that they do not attend to this kind of behaviour that much because of its general frequency, and, therefore, do not report on reaction tendencies which nevertheless might be observed by others. Still another explanation is the fact that this part of the study was conducted in northern Italy and that a southern sample would behave differently as is suggested for the decoding of non-verbal cues by Giovannini & Ricci Bitti (1981).

The trend for psychology students to report more symptoms than other students was significant but not as strong as expected. Generally, the strongest effects for internalising tendencies came from country-specific cultural differences, whereas for externalising tendencies, sex effects were stronger.

As an open question, there remains the problem of defining the various forms of reaction tendencies. Sensitising, for instance, is traditionally defined as a coping strategy with regard to anxiety. Repressors are persons who defensively avoid the experience of anxiety, whereas sensitisers are hyper-vigilant against anxiety-linked cognitions (Byrne, Barry, & Nelson, 1963). These individual differences in coping with anxiety are also to be seen in relation to social desirability. Male repressors, for instance, exhibit a discrepancy between low self-reported anxiety and high heart rate and facial display of anxiety (Asendorpf & Scherer, 1983).

In our study, the situation was quite different since emotions other than anxiety were considered. Moreover, self-reported reactions were taken as an indicator for sensitising or repressing tendencies. It has been shown in other studies that repressors tend to react more strongly to anxiety-provoking stimuli despite their lower anxiety values (Weinberger, Schwartz, & Davidson, 1979). In our study, sensitising correlated with the intensity of the experienced emotions. So, the relation between intensity and sensitising might be spurious. On the other hand, it might be argued from averaging over the emotions that the intensity of the experienced emotion is indeed associated with more self-observed reactions. Moreover, there could even be some kind of interconnected feedback loop, whereby the perceived reactions intensify the emotional experience, as has been proposed by Tomkins (1980) for facial feedback.

Interestingly, there was a moderate correlation between internalising and externalising reaction tendencies. This might indicate that they are not totally independent of one another on the one hand and cannot be seen as contrasting poles of a continuum on the other hand.

Our approach in defining and assessing sensitisation, internalisation, and externalisation by the use of self-reported physiological, bodily, and vocal reactions is in accordance to the act-frequency approach to personality (Buss & Craik, 1983). In our study, individual differences in these variables could be traced to cultural and sex differences and also, where associated, with different coping and control strategies. Problems arising from the nature of self-reports are still open to discussion. In order to study these reactions further, one would need direct observations of the reactions.

11 The effects of social factors on emotional reactions

Elisha Y. Babad and Harald G. Wallbott

11.1 Social aspects of emotion

This chapter is devoted to a 'social analysis' of the experience of emotion. Taking a social-psychological stance, we pose in this chapter some questions regarding the social aspects of emotion and examine the relevant data from the various countries in this study.

Emotion and emotional experiences must be understood, at least partly, as social phenomena. Emotions are most often enacted in social contexts, constituting an integral part of the social interaction process. People transmit to each other and receive from each other affective messages, and emotions play a major role in influencing attitudes and values, social cognition and social behaviour. In fact, ongoing, continuing relationships between people cannot be described without affective elements.

Analysis of the social aspects involved in the experience of emotion can focus on the emotions themselves and the ways in which they are experienced, on social and non-social antecedents of emotions, on verbal and non-verbal reactions, and on the control of emotion. Sociologists such as Kemper (1978) and Hochschild (1979) consider emotion, and particularly the control of emotion, to be a central factor in social interaction. The German sociologist Elias described the history of human civilisation as a history of affect control and regulation (1977). In his view, higher levels of civilisation call for higher levels of emotional control. Scherer, Summerfield & Wallbott (1983) quoted Aristotelian philosophy, stating on this point that if one wishes to be considered wise and socially skilled, one should show appropriate emotions in appropriate fashions in appropriate situations.

According to Ekman (1972), the control and regulation of emotions must be considered within the social context of the emotional situation. He described what he called 'Display rules' – socially learned norms that govern and regulate the expression of emotions within their social context. Ekman focussed on display rules related to the control, masking, and blending of facial expression, but such rules apply as well to other emotional expressions, for example vocal behaviour, verbal behaviour, body language, and interpersonal behaviour. On a more abstract level, display rules govern the amount and types of control employed by people when coping with emotional situations.

In this chapter we examine the social aspects of emotion in several ways. First, the 'social versus non-social' distinction can be applied to typify the emotions themselves. Are all emotions 'social' to the same extent or are some emotions *a priori* more social than others? A possible common-sense hypothesis could view joy and anger, for example, as more 'social' emotions than sadness and fear. But different emotions might carry quite different social meanings and might be 'social' in different ways. If emotions indeed vary in their social meaning as well as in their level of sociability, we must define this sociability in terms of the operational dimensions and variables used in this study and examine the empirical findings, which will confirm or disconfirm the hypotheses about the influences of social factors. We also focus on the characteristics of the people involved in the emotional situations and their influence on the experiencing of the various emotions, on the social and non-social antecedents of the emotions, and on the individual tendencies to experience emotions in a more social or less social way. Finally, taking advantage of the wide cross-cultural scope of this study, we examine the confirmation or disconfirmation of some commonly held stereotypes about different European nations and regions, as expressed in the subjective reports of our respondents.

Emotion and social interaction

What are the social characteristics of the experience of emotion? Social factors that might influence both the experience and the types of control employed to cope with the various emotions include the number of people involved in the situation and the degree of familiarity we have with them. Ekman & Friesen (1969a) argued that emotions and emotional reactions are often less controlled when one is alone or in a large, anonymous mass of people ('non-social' setting) than when one is in a dyad or a small group of people ('social' setting). Moreover, the control of emotion might also vary as a function of familiarity, less (or more) control being called for when one is with familiar people. Such variables, together with more specific knowledge about the role of these 'others' in influencing a person's experience of a particular emotion, define the social context and social support involved in these situations.

It is important to distinguish between the various emotions (joy, sadness, fear, anger) in terms of interaction and social support. Social support and familiarity might vary in their significance for different emotions, much as social interaction might play a different role in attempts to cope with the different emotions.

Social and non-social antecedents of emotional situations
The sociability of an emotional situation is indicated not only in the characterisation of the people involved in the situation, but also in the antecedents that preceded, and caused, the emotion. Obviously, the sociability of the antecedents and the sociability of the context of the actual experience are strongly related. However, despite this intuitive affinity, the two are far from identical. Sometimes the emotion is experienced in a social context (say, with a small group of familiar people) but the antecedent is non-social, while at other times the antecedent is social, but the emotion is experienced in a non-social context. Being frightened by a falling rock while mountain-climbing with a group of friends is an example of the former, while receiving a letter with bad news about a loved person and reading it alone is an example of the latter. Therefore, it is important to supplement the comparison of emotions with respect to the people involved in the situation with an additional examination of social and non-social antecedents of these situations.

Personality differences
The analyses and comparisons proposed thus far in this chapter (e.g. antecedents, familiarity, etc.) consider each emotion separately, and compare it to the other emotions. However, the data can be viewed from a different perspective – one emphasising systematic individual differences and consistent individual, or personality characteristics. Even if we assume that there are differences for the four emotions in the meaning and significance of social factors – and most of the analyses that we present are intended to examine these differences empirically – there might be some significance in the tendency of particular individuals to describe more social or more non-social emotional experiences. The four emotions considered in this study created a five-point scale for characterising individuals by the number of social or non-social situations they described.

   This approach to individual differences is more in a personality than a social-psychological perspective, and really not a focus or original intention of the project. This can be seen from the fact that no personality questionnaires were administered to all the respondents, and that only demographic information was available on all the subjects. However, some personality measures were available on some of the subjects, making it possible to compare the tendency to describe more or less social situations with other personality attributes on a sub-sample at least.

   As for the sample-at-large, some interesting comparisons could be made using the available background information. For example, it might be quite interesting to test whether females tended to describe more social situations than males, or whether large-city dwellers tended to describe less social situations than people coming from smaller, less alienated and anonymous places of residence (Milgram, 1970, 1977; Newman & McCauley, 1977). Another interesting avenue of investigation is to examine country differences in the tendency to describe more or less social situations. Commonly held stereotypes might describe Israelis or Italians as more socially orientated than German or Swiss people, and such differences can be readily checked in the available data.

National stereotypes

A study with parallel data-files on subjects from eight countries responding to the same questionnaire provides a rare opportunity for focussing on stereotypes. A major intention of this study was to compare reaction patterns in a cross-cultural perspective and to identify national differences (emics) and commonalities (etics) in the experience of emotion. But it is possible to approach the data from another perspective as well. What we had in mind was a theoretical social-psychological approach to the issue of national stereotypes.

Members of every nationality and citizens of every country hold stereotypes about themselves and about other groups. Many stereotypes are commonly held and accepted by all groups (although perhaps with the exception of their actual subjects or 'victims'). It is obvious that all stereotypes are over-generalisations and therefore constitute distorted pictures. Stereotypes thus vary in their level of validity, some being utterly (and often viciously) wrong while others might be construed as relatively valid characterisations of particular groups.

The fact that this study was not meant to focus on stereotypes at all makes it particularly appealing to examine the confirmation or disconfirmation of national stereotypes by the data. Latins are stereotypically held to be temperamental and very verbal while jokes are told about the silence of the British; Germans and Swiss are often characterised as being extremely serious and responsible; Israeli 'Sabras' as being tough and thorny; and French people as being refined in cuisine and love; and it was possible to use various parts of our data to see whether such images were confirmed in any way. The self-reported descriptions written by the respondents provided a wealth of information about their choice of contents, the types of antecedents that would cause particular emotions, their typical ways of reacting to these situations, their verbal, non-verbal, and physiological coping mechanisms, and so on and so forth. So, would the Latins indeed turn out to be more talkative than the British, or would the Germans show more achievement-oriented affect?

We approached this examination of stereotypes with great curiosity and

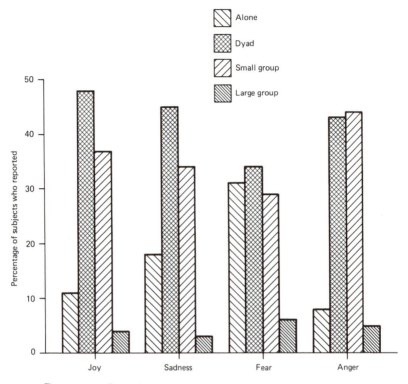

Figure 11.1   Group size

great caution. Self-reported descriptions of emotional experiences are hardly the kind of data used in stereotypy research, and the evidence can be interpreted in contradictory ways. For example, if the British subjects were to be found reporting an excessive amount of talking, that could be interpreted as disconfirming a stereotype, but it would also be possible to offer an alternative explanation that confirms the stereotype: it would argue that British subjects do not really talk more, only that their low baseline for talking makes 'normal' talking more salient and therefore worthy of particular reference when reporting their experience.

11.2 Findings on social interaction: group size and familiarity

To test the extent to which the characteristics of the other people involved in a situation influence the way in which an emotion is experienced, we examined for each of the four emotions the relation between group size and familiarity and variables such as the duration and intensity of the emotion, the amount of verbalisation, and the amount of control of symptoms/reac-

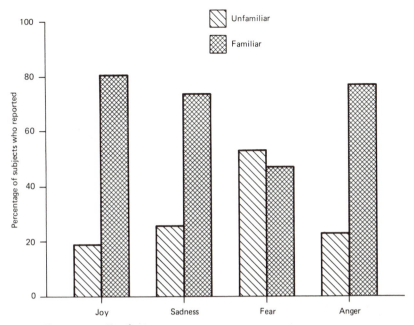

Figure 11.2 Familiarity

tions and of verbalisation. 'Group size' was divided into 'social versus non-social interaction': the coding 'social interaction' combined the dyad and small group categories (2 and 3), while 'non-social interaction' consisted of the 'alone' and large group categories (1 and 4), where there is no (or less) possibility for social interaction with others. Respondents also described for each emotion whether it was experienced with familiar or unfamiliar others, and this variable was labelled 'familiarity'.

The observed frequencies of group size and familiarity for the four emotions are shown in Figures 11.1 and 11.2. The data for all eight countries were combined, and we have not discussed cross-national differences in this section.

The data presented in Figure 11.1 show considerable variation across the categories and across the four emotions. Looking first at the group size categories, we see that large group situations were quite infrequent, while dyad and small group situations ('social interaction') were very common. The most notable difference was found for the 'alone' category: almost a third of the fear incidents had been experienced alone, while joy and anger were rarely experienced alone.

These data lead to the following conclusions: (1) all emotions are mostly experienced in a social context, and rarely in mass situations; (2) joy and anger are relatively more 'social' than the other emotions; and (3) fear is quite different from the other emotions, being experienced more frequently alone and in a non-social context (see also Chapters 5 and 9).

The data for familiarity presented in Figure 11.2 show a similar picture. Fear stands out from the other emotions in that it was experienced more frequently in the presence of unfamiliar people, while the other emotions were mostly experienced in the presence of familiar people. Thus, fear can be described as being a relatively 'non-social' emotion, while the other emotions are largely 'social'.

We computed a series of ANOVAs for the different reaction variables, using group size (from 1 = alone to 4 = large group), social support (familiar vs. unfamiliar people), or social versus non-social interaction (dyad + small group vs. alone + large group) as the independent variable in each ANOVA.

Duration

For three of the four emotions, duration did not vary as a function of group size, familiarity, or social versus non-social interaction. For sadness, all three ANOVAs yielded significant results, showing sadness to be of longer duration in a social context, and of shorter duration in a non-social (i.e. alone or in a large mass of people, with unfamiliar people) context.

Intensity

The results for intensity were very similar to those found for duration: for joy, fear, and anger, the intensity of the emotion did not vary as a function of the social versus non-social distinction. For sadness, all three ANOVAs yielded significant results, showing that sadness is experienced with greater intensity in a social context (i.e. in a dyad or a small group of familiar people). The other emotions seemed to be experienced with equal intensity in social and non-social situations.

Amount of verbalisation

Here most results were highly significant but the major explanation is rather trivial: one verbalises less when one is alone or in the company of unfamiliar people. Or, conversely: one verbalises more when one is not alone, and especially with familiar people. Obviously, this is true for all four emotions without distinction. However, there was an interesting distinction for group size across the emotions. While the smallest amount of verbalisation was reported for the 'alone' category for all four emotions, the largest amount of verbalisation was reported for the large group category for fear and anger, but for the dyad category for joy and sadness. Thus, joy and sadness seem to be more 'private' emotions in terms of the amount of verbalisation (sharing joy and sadness with one familiar person), while in fear and anger there is more verbalisation when more people are around. In other words, one is more apt to verbalise fear and anger in a mass situation than to verbalise joy and sadness.

Control of verbalisation

Here the results are quite complex and rather interesting. But first we should report a trivial finding which complements the previous report on the amount of verbalisation: for all four emotions, subjects reported the least amount of control of verbalisation when they were alone. Since subjects tended not to verbalise their emotions when they were alone, obviously they needed to exercise less control over these non-occurrences. A more interesting question is when do people exercise the highest degree of control? We found that for joy, sadness, and fear the highest control of verbalisation was exercised in large group, or mass situations, while for anger the highest level of control was exercised in small group situations. It is easy to understand why people will make an effort to control their verbalisation about their intense emotional experiences in the presence of many people. For anger, though, the picture might be different. It might be more dangerous in terms of the social consequences to express uncontrolled anger in a small group than in a mass situation, where the anger does not have a clear and identified victim.

With regard to familiarity, we found differences across the emotions in the control of verbalisation. For fear, verbalisation was equally controlled whether the other people present were familiar or unfamiliar. This is not surprising if we remember that fear differs from the other emotions in the high proportion of its incidence in the presence of strangers. For the other three emotions, the pattern was not uniform: verbalisations of joy were more controlled in the presence of unfamiliar than of familiar people, while verbalisations of sadness and anger were more controlled in the presence of familiar people. It seems to us that the explanation for this interaction is again related to social consequences: one can readily share intense joy experiences with familiar people without control and that is socially acceptable. But expressing uncontrolled anger and uncontrolled sadness toward familiar people might be less acceptable and more costly – uncontrolled anger can spoil the relationships with familiar people, while uncontrolled sadness is something that one's friends often cannot cope with!

Control of physiological symptoms/non-verbal reactions

In contrast to the control of verbalisation, the control of reactions/symptoms is less affected by social aspects. Significant correlations were obtained for sadness only. For joy, fear, and anger, the control of symptoms was unrelated to group size, familiarity, or social versus non-social interaction.

In sadness situations, symptoms/reactions were controlled least when subjects were alone, and most when they were with more than two people (i.e. small or large group). Greater control of sadness reactions was used in the presence of familiar, as compared to unfamiliar people.

To understand the greater importance of control in sadness situations, we must consider the nature of the more prevalent reactions for each emotion. For joy, the major reactions were smiling and laughing, and there is generally no need to exercise control over the types of reactions in joyous situations. For fear and anger there was no particular type of perceivable behaviour that was far more prevalent than other reactions. Fear was characterised by internal physiological reactions that are not visible to outside observers, while for anger the most important reactions were changes in voice quality. Therefore, subjects probably saw no need to differentiate levels of control over symptoms/reactions for these emotions. The case is different for sadness, where the predominant reaction was crying. As Scherer (1977) pointed out, crying is a 'non-negotiable' reaction that cannot remain uncontrolled in social situations. Therefore, control of sadness symptoms/reactions was greater as a function of the number of people involved in the situation.

Review of individual emotions

We now briefly summarise the accumulated findings for each emotion.

Joy was found to be an essentially 'social emotion' in terms of group size, social support, and social versus non-social interaction variables. The duration and intensity of joy were found to be unrelated to these social aspects. In terms of verbal expression, it was found that joy was verbalised most in social settings – dyads and small groups of familiar people. It was also found that, for this emotion only, subjects reported exercising less control of verbalisation and of symptoms/reactions in the presence of familiar than in the presence of unfamiliar people. Thus, as a social emotion, joy is more private and intimate, but it is not felt necessary to control or limit its expression in intimate settings.

Sadness was also found to be essentially a 'social emotion', although less so than joy and anger. Sadness was experienced mostly in social settings and with familiar people, but, more than for joy and anger, it was experienced in 'alone' situations as well. For sadness, the social aspects were most strongly related to the variables under investigation. Unlike the situation for the other emotions, the duration and intensity of sad experiences are related to the social aspects – greater intensity and longer duration were reported for these experiences in social, compared to non-social settings. Sadness was also more verbalised in a social setting (dyad and small group) and in the presence of familiar people, but in these settings more control of verbalisation and of symptoms/reactions was exercised. We suggest that the greater demand for the control of the emotional expression of sadness in social settings stems not only from its greater duration and intensity in social interactions, but also from the special 'non-negotiable' nature of the predominant expression of sadness: crying.

Fear was found to be the least social of the four emotions. It was experienced alone more often and in a dyad or small group less often than the other emotions, and it was experienced more in the presence of unfamiliar than in the presence of familiar people. Since fear is more non-social than the other emotions, it is not surprising that the social aspects were found to be largely unrelated to the dependent variables for this emotion. The duration and intensity of fear were unrelated to group size, social support, and social versus non-social interaction. Fear was more verbalised but also more controlled in large group situations. In addition, fear was verbalised more frequently in the presence of familiar people than of unfamiliar people, but the control of verbalisation was unrelated to familiarity. Finally, the social variables were found to be unrelated to the control of fear symptoms/reactions, and we suggest that this is due to the fact that fear reactions are more physiological and internal than reactions for the other emotions, and are not readily visible to other people.

Like joy, anger is clearly a social emotion, experienced mostly in social settings (dyads and small groups), mostly in the presence of familiar people, and seldomly alone. Anger is not a particularly private emotion, and was strongly verbalised in large group situations. When anger is expressed in large group situations, the angry person does not exert much effort to control the angry verbalisations. However, in more intimate social settings and in the presence of familiar people, more control of verbalisation is exercised, and we suggest that this control prevents negative social consequences to anger. Finally, since no prevalent physical symptoms – except for voice changes – are characteristic of anger, the level of control of symptoms/ reactions was found to be unrelated to the social aspects under investigation.

11.3 Findings on social and non-social antecedents

Section 11.2 deals with the characteristics of people involved in the emotional situation: how many people were involved and how familiar were they to the respondent. This section deals with the antecedents of the emotional situations and their level of sociability. It is reasonable to expect probable combinations of antecedents, group size, and social support that are either totally 'social' or totally 'non-social'. In other words, social antecedents will more probably lead to a social experience. And yet we point out in Section 11.1 that social antecedents can sometimes lead to a non-social experience or that non-social antecedents can lead to a social experience.

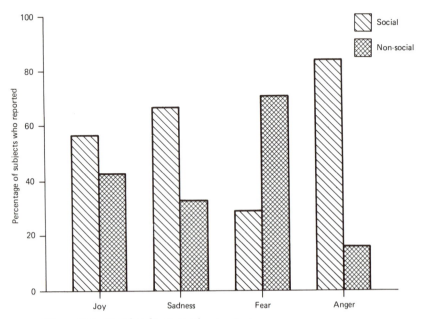

Figure 11.3   Social and non-social antecedents

Distinguishing between social and non-social antecedents of emotions can add to our understanding of the nature of emotion. Examination of group size and familiarity (see Section 11.2) showed fear to be a relatively non-social emotion and joy and anger to be highly social emotions. Is this also true in terms of the events that cause these emotions? Are there particular social or non-social events which tend to create particular emotions? And finally, how are aspects of the actual experience of emotion (duration, intensity, verbalisation, control) related to, and influenced by the social or non-social nature of these antecedents?

The first step we took in trying to answer these questions was to divide the entire list of antecedents in the codebook into social and non-social categories. About half of the listed antecedents were social, and the other half were non-social. Social antecedents included relationships (with friends, family, acquaintances), group behaviour, temporary and permanent separations and meetings, the appearance or departure of persons (through birth, death, etc.), meeting strangers, and being victims of injustice caused by other people. Non-social antecedents included news, achievement-related causes (success, failure), formal rituals, 'body and mind centred' phenomena (sickness, pain, physical harm, food, nature, art, material goods, etc.), traffic-related antecedents, the supernatural, the risk and external forces.

The proportions of social and non-social antecedents reported for the four emotions are shown in Figure 11.3. The data are based on the total sample, with no distinction for the various countries. As can be seen from the figure, the emotions differed greatly in the sociability of their antecedents. Fear was clearly again a non-social emotion, while anger had a very high proportion of social antecedents. Thus, our previous conclusions are confirmed and sharpened by these data.

While joy and anger were grouped together as the most social emotions in the previous analysis, here we find joy to have been somewhat less social than anger. Examining the specific social and non-social antecedents for joy, we find that almost half of all joy antecedents were concerned with relationships (22%), temporary meetings (15%), and acquisition of new friends (4%). Most of the non-social antecedents (and about a third of all joy antecedents) were related to achievement and success (15%), mind and body pleasures (10%), and good news (8%) (see Chapter 4).

A similar analysis of the specific antecedents of sadness shows that the predominant social antecedents were relationships (26%), death (21%), and temporary and permanent separations (13%). The most prevalent non-social antecedents were bad news (9%), pain and sickness (9%), and failure (7%). As for anger, here only clear and frequently used categories of social antecedents could be identified: relationships (37%), anger at strangers who did not behave well and were inconsiderate (18%), and anger at people who took advantage, caused an injustice, or victimised the respondent (18%). No clear non-social antecedents of anger could be identified.

The non-social nature of fear is expressed not only in the extremely low proportion of social antecedents, but also in the salient lack of 'relationships' antecedents (only 4%). The social antecedents that were mentioned for fear consisted mainly of fear of attack by strangers (14%) and fear that familiar persons might die (5%). The prevalent non-social antecedents included traffic (20%), fear of the unknown (13%), fear of failure (12%), phobias and fears of external forces ranging from the weather to faulty machines (10%), and body-related fears (7%).

Using social versus non-social antecedents as an independent variable, and looking again at duration, intensity, verbalisation, control of verbalisation, and control of symptoms/reactions, most comparisons yielded results of greater significance (longer duration, more verbalisation, etc.) for social than for non-social antecedents. The patterns of these results were in line with those of the findings on group size, familiarity, and social versus non-social interaction.

For joy, situations with social antecedents were more intense than situations with non-social antecedents. For sadness, social antecedents resulted in longer and more intense experiences. Experiences of fear were longer when they had social antecedents, and only anger was unrelated to social versus non-social antecedents.

For joy, fear, and anger, respondents reported a higher level of verbalisation in situations with social antecedents. This was not the case for sadness, but subjects reported exercising a higher degree of control of verbalisation and of symptoms/reactions in sadness situations with social antecedents. For joy and fear, the higher level of verbalisation in social situations did not lead to a higher level of control of verbalisation, while for anger there was more control of verbalisation following social antecedents. Finally, there were no differences in the control of symptoms/reactions for these three emotions.

To summarise these results by emotion: experiences of joy were more intense when they had social antecedents, and respondents reported having verbalised more in these situations. There were no differences for the control variables. Experiences of sadness were longer and more intense following social antecedents, and respondents employed more control of verbalisation and of symptoms/reactions. Fear experiences were longer following social antecedents and respondents verbalised more in these situations, but there were no differences in the control variables. Experiences of anger were neither longer nor more intense following social antecedents, but respondents verbalised their anger more and controlled their verbalisation more in the social situations. These patterns quite clearly follow those of the results given in Section 11. 2.

Finally, we examined the prevalent physiological symptoms and non-verbal reactions reported for each of the emotions, and compared the proportions of their occurrence in situations with social and non-social antecedents. (Only differences larger than 5% between the proportions of a given symptom for social and non-social antecedents are mentioned.) For joy, the most prevalent reactions were laughing and smiling (about 40% of the reactions), but no differences were found for the specific antecedent groups. For sadness, crying and muscle symptoms were most prevalent, and both these symptoms were reported as occurring more often in social situations (37% vs. 22% for crying; 24% vs. 18% for muscle symptoms). In addition, 'general unpleasant rest sensations' were mentioned as occurring more often in non-social situations (21% vs. 15%). In fear situations, the prevalent reactions were 'muscular symptoms' and 'stomach troubles', and both differed for social and non-social antecedents: stomach troubles were more frequent in social situations (25% vs. 19%), while muscular symptoms like trembling were more frequent in non-social situations (45% vs. 33%). The most prevalent reaction to anger was 'changed voice quality', and it was mentioned as occurring more often in social situations (31% vs. 21%). In addition, 'changed movement quality' was also higher for social situations (11% vs. 5%).

These differences in physiological symptoms/non-verbal reactions are quite limited, and we believe that symptoms and reactions were largely uninfluenced by whether the antecedents were social or non-social. The largest, and probably most meaningful difference (37% vs. 22%) was found for crying in sadness situations, where most crying was reported for situations with social antecedents. This probably accounts for the significant difference found for this emotion in the control of symptoms/reactions.

11.4 Individual differences in the sociability of the emotions

Although this research project did not focus on individual differences, we defined a dimension of individual differences describing a person's tendency to describe social or non-social emotional situations. Using the distinction between social and non-social antecedents discussed in Section 11.3, we counted for each respondent the number of emotions with social antecedents. The range of this frequency scale was 0–4, with 0 describing an extreme non-social tendency, and 4 describing an extremely social stance. The distribution of subjects on this scale was uneven ($0 = 16$; $1 = 117$; $2 = 309$; $3 = 255$; $4 = 77$), with a mean of 2.34 'social' situations per subject. For the purposes of the present analysis, the values 0 and 1 were combined to form a 'low' category, and the values 3 and 4 were combined to form a 'high' category.

A series of ANOVAs were computed, using this dimension of individual differences. The first ANOVAs analysed demographic information: age, the number of brothers and sisters, the number of years spent at the university, the place where the subject had spent most of his or her life, and social class. None of these ANOVAs yielded significant differences, indicating that the tendency to experience emotions more socially (or rather, to report more social emotional situations) is unrelated to these demographic indices. As for sex, the analysis yielded a highly significant value, with females reporting more social antecedents to their emotional experiences than males.

It is hardly surprising that the females' emotions were more socially oriented than those of the males. However, we can only speculate about the reasons for this difference. Females might simply be more 'social' than males, or they might be more sensitive than males to social-emotional cues, or they might be more highly motivated than males to maintain social relationships, attaching more affect to interpersonal issues. It might also be the case that males are more egocentric (or even more egotistical) than females, therefore describing more situations centred on the self and less situations dealing with others.

The next series of ANOVAs analysed the relations between the tendency to describe more social situations and the averaged values for the duration and intensity of an emotion, verbalisation, and the control of verbalisation and of symptoms/reactions. Unlike the previous analyses of these variables, which were intended to distinguish between the four emotions, here the average value (say, average duration) for each person across all four emotions was used. Subjects who tended to describe more emotional situations with social antecedents also reported a longer duration of emotional experience, a higher average intensity of emotion, verbalised more and also exercised more control over their verbalisations. In line with earlier findings, no significant effect was found for the control of symptoms/reactions.

Thus, very 'social' subjects experienced their emotions more intensely and with longer duration then 'non-social'subjects, they spoke more during these experiences, and tended to control their verbalisations more.

Finally, we asked whether subjects from the different countries in the sample would differ in this tendency to report social-emotional situations. We found that there were country differences, with German-speaking subjects (German and Swiss) showing the highest tendency for social situations (mean number of social situations reported: 2.5), Israeli and Italian subjects showing the lowest tendency for social situations (2.1), with French and Spanish subjects (2.2) and Belgian and British subjects (2.3) in between these extremes.

It is not easy to explain these cross-national differences. Commonly held stereotypes would not predict German-speaking people to be more socially orientated than Mediterranean people. On the contrary, intuitive notions would probably hold Italians to be more socially orientated than Germans. Examination of the prevalent antecedents reported from each country shows that Israelis mentioned news, achievement, strangers, and justice (mostly non-social antecedents) more often than subjects from other countries, and social antecedents such as relationships, temporary and permanent meetings and separation less frequently than subjects from other countries. This would account for the low social value found for Israel, but it does not conclusively show Israelis to be less social. It could mean that other salient concerns overshadow the social orientation when one is asked to describe one situation for each emotion.

11.5 Confirmation and disconfirmation of national stereotypes

The last discussion in this chapter is also the most speculative: all the data can have two or three plausible interpretations. We said earlier that the very fact that there was no intention of analysing national stereotypes in this study and that the self-report descriptions used in this project are hardly appropriate data for stereotypy research made it more exciting to use the data to examine the confirmation or disconfirmation of stereotypes, that is to see whether the self-reports of subjects from different countries follow some of the commonly held notions about the people from these countries. But the ancient saying that 'exceptions might only prove the rule' could be relevant here, leading us to except disconfirmation of stereotypes to be the rule rather than the exception. That which is less conventional and more unusual can gain high salience, and by this argument respondents would describe emotional situations that deviate from the common stereotypes. It is known in the literature on stereotyping (see e.g. Babad, Birnbaum, & Benne, 1983) that definitions of people by self and others tend to under-estimate commonalities and overestimate the unique and the different. Therefore, data that do not follow stereotypic conceptions would not necessarily negate these stereotypes.

The last finding reported in the last part of Section 11.4 exemplifies the problems involved in interpreting these data in terms of stereotypes. On the face of it, the findings showing the greater social orientation of German-speaking subjects compared to Israelis and Italians disconfirmed widely held stereotypes. But there might be special contingencies – ranging from the political situation to the specific wording of the translated questionnaire – that might influence and distort the overall pattern of the different factors. Moreover, the overriding phenomenon emerging out of this entire project is one of great international commonality in the experience of emotion. In the language of cross-cultural research (see Segall, 1979) the *etics* in the experience of emotion are far more powerful and dominant than the *emics*. The correlations between antecedents or other groups of variables for the different emotions among the various countries are extremely high (maybe excluding Israel, where the patterns are slightly different), and differences in frequencies or means, even if statistically significant, do not reflect great effect magnitudes. Thus, it is somewhat difficult to discuss stereotypes, which stress differentiation, when the overall picture shows much uniformity.

Despite all this, it is exciting to compare the patterns emerging from this study for the different cultural groups to the commonly held images of these groups, particularly if this analysis is taken with a grain of salt and more than a grain of doubt. In fact, in Section 11.4 we examined not only the image of Israelis and Italians ('Mediterraneans') as being more socially oriented than the Germans and the Swiss ('German-speaking'), but also the image of women being more socially oriented than men. The first stereotype was disconfirmed, the second was confirmed.

On the basis of commonly held images of different cultural groups in Europe, a picture of predictions could be drawn for various aspects in this study. The German and the Swiss would tend to be hard-working and achievement-oriented, paying less attention to relationships and social aspects. Southern Europeans would pay less attention to work and achievement and focus much more on social relationships. This would be due to the stronger family ties, family structure, and recreational patterns in countries such as Italy. Northern Europeans would be more reserved socially. Other stereotypes focus on the expression of emotion. Some groups are held to be cool and reserved, while others are perceived to be temperamental, uninhibited, and highly expressive. Images of Italian women crying at funerals or Italian men engaged in loud discussions or quarrels in streets and market places and 'palavering a lot' would be contrasted with the British (and possibly German) tendency to control the expression of emotion and appear cold, aloof, and unemotional. This would be indicated in differences in the reported intensity of emotion, of the amount of verbalisation, and of the control of verbalisation and other reactions. Israeli subjects would be expected to differ from the other European groups. Israel's location in the Middle East makes it a 'non-European' country, and the continuous war and conflict would certainly tend to influence how the Israelis experience their emotions. In addition, the images of the collective life on the Kibbutz, the camaraderie among soldiers facing dangers together, and the recent creation of a viable state out of groups of victimised immigrants coming from many countries, lead one to expect Israelis to stress relationships, cohesion, and national unity.

Some of these stereotypes were confirmed, but most of them were disconfirmed by the respondents' reports. The German and Swiss subjects mentioned relationships antecedents more than the other groups, while the Italian and Spanish groups mentioned achievement situations more than the other groups. The German and Swiss subjects mentioned achievement the least often of all the groups, while the Spaniards and Israelis scored lowest in the relationships category (see also Chapter 5).

The Italian, British, and Spanish subjects reported the highest average intensity for all four emotions. Subjects from West Germany, Belgium, Switzerland, and France reported a lower intensity, and the lowest intensity was reported by the Israeli subjects. Probably the most surprising elements here are the high emotional intensity reported by the British and the low intensity reported by the Israelis.

The British were surprising in the amount of verbalisation as well. The highest levels of verbalisation were reported by the Swiss, British and Italian subjects, and the lowest levels by the French and Belgian subjects. The least amount of control of verbalisation was reported by the Italian, Spanish, and Swiss subjects, and the greatest amount of control by the Belgian, French and German subjects. As for the control of physiological symptoms/non-verbal reactions, the least amount of control was reported by the German,

Swiss and Italian subjects, and the most by the Belgian, French, and British subjects (see Chapters 7 and 8).

The picture that emerged for the Italians is surprising in terms of achievement orientation and relationships, but fits the stereotypic picture for the other variables: the Italians were more verbal and exercised less control over their verbalisations and their reactions than did the other nationalities. In addition, we also found that the Italians and Spaniards reported more situations taking place outside, while the Belgians and Germans reported more situations taking place inside. The picture that emerged for the British is somewhat surprising, in that the British reported a very high level of verbalisation. This goes against the image of and the numerous jokes about Britons speaking very little. On the other hand, the high level of control of symptoms/reactions found for the British group is in line with held stereotypes. The findings about the Swiss subjects were very surprising. Contrary to stereotypic expectations, the Swiss mentioned relationships most often and achievement least often. The Swiss reported a high amount of verbalisation, and a low level of the control of verbalisation and the control of symptoms/reactions. In fact, it might be suggested in light of the findings that Switzerland emerges as a 'Southern European' country rather than a 'German-speaking' country. If we had used multi-dimensional scaling techniques to draw the 'map' of Europe according to the findings in this research, the emerging map would probably be quite different from what is found in the atlas.

The Israeli group emerged as being quite different from the other European groups (see Appendix A8). The reported intensity of emotional experience was the lowest of all the countries; Israelis mentioned relationships and groups least frequently, and were very high in the categories 'news', 'impact of strangers', and 'death'. Some of this might not be surprising if one remembers the unique conditions of living in Israel. In fact, opinions are divided as to whether Israel is in fact a European country. In terms of the Eurovision song contest and the basketball championship games, Israel is part of Europe. In terms of international soccer and in the minds of geographers, Israel is part of Asia. And Israel's population is a mix of people of European, American, Asian, and African origin.

In summary, it is clear that some of the observed patterns in this study did not follow the expected stereotypic predictions for subjects from the different countries. It is true that overall there were more commonalities than differences, and the different nationalities were more similar to each other in the observed patterns than might have been expected. But where differences between countries did exist, they rarely followed the commonly held stereotypes. Maybe the implication should be that long-held stereotypes must be revised. Or one might even dream that stereotypes will disappear into oblivion. However, the picture is not that simple. As cognitive organisers of a person's social world, stereotypes are not likely to disappear, and it is known that stereotypes are extremely resistant to disconfirming information.

The setting of writing open-ended essays describing emotional experiences is not the most appropriate one for the study of stereotypes. Self-report does not necessarily reflect valid 'reality'. The responses reflect what people say about their behaviour, not their behaviour itself. It is quite conceivable that people's reports deviate from or even contradict, what they actually do: the British subjects might have emphasised verbalisations because they did *not* verbalise very much and their baseline was so low as to make any verbalisation seem more intense. Or the Southern Europeans might have stressed achievement situations because they are *not* achievement-orientated, and so made any achievement situation salient in an exaggerated way. Or the Swiss might have accentuated in their self-reports unique facts that are *not* characteristic of the Swiss.

Given sufficient time, stereotypes can change, especially in the light of accumulated disconfirming information. To give one example, Japanese workmanship was considered of the worst quality in the 1950s. The label 'Made in Japan' was simply derogatory then. Today, following great changes in quality control and in Japanese industry in general, Japanese workmanship is highly regarded all over the world. The Princeton studies (Karlins, Coffman, & Walters, 1969), in which a series of national stereotypes were investigated three times over a span of 36 years, showed that the contents of specific stereotypes may well change over time, but that the basic phenomenon of stereotyping remains unchanged.

Europe has changed in the last decades, and stereotypes are bound to change as well. Many factors combine to diminish the sharpness of stereotypic distinctions: the Common Market, the easy access and movement among countries, and the impact of television, which serves as a great equaliser even if at times it promotes national stereotypes. It is not inconceivable that we are witnessing the emergence of a more global 'European' entity that differs from the 'American' or the 'Japanese'entity, but is moving toward more uniformity within it.

12 Emotion experiences across European cultures: a summary statement

Klaus R. Scherer

When we embarked on this work in 1979, there was little in the literature that could have helped us to formulate specific hypotheses concerning the nature of everyday emotional experiences. The intent of the study was clearly exploratory – an attempt to gather information concerning situations that regularly evoke specific emotional responses and to assess the nature of the corresponding bodily and behavioural reactions. The presentation of the data from this questionnaire study with 779 respondents in eight European countries fills a whole monograph and yet we are painfully aware of the fact that our analyses have not done justice to the richness of the material that was collected. There is still much that could be used for carrying out additional analyses, particularly of a more qualitative kind.

At the same time we realise that although the patterns of results that we present in this book may be interesting and stimulating, their status as evidence is limited. Since very few of the differences or trends that we have reported were formally or even informally predicted, the use of significance tests can only be regarded as an attempt to guard against the interpretation of trivial differences. We had hoped from the beginning that the results from this study would be able to serve as a point of departure for future studies in this area. Therefore in this summary we have presented patterns of results in the form of hypotheses to be tested in further work. In doing this, we have taken advantage of the licence that a concluding chapter affords, and have gone beyond the data at times to explore speculatively the direction that the results point to.

This summary is organised along the lines of the major issues touched on in the original questionnaire. Even though the shorthand labels for the emotions are used, as throughout the monograph, it should be recalled that subjects were given two labels for each emotion in the original questionnaire, suggesting a broader range for each of the specific emotions (i.e. joy/happiness, sadness/grief, fear/fright, anger/rage). It may be important to keep in mind while evaluating some of the patterns of results summarised in this chapter.

12.1   Frequency of occurrence of specific emotional events

In a questionnaire study of the kind conducted here, which collected actuarial data, it is interesting to assess the rate or frequency with which events leading up to specific emotions occur. The format of our questionnaire was not particularly suited for this, since we just asked the respondents to report one situation each for the four major emotions that had happened during the previous four weeks. In doing so we had assumed that almost everybody would have a sufficiently intense experience of the four emotions within the course of those four weeks. Apparently, this was not the case. Since we asked how long ago the respective event had happened and since the respondents varied widely in terms of the recency of the reported events, we could at least estimate the average frequency of specific emotional experiences that were intense enough to be stored in the long-term memory. Clearly, this can only be a very rough estimate since there are likely to be strong individual differences in terms of how hard the respondent tried to remember an emotion-eliciting event in the recent past rather than just writing down a notable event that happened years ago and that came readily to mind when the emotion label was encountered. It is hard to believe that the respondents reporting sadness events which happened years ago had not been sad since.

Yet, on the average, and given the large number of respondents, it might be legitimate to hypothesise about the frequency of emotional incidents with threshold intensity. One of the four kinds of emotion had occurred within at least several months for almost all of the respondents. Thus, it is probably safe to assume that every few months we experience emotions of sufficient intensity to allow us to retrieve the situation from memory with ease at a later date and to describe it in detail. Anger and joy seemed to occur most frequently: for three-quarters of the respondents the respective situation had occurred within the last four weeks and, particularly for anger, almost half of the respondents had had such an experience in the last four weeks. For sadness and fear, on the other hand, only two-thirds of the respondents reported an incident that had occurred within the last four weeks. One might assume, therefore, that these emotions are somewhat less frequent than anger and joy, although about a third of the respondents reported a sadness or fear incident within the last week. Generally, however, we might be justified to hypothesise the following rank order in terms of frequency of occurrence of situations eliciting the respective emotion:

anger > joy > sadness > fear

Obviously, the intensity of the respective emotional experience has to be controlled for if the actuarial frequency of different emotions is to be studied empirically in a serious way. Since the intensity of the emotional experience is directly dependent on the subjective evaluation of the situation, this is no easy task. As the intensity of the experience most likely affects the conditions of memory storage of the event as well as the ease of retrieval, it may be necessary to use more direct measures of memory retrieval to explore this issue.

12.2 Types of antecedent situations

What types of regularly occurring situations or events are likely to provoke the four major emotions? Which are the central features or life circumstances involved? In trying to answer these questions we are of course bound by the limits of the coding scheme for antecedent situations which we developed in the course of this study. As described in Chapter 3, our procedure in developing this scheme was rather eclectic and orientated toward face validity, particularly in terms of how well we were able to categorise the situations reported in the large-scale pilot study conducted beforehand. This inductive procedure has its advantages in that it protects one from adopting a level of abstraction that might be too far removed from reality.

As shown in Chapter 4, some types of antecedent situations occurred remarkably more often than others for the specific emotions: for joy these were 'relationships with friends', 'meeting friends', and 'success experiences'; for sadness 'problems with friends', and 'death of friends'; for fear 'traffic', 'physical aggression by others', 'fear of unknown', and 'achievement-related situations'; and for anger 'failure of friends, others, and relatives to conform to social norms' and 'inappropriate rewards for self'.

On examination of these types of antecedent situations, it becomes obvious that what underlies virtually all of the categories is a need, motive, goal, or expectation that is of primary significance for the individual and thus highly ego-involving. Following Frijda (in press), we have chosen the term 'concern' as a more general description of the state of psychological striving that underlies the respective emotions.

What, then, are the primary concerns that seem to have been affected in the situations reported by the large majority of our respondents? It seems possible to identify three major types of concerns: person concerns, relationship concerns, and social order concerns. Person concerns concentrate on the individual, both in terms of the physical body and the psychological identity, that is the self. The primary concerns here are survival and bodily integrity, that is freedom from pain or injury and fulfilment of the basic needs for nurture, warmth, and protection as well as of higher needs, particularly the intactness of the self-concept and the bolstering of self-esteem.

Relationship concerns reflect the fact that humans, like many other mammals, are social animals. From birth, they are dependent on close relationships with nurturant others, in dyadic and later in group relationships. Concern here is with the establishment, the continued existence, and the intactness of a relationship as well as with its prevailing atmosphere or the integrity of and cohesiveness within social groups. It is rather well-established by now that such relationship needs are central components of the motivational make-up of most social animals.

Social order concerns are more difficult to define briefly. They involve the sense of orderliness and predictability within the social environment and include phenomena such as norms and justice. In other words, individuals have rather strong feelings about what ought to happen in social encounters and how social structures ought to be organised. They assume that others, just as themselves, follow implicit or explicit norms and, in particular, that they themselves will be treated justly and fairly (see the large literature on justice in social psychology, e.g. Deutsch, 1983).

Clearly, these three concerns are not independent of each other. For example, in many ways self-concept and self-esteem are bound up with the nature of dominant relationships. Similarly, individuals import social order concerns to relationships and groups where they are most likely to be monitored. At the same time, it is possible to conceive of a differential centrality of these concerns almost in terms of an onion-like model with person concerns being most central and relationship and social order concerns increasingly more peripheral. To some extent, one could speculate that there is a dimension which has a more biological aspect in the centre of the onion and more cultural aspects as one gets closer to the periphery.

Are the emotions evenly distributed across these patterns of dominant human concerns? Our data seem to indicate that this is not so. On the contrary, one could hypothesise that person concerns, particularly bodily intactness and welfare (e.g. avoidance of injury or death and satisfaction of needs) and self-esteem (as in achievement situations) give rise mainly to joy and fear, depending on whether the goals concerned have been attained or are endangered. Relationship needs, on the other hand, are particularly prone to lead to joy or sadness experiences, depending on how well things go in the relationship or group. Social order concerns are different again and seem to be the main domain of anger situations as exemplified by cases in which the social order is disrupted by inappropriate, norm-violating, or unjust behaviour.

These findings suggest that at least the emotion labels in our language, if not the underlying emotional experiences themselves, are to some extent linked to specific central concerns of the individual. It is instructive to try to assess to what extent a similar pattern holds for animals. It seems reasonable to assume that the status hierarchy in many animal groups could be considered to be linked to a rudimentary sense of social order, with anger-like states resulting when this rank order is threatened by a challenger. Similarly, the search for the emotion of sadness in animals, the existence of which is often debated, could be guided by the notion that this state is particularly linked to relationships and group cohesion. Averill (1968) has argued, in fact, that the adaptive function of grief is to ensure group cohesiveness in species where a social form of existence is necessary for survival. There would be no problem in finding animal equivalences for the person or organism-centred concerns as far as danger is concerned. At the other extreme quiet happiness could be related to comfort states which can be found in quite a few species of animals. To what extent joy is also present is an interesting issue. In humans, exuberant joy seems to be mainly related to self-concept or self-esteem related events and there is the strong possibility that this aspect of organism-centred concerns is less developed in most animals.

Another intriguing issue for further research is the following question: To what extent are experiences of joy or happiness that have been produced by relationship experiences different from those that are related to person concerns? (Joy being the only emotion which was apparently produced by two of the major concerns.) It seems possible that even though we use similar labels, the underlying states are actually quite different.

In the light of the possibility that an emotional experience takes on a special flavour depending on the concern by which it is evoked, it is interesting to look at the results obtained in our study for fear. As mentioned in Chapter 2, in the English version of the questionnaire we had provided the labels fear and fright for this range of emotion. However, since the difference between these two terms was difficult to render in some of the other languages, terms closer to 'anxiety' were used in some of the translations (e.g. the German *Angst*), even though many emotion theorists claim that fear and anxiety are very different emotions. We decided that ·since in popular usage the distinction is not always drawn very precisely, it might be better to invite reports of emotional experiences from what might be a continuous domain in lay psychology. Looking at the antecedents of the situations reported, it would seem possible to reserve the label 'fear' for those situations which are relevant to those person concerns related to the physical aspect of the self, that is particularly survival and freedom from injury, whereas anxiety might be the term used when there is danger to the self in terms of self-concept or self-esteem which affects the long-term welfare of a person (as for example in achievement-related situations). This distinction might encompass other criteria that have been proposed, such as linking fear to specific dangers that are imminent and anxiety to more unspecified dangers in the future. One could argue that threats to the body are likely to be much more immediate and specific than the multiple sources of threat to the self. Obviously, this issue is far too complicated to be dealt with in a satisfactory manner in the present context. However, the results of our study seem to suggest that it would be profitable to use the criterion 'type of antecedent concern' as one of the variables in the discussion of the differences between fear and anxiety.

Much of the foregoing discussion has been highly speculative in nature. At the same time, the consistent occurrence of these concern-related antecedents seems to encourage further theorising and research in the direction of linking specific motivational syndromes or concerns to specific emotions.

To conclude this section, it is interesting to compare to what extent respondents described direct experiences, that is events that had happened to *them*, as compared to emotional experiences that had occurred as a result of empathy with an event that had befallen *someone else*. Only for sadness did we find an appreciable number of respondents, about 20%, who reported the emotional experience as a result of feeling *with* another person. This seemed to be particularly pronounced for death and the end of relationships as a source of sadness in someone else. Again, it is interesting to speculate why this should be so. Is it that the sad event is affecting the relationship with the person who is experiencing it? Or is it that we consider relationships so highly important that we are impressed by our own vulnerability if something happens to someone else's relationships? In any case, it would seem worthwhile pursuing the issue of differential empathy with different emotional states.

12.3 The ecology of emotional experience

In addition to the kind of antecedent event giving rise to an emotional experience, we were interested in the location of the incident and in the type of other persons involved, that is the physical and social ecology of the emotional experience. As one might expect from the importance of relationships for many of the emotional experiences, most events had taken place inside familiar places, presumably the home or the work place, except for fear, which usually took place outside or in unfamiliar surroundings. It is interesting to note that fairly few fear antecedents occurred inside familiar places; this might be an indication that in most of these, presumably public institutions, restaurants, etc., one tends to find fairly structured, role-governed interactions that only occasionally acquire emotional significance. Joy or happiness occur fairly frequently in those contexts and it is not quite clear why this should be so. It has been surprising to us that relatively few anger experiences were reported as taking place *inside* unfamiliar places, even though we often talk about angry reactions to civil servants, shopkeepers, etc. However, the actual incidence seems to be fairly low: according to our study it is either relatives and close friends or total strangers on the street who arouse our anger.

We found similar tendencies for the social ecology of emotional experience. Only in fear situations were people more frequently alone or together with unfamiliar others (which, incidentally, may well add to the fear response). To some extent this was also true in sadness, possibly because of the frequent antecedent pattern of separation and the break-up of relationships. In most of the other cases, however, the respondents experienced emotion while with others in dyadic relationships. Very often these others were familiar friends or relatives. This again demonstrates the essentially social nature of most emotions, not only in terms of the antecedents, but also in terms of the settings in which emotional experience unfolds.

12.4 Subjective feeling states

We asked the respondents to provide a detailed verbal description of their emotional experience. The extent to which this opportunity further to qualify verbally the emotion description was used shows that the broad labels which we had used as elicitors did not do justice at all to the special nature of the emotional feeling. Many respondents wrote rather lengthy descriptions, using a variety of emotion terms in an attempt to get at the subtle characteristics of their unique experience. On reading these descriptions, it became quite clear that many respondents had trouble in rendering verbally the quality of the feeling. The descriptions that were provided, however, were highly differentiated and of an enormous richness. It remains for future, more qualitative analyses to use this interesting material.

In the present monograph we analysed statistically the intensity of the emotional experiences, which we assessed by a ten-point scale, and the duration of the emotional feeling, which we measured by coding the free response into a five-point scale (with specific time period indications for each category). The intensity data were somewhat difficult to evaluate since we asked for reports of *major* emotional events in the questionnaire. Presumably, all of these were characterised by a fairly high intensity. It is thus not surprising that the mean intensity reached 7.3 on the scale from 0 to 9.

In spite of this obvious floor effect, we found an interesting difference between the emotions: anger experiences were reported to be significantly lower in intensity than the other emotional experiences. There are a number of possible explanations for this. One possibility is that anger situations, as shown in Chapter 5, seem to occur more frequently than other situations with an intensity reaching the threshold required to enter the long-term memory. Since one might assume that the intensity distribution is skewed toward the lower end, it would seem likely that more instances with lower intensity should be reported at a given point of questioning. Alternatively, it would seem possible that the experienced and/or reported intensities are lower because of the strong social control of anger (see below). Finally, a third explanation could be derived from the discussion about concerns above. If indeed social order concerns are relatively less central to the individual than the person and relationship concerns, one might assume that the experienced intensity of emotions related to that concern are likely to be lower. In any case, we believe that this may be a rather stable effect and would suggest the hypothesis, to be tested in further studies, that anger experiences are on the whole, significantly lower in intensity than the experiences of joy, sadness, or fear.

The duration of the emotional experience is of particular interest, since it relates to the important conceptual issue of distinguishing between emotions and moods. In this study we found highly significant differences in the reported duration for the four emotions (see Chapter 9). Based on this pattern of data we would suggest the following hypotheses for future research:

> Fear lasts from a few seconds up to a maximum of an hour. The assumption underlying this hypothesis is that fear is an emergency response par excellence which is usually provoked by an immediate stimulus event requiring flight or submission to the aversive consequences. It is likely, then, that this very high-intensity emotion will be rather short-lived and could not be endured for longer periods of time. Obviously, this is not true for anxiety (see discussion above).

> Anger lasts from a few minutes up to a maximum of a few hours. The assumption here is that this emotion is fairly transient, since it is mostly related to discrete events that require either coping or internal adaptation. It would seem unlikely that anger will persist if the person is no longer exposed to its object or constantly reminded of it.

> Joy lasts from about an hour to a maximum of a day. It is to be expected that joy is a more lasting emotion because of the significant concerns relating to the self or to salient relationships.

> Sadness lasts from about a day to several days. The assumption here is that in most cases important relationship concerns underly the occurrence of this emotion, and that extensive 'grief work' is required for adapting to the changed situation.

These predictions are meant to cover the majority of the respective emotional experiences with the clear acknowledgment that there may be exceptions in terms of shorter and longer durations. One would assume generally that the range of durations is determined by the centrality and long-term significance of the respective concern.

Many theorists might find it difficult to envisage emotions lasting for longer than several hours, and would perhaps raise the question about the difference between emotions and moods. Ekman (1984) argues that facial muscle action rarely lasts for longer than four seconds and that even slower systems, like the autonomic system, are unlikely to be affected for more than a few hours. He proposes to call anything that transcends the possible duration of changes in these organic sub-systems a 'mood'. Our respondents, however, frequently reported the duration of joy and sadness (and in some cases even of anger and fear) to be longer than a few hours. Do we have to assume that the original emotions blend into happy and depressed moods, respectively, without the respondents noticing or acknowledging a difference in their reports? One might argue that unless the respondents themselves notice a qualitative change in their feeling about the event, one should not distinguish between emotion and mood. However, even if one does agree that the distinction between emotion and mood depends on the length of time for which changes in the organic components last, it may be difficult clearly to demarcate the change from emotion to mood. There is no all-or-nothing pattern in the presence or absence of organic changes; on the contrary, there is probably a gradual decrease in the number and intensity of symptoms in the various sub-systems. It will be difficult to decide what the critical level required for an emotion is. This question hinges on the necessary and sufficient requirements for a definition of 'emotion'.

One could argue that most theorists want to use the term 'emotion' when attention is turned to the emotion-eliciting event, when there is a specific feeling state related to the evaluation of this event, and when there are persisting changes in the physiological and expressive sub-systems. The term 'mood', on the other hand, can be taken to refer to the general 'tuning' of the organism to respond to particular antecedent events or to relive past situations. Mood could also be accompanied by persisting changes (probably at fairly low levels) in organic sub-systems and possibly unconscious concern with specific events. Contrary to emotional experiences, however, we would not expect conscious focussing of attention on either the eliciting event, or a specific feeling state, or a specific proprioceptive feedback of physiological or expressive symptoms. Using this distinction, it would seem to be possible to account for the presence of an emotion of several days, as in sadness, in those cases where the respondents are likely very frequently to re-experience the original event and their reaction to it in such a way that the conscious attention is almost continuously turned toward that situation. While it is unlikely that no other foci of attention, such as practical concerns of living, intervene, a conscious focussing on the emotion-eliciting event and reaction could persist to a point where at least subjectively continuity of the emotional experience is seen.

The theoretical approach adopted here assumes that there is a 'natural' time course for specific emotional experiences linked to specific types of events and functions of adaptation. This implies also that there is a steady decrease in the intensity of the feeling and the severity of the symptoms and a slow return to a balanced state or baseline unless this is interrupted by a re-experiencing of the earlier event and the reactions to it, or the re-enactment of the total emotional experience. It has been argued elsewhere (Scherer, 1985) that if a return to baseline or a change to a new balance at a different level does not occur, we should define the situation as one of 'emotional stress'. The lack of return to a balanced state could be due to (1) continuing stimulation, (2) a lack of coping potential, or (3) cognitive perseveration beyond the normal frequency of re-experiencing.

The patterns of duration of emotional experiences can also be related to emotional disturbance, for example, if the unbalanced state lasts longer than 'normal' or 'appropriate' given the circumstances of the original emotional experience (as judged by a social consensus of significant others). Abnormal duration is obviously only one indicator of emotional disturbance; others are the appropriateness of the type and intensity of the emotional reaction given a specific stimulation. Again, we cannot do justice to this complex issue within the confines of this chapter.

We have dwelt quite extensively on the issue of duration because of the major conceptual importance of this issue and because of the fact that the data set from our study and others like it might be able to provide a first approximation of what could be considered 'normal' or appropriate, given particular types of experiences. It can inform us about the nature of normative expectations that people in a culture might have concerning the appropriate durations for specific emotions.

12.5 Speech activity in emotional situations

While it is often assumed that non-verbal communication is the language of emotion, our results show that emotions are not generally silent. Joy and anger in particular lead people to be quite verbal, and often result in lengthy utterances or discussions. Sadness and fear, on the other hand, are experienced somewhat more silently with either no verbal response or just an exclamation. This may be partly due to the fact that people tend to be alone in sad and fearful situations (see Chapter 5) and partly to the fact that the duration, at least of fear, is rather short. In line with the earlier statement (see Chapter 11) that joy and anger seem to be more social emotions than sadness and fear, we would predict for future work that more social speech activity will be observed for those emotions. We had also asked our respondents to report *what* they said in the respective situation. Given the limited number of analysis techniques available in this area, again we have not so far examined this information systematically. However, reading through the verbalisations reported indicates that a qualitative analysis might yield important information on the cognitive processing involved in emotional experience.

12.6 Non-verbal reactions

Since virtually all of the questions asked in the questionnaire were open-ended, we obtained the results that were to be expected from this format. Not all of the respondents gave specific information on non-verbal reaction and the great diversity in the type of answers made it difficult to categorise the responses. We had decided on the open-ended procedure since we did not want to bias the results by suggesting specific reaction categories to the respondents through lists of behaviours to be checked. However, while we believe that the spontaneously reported patterns are more valid, the analysis suffered by requiring us to group the responses into a small number of fairly global categories in order to obtain frequencies that allow statistical treatment. Some of the results on the non-verbal reaction patterns to the four emotions are therefore not very revealing, and there is not much differentiation between the emotions.

We found, for example, that all four emotions were reported (by more than 5% of the subjects) to have led to changed voice quality, specific voice reactions, and changed facial quality. At most, it is interesting to observe the preponderance of voice reactions and the rare mentioning of specific facial movements. There were a few specific patterns: expressive hand movements occurred for all the emotions but sadness, emphasising the passive nature of this emotion and the reduced non-verbal activity generally. Very specific facial reaction patterns were reported for sadness and anger. Also, as one might expect, laughing and crying differentiated joy and sadness, respectively. Joy was characterised by approach behaviour and expansiveness while freezing was specific to fear. Specific non-verbal reactions for anger were changed movement quality and changed speech quality. Possibly, this was the case because of the social nature of anger and the important role of communication in response to anger situations. It is interesting to speculate about the evolutionary significance of the expression of anger for signalling purposes in socially living species. It is possible that anger, more than the other emotions, is central in communicating reactions to events (particularly the behaviour of others) and behavioural intention to the social surround.

12.7 Physiological symptoms

Because of the open-answer format, as for the non-verbal reactions, the physiological symptoms had to be combined into a fairly small number of categories, mostly referring to the bodily region or location of the experienced symptom, in order to obtain a sufficient frequency of observations for statistical analysis. Furthermore, individuals vary remarkably in how much attention they pay to internal symptoms (see Pennebaker, 1982; Shields, 1984).

Quite apart from these methodological problems, the status of the reports on physiological symptoms is quite uncertain since the debate on whether or not the different emotions are physiologically differentiated continues with unabated vigour. In addition to the well-known problem that people may often be wrong when reporting their internal states (see Pennebaker, 1982), the subjective report of physiological symptoms could be due to cultural or personal implicit theories or stereotypes. However, few of the studies that have attempted to look at subjective reports of physiological symptoms in relation to measured changes in the values of autonomic response systems have dealt with real-life emotions characterised by very intense feelings such as were reported in this study. We have to presume then, that the issue of whether the different emotions are indeed characterised by highly specific patterns of physiological changes and whether individuals can accurately report on these changes is still unsettled and, to some extent, a matter of conjecture.

It is difficult to believe that there is no such differentiation at all and that people are generally wrong in noticing what is going on inside their body. Of course, they do not have the technical vocabulary that is required to describe precisely the processes that are actually occurring. Nevertheless, the subjective reporting of physiological symptoms may at least give us some hunches as to what the underlying patterns might be. We feel encouraged in this belief by the findings in the present study (see also Shields, 1984). Since we had a large number of subjects it is possible to disregard some of the more isolated reports and to concentrate on the basic changes that were described by a fair number of subjects in all of the cultures studied. In spite of the large potential for error in the results we obtained, given that some respondents may not have reported symptoms they really had or may have misreported some of the symptoms, we propose the hypothetical predictions given in Table 12.1: these should be tested in further studies, either in terms of objective measurement or in terms of self-report.

While the predictions are mainly based on the data from the present study, they are also motivated by theoretical considerations (see Scherer, 1986). For example, one could predict an increase in cardio-vascular activity to be

Table 12.1. *Predictions for differential physiological symptom patterns*[a]

	Emotion			
Symptoms	Joy	Sadness	Fear	Anger
Cardio-vascular activity	+	?	+	+
Striated muscle tone	+	−	+	+
Gastric disturbance	o	+	+	+
Skin temperature	+	o	−	+

[a] +, increase; o, no change; −, decrease; ?, no prediction.

primarily due to the arousal produced by a mismatch between an actual state and an expected state, such as might occur for joy, fear, and anger. Such a mismatch occurs for sadness, too, but in sadness situations the event and its consequences cannot be controlled and the person's coping potential is reduced to passive acceptance of and internal adjustment to the new situation. Therefore, we would expect a decrease in striated muscle tone for sadness as compared to an increase in this action-oriented somatic system for joy, fear, and anger, where some action is likely to occur.

For all three negative emotions (sadness, fear, and anger) there is a need for adjustment or adaptation either through internal means as in sadness or through external action as in fear and anger. One could hypothesise therefore, that because of the disturbance of the homeostatic regulation of the internal milieu there is an interference with the smooth functioning of the internal systems, and particularly of the gastro-intestinal regions.

The temperature of the skin distinguishes mainly between anger and fear (see Ekman, Levenson, & Friesen, 1983, for similar results). This effect might be due to the differential involvement of adrenaline and noradrenaline secretion and to differences in the regional blood flow (see Scherer, 1986).

This discussion of physiological concomitants of emotion had to be extremely general. Also, we did not want to venture too far from the rather gross pattern of predictions that the present data set suggests. With an increase in our knowledge about the physiological components of emotion it will be necessary, of course, to develop more precise predictions concerning the details of these processes, such as the complex relations between heart rate, blood pressure and other parameters related to cardio-vascular activity, to pick just one example.

12.8 The control of emotional reactions

Much has been written about the social control of emotion and individual attempts at regulation of the emotional experience, but there are very few empirical data. In this study, we wanted to make a first attempt to understand this phenomenon, if only by asking a rather general question concerning the type of control that respondents had attempted to exert and making the request that respondents should indicate on a rating scale how much control they tried to use. We distinguished between the control of verbalisation, a type of behaviour that is highly subject to normative constraints, and the control of non-verbal reactions and physiological symptoms, which are less obviously monitored by the social environment. On the basis of our findings we would predict that people do attempt to control sadness, fear, and anger across all response modalities whereas they are much less concerned with the control of joy. Interestingly, there was a difference between anger and the two other negative emotions in the amount of control of verbal behaviour: the rated degree of control was highest for anger. It is quite possible that this shows the influence of social sanctions connected with a public display of anger or the desire to avoid an escalation of conflict. This would seem to be in line with what has been suggested in Chapter 11 concerning the rather intricate role of anger in social interaction. It may be a safe prediction that for all types of non-negotiable behaviour, particularly verbal behaviour, anger will be highly controlled.

There was an interesting dependence on the social context for this finding. Whereas for all the other emotions there was more control of verbal behaviour in large groups, control of the verbal expression of anger was greatest in *small* groups. Furthermore, there was more control of sadness and anger in interaction with familiar others, that is friends and relatives, as compared to interaction with unfamiliar others, whereas for joy this was not the case. It would seem possible that in the case of anger this was due to the fact that open expression of anger is perceived to be very dangerous for the continuing existence of a relationship or for the atmosphere within it and that one tries to protect others from the effect of sadness (particularly given the role of empathy described in Chapter 5). It is particularly interesting in this connection that even the internal symptoms are more controlled for sadness when one is together with familiar others. This may serve to prevent 'emotional contagion', given the presumed empathic responsiveness of others to sadness.

12.9 Individual differences in emotional experience

In our questionnaire we asked many questions concerning the family background and the geographical origin of our respondents (see Appendix B). Surprisingly, none of these variables yielded much in the way of differential effects. In addition, there were rather fewer sex differences than we had expected. From data thus collected, and assuming that the differences we found were not exclusively due to reporting bias, we would hypothesise that females are generally more expressive than males, particularly in the face, across all the emotions. Males are likely to be more stoical, experiencing more pleasant rest sensations in joy and more unpleasant rest sensations in sadness. We would predict also that females are in general more sensitive than males to both their internal symptoms and their behaviour, particularly in fear and sadness.

It is interesting to speculate on whether these sex differences are due to a higher sensitivity to emotional experiences or whether they are related to the fact that females suffer more in negative emotional situations. There are some reports about women being generally more negatively affected by stressful life events than are men. And in our study it was in fact only for sadness that we found non-trivial sex differences in the subjective feeling state, with women reporting a tendency toward a higher intensity and a significantly longer duration of the emotional experience than men. This could be due to a number of factors. For one, it is possible that the central concern of relationships is much more important for the definition of a woman's self (for example, women seem to be involved in more social activities than men (Kessler & McLeod, 1984)). Women may thus evaluate changes in relationships as being more serious than men do and experience more intense emotional effects. Alternatively, if women generally express their affect more strongly than men, one could expect them to have increased subjective suffering if one subscribes to a proprioceptive feedback theory concerning the relationship between motor expression and feeling.

We did not use personality scales to try to assess individual differences between respondents (except in the German and Swiss samples, see Appendixes A3 and A5). However, we did split the respondents into three groups depending on how many symptoms they reported generally (sensitisers) and whether they tended to report internal physiological symptoms (internalisers) or external behavioural reactions such as verbal and non-verbal behaviour (externalisers). On the basis of the findings of our study, sensitisers and internalisers are predicted to experience more intense emotions and at the same time to engage in more control of both verbal behaviour and non-verbal behaviour and physiological symptoms than externalisers. It will be interesting to examine whether these are indeed stable personality differences and whether they are related to a repression–sensitisation dimension or to self-monitoring (i.e. objective self-awareness, self-consciousness). Of course, there is still the possibility that those who had more intensive experiences also reported more symptoms. However, since the tendency was visible across all the emotions, it is unlikely that there were respondents who by chance had more intense experiences for the emotions studied here.

12.10 Cultural differences

When we originally embarked on our study, we had expected rather sizeable intercultural differences. Indeed, the interest in possible differences in the emotionality of various European cultures was one of the major incentives for the cross-cultural aspect of the study. In evaluating the data, we were surprised to see how similar both the antecedents and the reponses for the various emotions were across all the cultures. The differences that we did find are very hard to evaluate systematically, particularly since we have to confess to not yet having developed a systematic framework for cross-cultural comparison. What is missing is a theoretical structure, supported, by anthropological work, concerning the major areas in which emotionality is likely to differ in different cultures depending on factors such as values, life-style, and patterns of interaction.

Although there were fewer cross-cultural differences than we had expected, there were several interesting results concerning specific aspects of emotional reactivity in the various countries. Examples are the predominance of basic pleasures reported by the British, the high incidence of closed-in, interior settings for emotional situations in Belgium, and the unexpectedly strong emotionality of the Swiss. It would also be very interesting to pursue the issue of differences between Arabs and Jews in Israel, the issue of potential differences between 'Northerners' and 'Southerners', the interesting issue of high achievement motivation in the southern countries, and a number of other patterns of this sort. Since none of these differences was predicted, we have been hesitant to place too much emphasis on these data in the preceding chapters. A somewhat more detailed discussion can be found in the 'Notes on results for specific countries' in Appendix A.

12.11 General conclusion

While the present study had obvious limitations because of its exploratory nature and the reliance on self-report, the results do suggest a number of interesting leads for further research in this area. We believe, on the basis of our preliminary findings, that it will be possible to examine the process whereby specific antecedent situations produce emotional reactions and also the nature of the reaction patterns in more carefully designed studies, in terms of both self-report and objective measurement in observational studies. In further self-report studies it would seem to be of particular interest to focus much more specifically on the patterns of stimulus evaluation that determine the response to a specific event. As has been shown early on by theorists such as Arnold (1960) and Lazarus (1966), information about the way in which the individual evaluates a particular event or situation with respect to his or her values or goals is central to an understanding of the nature of the emotional reaction. More recently, a number of theorists have proposed more detailed features or dimensions of this evaluation process. Specifically, Scherer (1981b, 1984) has argued for a sequence of stimulus evaluation checks which would serve to determine the significance of a particular event in the light of an organism's motivational state and coping potential. In a new interculturally comparative questionnaire study involving samples from all continents, we are now attempting to obtain self-report data concerning specific details of this evaluation process as well as to replicate some of the patterns of findings that have been reported in this monograph.

Given the enormous logistic problems one has in trying to get respondents that are comparable across many sets of cultures, this new study is also being conducted with students. Clearly, it is essential for future studies to obtain respondent populations that represent a broader sampling of the people in a society and at the same time provide a better representation of the life events that are likely regularly to evoke emotional reactions. As mentioned before, it will also be essential to be more specific about our predictions concerning the differences between the various kinds of social groups being studied, as well as about cultural effects on emotional experience. This can be done fruitfully only when we have a better grasp of the way in which individuals evaluate events that are of central importance to them. Thus, while we clearly need more data we also urgently need more theory.

Appendix A
Notes on results for specific countries

Introduction

This Appendix contains a rather unusual set of material for a research monograph – a series of 'country notes'. These consist of a wide range of material that, for various reasons, does not fit squarely into the main chapters of this monograph. In many cases, the main purpose of the country notes is to discuss specific aspects of the results in a particular country, for example a major difference between a particular culture and the total sample or differences between sub-samples within a country (e.g. Paris vs. Lyon or Israeli Jews vs. Arabs). In other cases, additional material that was gathered in a subset of the countries is presented, for example personality measures in West Germany and Switzerland. In still other cases, the investigators in a particular country tried out a novel analysis procedure, using a different theoretical approach (e.g. in the case of our Spanish collaborators), and this is presented in the country note.

Apart from the cuts that were required to keep the volume within reasonable bounds, the editing of these 'country notes' has been minimal in order to preserve the idiosyncrasies and the special approach of the individual authors. These notes are therefore very heterogeneous, but we feel that this part of the monograph provides some of the flavour of this intercultural research collaboration that may be absent from the more formal chapters in the main part of the volume. Since the authors were encouraged to sprinkle examples liberally into the text of these notes, the reader may here find some of the 'meat' that might be missing in the reports of the statistical analyses given in the main chapters.

While it has been difficult to avoid repetition altogether, an attempt has been made to have as little as possible. Consequently, some of the results that are mentioned in more detail in the main chapters (or in Scherer, Summerfield & Wallbott, 1983, for the earlier study) are only hinted at in the country notes. Similarly, tables and figures are used only in those cases where the information cannot be found elsewhere in the volume. References cited in this Appendix are included in the list of references.

A1 The British case: the pleasures of life and the art of conversation

Angela B. Summerfield, Robert J. Edelmann and Elizabeth J. Green

A1. 1 Traditions of emotional expressiveness in Britain

Wel loved he garleek, oynons
and eek lekes,
And for to drinken strong
wyn, red as blood

GEOFFREY CHAUCER,
1340–1400

I sing of Youth, of Love and
have Accesse
By these to sing of cleanly –
Wantonnesse

ROBERT HERRICK,
1591–1674

Has the English temperament changed since Herrick or Chaucer?

In a classic study by Katz & Braly (1932) the English were characterised as being sportsmanlike, intelligent, and conventional, a stereotype of the British generally that seems to have persisted over the years. The literature on British emotional expression is also largely based upon stereotypes. Harper, Wiens & Matarazzo (1978) stated that the British are noted for their 'understatement' of emotion. This latter point is based upon Ekman's (1972) notion of display rules (i.e. socially learned, culture-specific) which can modify facial expressions. Deintensification of emotions, as in 'the stiff upper lip' is suggested as a typical characteristic of the British. Whether this is actually the case in reality has yet to be tested, although evidence from the study of other non-verbal behaviours does tend to suggest that the British may be rather 'under expressive'. As Jourard (1966) noted when observing the amount of touching between pairs of individuals in coffee houses, Puerto Ricans touched 180 times in an hour, the French ten times, Americans twice but the British not at all.

The characteristics of the British sample in our study have already been described in the main chapters of this monograph. Nevertheless, certain key characteristics deserve re-emphasis here. The majority of subjects in the sample were studying at one of two institutions within the University of London. Only approximately 7% of the relevant age group receives a university education in Great Britain, so becoming a student reflects a significant intellectual and social achievement. Most had come to London to study and were living away from their parental home. A quarter had come from families where their father was a manual worker and the great majority had mothers employed outside the home. Such people are not typical of their age group. They are also not typical of university students in many other parts of Europe, where different methods of selecting and funding the recipients of higher education prevail.

The data from this British sample and from the 'pilot study' sample (see Chapter 2) were collected at different times of the year – the pilot study data in January, just after the Christmas vacation, and the British sample data between April and July. This allows the interesting possibility that seasonal variations in emotion may have influenced the data. Research with psychiatric patients has indicated that there are reliable seasonal changes in mood, at least for certain clinical populations. The incidence of admission for psychotic depression, for example, appears to be particularly high in the late winter or early spring although a peak in autumn has also been observed by some authors (e.g. Eastwood & Stiasny, 1978). Variations in admission for mania appear to show even more reliable seasonal patterns with a peak in the summer months being reported by several authors (e.g. Myers & Davies, 1978).

Seasonal variations in suicides have been noted in a number of reports reviewed by Parker & Walters (1982). Swinscow (1951) examined suicides by month in England and Wales for the years 1921–48 and found that they peaked in the period from spring to midsummer, while Lester (1971), studying the suicide rate in New York State, found peaks in May and October. Meares, Mendelsohn & Milgrom-Friedman (1981) examined monthly suicide data in England and Wales between 1958 and 1974 and found that male suicides peaked in April–May while there were two peaks for female suicides, in March–April and October–November.

Possible biological influences on seasonal mood variations have been suggested by several authors. One theory, which has gained some measure of support, involves the pineal gland, which is known to influence circadian and seasonal rhythms in mammals. Light has an effect on the pineal and it is believed that it causes a reduction in melatonin secretion (Lewy, 1983), thus exerting inhibitory effects on gonadal and thyroid function (Wurtman, 1977). It has been suggested that the rapid increase in luminance caused by the early spring sunlight after several months of winter darkness stimulates the pineal and thus increases a person's vulnerability to certain affective disorders at this season.

Clearly, this work with psychiatric patients and suicides refers to mood swings which are abnormally large and dramatic and it is unclear to what extent more normal mood swings are influenced by seasonality. However, some work using normal subjects' self-reported mood changes has suggested that seasonality can also exert an influence on non-clinical populations. Whitton, Kramer & Eastwood (1982), for example, identified two distinct groups within their subject population. One of these, but not the other, showed periodicity and an influence of climatic variables on the mood data. While we could not pursue this issue in a systematic fashion on the basis of the present data, it would be an interesting area of study in future research.

In this country note we place most emphasis on the results from the main questionnaire as reported in this monograph (Study 2), but compare these findings with those of the earlier study (Study 1) reported by Scherer, Summerfield & Wallbott (1983) for the reasons mentioned above. The 64 subjects in Study 2 were drawn from a similar population to the one from which the 154 subjects in Study 1 were taken.

A1.2 Situations causing Britons to experience emotion

The British results from the two studies can be described best by considering each emotion in turn. The results given refer to Study 2 unless otherwise stated.

Joy. A constellation of factors appear to be associated with the rather low-key nature of British joy. These can best be considered by focussing on the types of situations which were described as antecedents. Twenty-three per cent of the subjects gave responses in the category 'body-related basic pleasures' when describing what had made them happy. This category refers to the pleasures of the senses, for example, food, drink, sexual experiences, and physical exercise (for details see Chapters 4 and 5). This finding is consistent with the results of Study 1, in which basic pleasures were also the most common antecedent. This preoccupation with sensual pleasures was quite uncharacteristic of subjects from other locations.

Examples relating to food from Study 1 included:

> 'Went out for pleasant but expensive meal.'

> 'Black pudding for breakfast.'

> 'Just that everyone was back at College and everyone went out so that the pub was really packed and everyone was really drunk and happy.'

Other forms of physical pleasure were also referred to. A subject described a dance class:

> 'I managed to get the steps in a routine...it produced a nice sense of pleasure and elation.'

And subjects in both studies referred to sexual happiness, often simply by saying, as in the case of this subject from Study 1:

> 'We made love.'

The British sample displayed an average incidence of references to relationships with friends but those descriptions often overlapped with those of 'basic pleasures':

> 'It was my boyfriend's birthday and we sat in bed all morning and I got him lots of presents which he was opening. We drank lots of tea and ate birthday cake.'

> 'Met girlfriend after being out of the country for four weeks. I ran, laughed and hugged.'

It is not clear from these data whether subjects de-emphasise friendship in comparison with the samples elsewhere, or whether they are simply more explicit and less euphemistic about their relationships with the opposite sex, leading to a coding of the item as 'basic pleasure' rather than 'relationships with friends'.

Success was not a preoccupation of the British sample. Only 16% of the subjects referred to it in both studies and many of these gave examples which were unrelated to their academic work:

> 'I received a good result on a statistics examination.'

contrasts with sporting preoccupations:

> 'scored a try'

and:

> 'I reached a typing speed of 65 words per minute.'

> 'When I first taught Rebecca (very backward academically) she described the position of Blackpool on a map of the UK as "Up the world". When I gave her a test after a six-week project on the UK and Europe, she positioned the major cities and towns in the UK and also European countries correctly.'

In Study 2, in contrast to Study 1, relationships with relatives were also described (13%):

> 'I took my fifteen-months-old daughter to her nursery school...for the first time since her attendance she displayed an understanding and willingness to be left. She kissed me, walked straight to her caregiver, climbed on her lap, kissed her, waved, turned to me and said goodbye.'

An examination of individual differences in the data revealed some systematic variations. Sixty-five per cent of the references to relationships as antecedents were made by women, and on a breakdown of social class, 65% were made by subjects of white collar origin. The majority (60%) of references to news as an antecedent were made by men. The only antecedent category for which subjects of blue collar origin predominated was achievement (56%). Psychology students differed from the rest in emphasising relationship factors as antecedents.

Sadness. Our subjects were as definite in describing sadness as they had been in describing joy. The most common antecedent of sadness in Study 2 was bereavement, possibly explaining the high degree of intensity reported for the emotion in this study relative to that reported for Study 1, with 25% of subjects reporting the death of someone close to them or occasionally the death of a pet or a plant:

> 'The totally unexpected death of a much-loved uncle. A great part of my grief was for the sadness of my aunt.'

> 'I was lying in bed looking at a picture of my brother who died when he was 21, trying to tell him what I was feeling, thinking about him and my frustration at him not being there.'

Bereavement was the third most common antecedent of sadnesss (12% of subjects) reported in Study 1, possibly because the shorter time period reduced its incidence.

Problematic relationships with friends were reported by 14% of subjects in Study 2:

> 'A friend with whom I had been having a casual relationship (sex). I heard through the grapevine that he was very depressed – this made me react emotionally for a number of reasons. I talked it over with my flatmate and ended up in tears. I was very surprised at the reaction I had.'

The theme of loss in relationships (77% in Study 2) recurred in both studies, as demonstrated by these quotations:

> 'Heard I'd lost my girlfriend,'

> 'My aunt and her family moved to France.'

A related and recurrent theme was that of leaving home for many students who were 18 or 19 years old:

> 'I was homesick.'

Nineteen per cent of subjects in Study 1 reported failure and frustration as a cause of sadness, but this was mentioned by only 8% of subjects in Study 2. Only 2% of subjects in Study 2 referred to depression or a sense of alienation:

> 'Nothing specific, free-floating anxiety which occasionally fills one's awareness.'

Eight per cent of subjects reported that bad news from the media had made them sad. The following report on the war between Britain and Argentina in the South Atlantic is an example:

> 'I read an article in a newspaper of a group of soldiers, one of whom had died as their tank landed on a mine bomb...I found out I had once seen the boy at a club meeting. He was only 20 years old.'

Again, substantial sex and social class differences were apparent. Seventy-one per cent of the references to relationships about temporary separation were made by women, as were 67% of the references to bad news. Sadness about bereavement was equally divided, between the sexes. Seventy-six per cent of the references to relationships and 10% of the references to achievement were made by subjects of white collar origin. Overall, if the reports of joy seemed to concentrate on some of the more superficial aspects of life, the reports of sadness gave a more consistent picture of real grief and of stoical attempts to deal with it often at a distance and away from familiar people and surroundings.

Fear. The reactions to fear appear to be complex and need to be interpreted in relation to varying antecedents. All subjects reported past situations, but 30% of subjects in Study 2 said they had imagined the problem. This is substantially different from the case for the other countries; in the other countries real problems were consistently described.

There was consistency in the main antecedents reported for fear in the two studies, except for one notable exception – fear of the supernatural. This featured only in Study 1, where 14% of subjects referred to it.

In Study 2 three factors, assault or physical aggression, failure and traffic each accounted for 20% of the antecedents. Fear of assault and physical aggression was described in relation to being followed or accosted by strangers:

> 'I was coming home late at night on the last tube at about midnight. I was in a corner on my own. A male got into the tube and sat next to me. He began to talk to me in a very aggressive and suggestive manner.'

'An elderly, very respectable-looking man carrying a brief case shouted "Pig" into my face as he left the bus. When I looked down out of the window he was standing on the pavement looking up at me – his face contorted with hate, first shaking his fist at me – then making the V sign.'

Traffic accidents were also reported:

'Was witness to a four car crash whilst walking home and one of the first on the scene. One car was in particular trouble, upside down and smoke pouring from the engine. A young man was trapped by his seatbelt to the ceiling. He was conscious and seemingly unhurt but panicking terribly. Against advice from others I kicked in the passenger door and crawled in and freed him and helped him out.'

The British sample was distinctive in the high incidence of fear of the supernatural as an antecedent in Study 1. This was sometimes the result of watching a horror film in solitude:

'Lying in bed at home and the place was creaking eerily.'

However, some subjects had become involved with the occult:

'Hearing tape of supposed "ghost" – my brother had been to a seance. I was alone in the house.'

Since these data refer to the Christmas period, it is possible that this reflects seasonal activities, such as telling ghost stories.

Female subjects showed substantially more fear of strangers (62%) of all incidents reported by females), of achievement-related situations (69% of all incidents reported by females), and of novel situations (88% of all incidents reported by females), than did male subjects. Subjects of white collar origin were more affected by bad news (67% of reports were by subjects of white collar origin), achievement-related situations (83% of reports), traffic (100% of reports), and risk-taking (75% of reports) than were subjects of blue collar origin.

Many subjects regarded the social environment, whether it were potential attackers or traffic, as a source of recent fear experiences. They seem to have perceived themselves as vulnerable in a social context which was unpredictable and threatening. In interpreting these results, it must be remembered that the subjects live and study in one of the largest cities in Europe, where there is a high incidence of urban problems.

Anger. Subjects in the British sample were quite clear about what made them angry. Fifty per cent of subjects in Study 1 reported that it was unreasonable behaviour to common property such as buildings, telephone boxes and common rooms in student accommodation. This was more than twice the incidence of this category in any other location. This was also the main antecedent category for anger in Study 2, being reported by 23% of respondents:

'I tried to phone a friend and the phone in the telephone box was broken.'

'The grill in our kitchen (in the student hostel) was dirty, the handle was missing and the tea cloth was missing.'

Such problems were often interwoven with relationship problems, as reported by 17% of the subjects:

> 'My flatmate...left her boyfriend and fellow flatmates to clear up her mess after her – always leaving the scene before anything could be said.'

> 'Myself and a friend had made an agreement that he would be able to stay in the flat alone or with another (in my deliberate absence) for one week, if I could have a similar separate week...However, during my week alone he arrived after two days without giving any explanation or apology.'

Some were dramatic. One subject reported that his:

> 'Room-mate brought his girlfriend to our room and started making passionate love while I was trying to work.'

Assaults and robbery were also mentioned as causes of anger, by 10% of subjects in Study 2:

> 'Two residents (of the hall of residence) were beaten up on the previous day by six youths. That evening a gang of a dozen or more youths attacked our hall, smashing windows and beating up two more members who are close friends of mine.'

The next most often mentioned category in Study 1 was unnecessary inconvenience (12%):

> 'My boyfriend brought home a relative of his to stay for a few months.'

but this was mentioned less often in Study 2 (8%).

The reports on anger echo those on sadness. Physical danger, assault, and lack of appropriate behaviour by other people provoked subjects in both cases.

A1.3 Discussion

The results of the two studies taken together show not only distinctive patterns of antecedents for each emotion, but also a considerable degree of consistency across the samples and studies. Joy is characterised by an emphasis on basic pleasures, followed by relationships with friends and success experiences.

The important role played by basic pleasures is unique to the British sample and there are a number of possible explanations. Firstly, most subjects were living away from home and therefore had opportunities to indulge in what they may have seen as previously forbidden delights of adult life, such as alcohol and sex. In addition, as we have suggested above, the British students may have been disposed to be frank rather than indirect about sexual relationships, thus influencing the categorisation of their responses as 'basic pleasure'. Since both British samples had a higher proportion of students from blue collar families than the samples from elsewhere in Europe, it is difficult to evaluate the extent to which this was compounded by social class, or indeed, the extent to which students of blue collar origin influence students of white collar origin. It is also not easy to evaluate whether joy in this context reflects the reduction of sexual and other basic drives or a more abstract pleasure in being alive and whether it originates from pleasure in the acts of eating, drinking, and sexual intercourse or in the social context in which they occurred. The results on sadness raise the question of whether personal relationships bring grief, as has been noted in the Belgian findings (see Appendix A6). These results do not provide a mirror image of the findings for joy.

The emphasis on traffic and assaults in the data for fear is partly a result of urban life and partly the consequence of civil unrest in Britain in a time of peak economic recession and unemployment. A similar pattern emerged for anger, with the emphasis on damage to public property, and a similar explanation probably holds.

The overall impression we received from the reports by the British subjects is that positive emotional experiences were mainly triggered by everyday events, while negative experiences were related either to loss, or to separation, or to actual or imagined physical damage to the individual. The relatively young sample in both studies therefore presents a picture of exploring early adult life on the one hand, and of using coping strategies in the face of social unrest and disruption of personal relationships on the other.

A2 The French case: emotion and rationality

Verena Aebischer and Jacques Cosnier

A2.1 Introduction

Social psychology was born when its originators' attention was caught by a paradox. Man as an individual would act in a rational manner and adjust his behaviour to socially acceptable norms. When in a group or crowd, however, he would stop reasoning and give way to his instincts, feelings, and emotions, and act in a heedless and destructive manner. The study of this conflict between rationality and instinct, between reflection and emotion inspired the pioneering work of Le Bon (1896), Tarde (1900), McDougall (1920) and many other social philosophers but found, somehow, no echo among the succeeding generations of researchers.

The eventual rehabilitation of emotion to its prominent position as a focus of research attention today does not come as a surprise, however. It is but an expression of a more general transition from one value system to another which culturally, politically, and socially heralds a new type of society. The social movements of the 1960s and 1970s, with their accompanying breakdown of the traditional ideologies, and their questioning of bureaucratic and technocratic optimism, have brought about new forms of action and a new appreciation of the world favouring a new outlook at man.

Thus society has discovered the importance of personal experiences, of a new sensitivity, and a new capacity for emotion.

One by-product of this more general phenomenon is the flourishing of therapy groups whose main purpose is to help man to shed the emotion-inhibiting chains acquired through education and to find himself and his feelings as a subject capable of expressing his anger, envy, jealousy, or sadness. Another one is the awakened interest of social scientists in the understanding of emotion as part of human reality.

French society, as is the case in most western societies, is certainly sharing in the change described above, that is the change from one value system to another, from an ideologically oriented perspective to one more concerned with people's concrete personal lives and needs, their sexuality, their bodies, and their personal and intimate relationships. Nevertheless, culturally, politically, and historically, France is also a country where traditions and institutions have a great hold and a not-to-be-neglected capacity to resist any change.

Bearing these considerations in mind, it is interesting to compare an analysis of what French students today recall when asked to write down some of their emotional experiences with an analysis of the recollections of students in other western countries.

A2.2 The nature of the French sample

Two different student populations took part in the French study, one in Lyon ($n = 85$), the second largest French city, which is situated in the southern part of France, and the other in Paris ($n = 64$), the French capital, which is situated in the northern part of France (see Chapter 2). Overall, the sociological composition of the French student sample as a whole was in many respects comparable to that of the generation of young people who, in all parts of the western world, had initiated alternative life-styles which valued feelings rather than ideology, and personal experience rather than political revolution. They were young undergraduate students (the Parisian sample was about two years older than the Lyon sample, which, on the average, was 21 years old). Most of them were single and unattached and came from French white-collar middle class families. With the exception of about one-quarter of the Lyon sample which was of rural extraction, the students had spent most of their lives in French urban surroundings (big cities or towns). Their mother tongue was French, but more than three-quarters of them (88%) were acquainted with the English language. About a quarter of the Parisian sample worked; all the others were full-time students. There were significantly more psychology students in the Parisian sample (56% vs. 37%), and significantly more students of natural sciences (44% vs. 28%) in the Lyonnais sample.

As the dependent variables showed little variation between the two French samples, the following sections will distinguish between them only when the differences were statistically significant or otherwise noteworthy.

A2.3 The activation of strong feelings within a familiar setting

It is interesting to note that the French student samples overall, when asked to think about situations that had triggered joy, sadness, fear, and anger often recalled emotions they had felt intensely in situations that, perhaps more so than for the other samples, had occurred more than several months ago, anger being an exception (see Chapter 4). This finding held above all for the students from Lyon who, for joy and sadness, significantly more so than the students from Paris, described situations from several months and even several years ago.

Strong feelings, so it seemed, rarely occurred without an audience except for fear, which, as in the other samples showed a pattern of its own. The emotions experienced by the French students mostly took place in private, inside, within the familiar setting of being with friends and family members. One or a very few people seemed to be the main antagonists who were either the cause or the witness of more or less controlled emotional outbursts. Joy in a dyad was significantly more important in Paris than in Lyon (64% vs. 33%), whereas in Lyon joy above all was experienced in small groups (39% vs. 23%). In both samples sadness was mainly experienced in a familiar setting. However, there were significantly more unfamiliar people involved in sadness experiences in Paris than in Lyon.

A2.4 Antecedents

As noted in the results chapters above, there were fewer intercultural differences for antecedents than expected. The French sample in particular generally corresponded well with the overall mean. Furthermore, statistical analyses yielded only very few significant differences between the Paris and Lyon samples. Consequently, we will describe only the major patterns of the French antecedents.

Close relationships. If emotion is part of human reality, we can say that friends and relatives keep this part constantly alive. Thus, be it in a positive or a negative way, French students experienced the greater part of their joy, anger, and sadness situations with their friends and relatives. The joy often consisted of having a good talking or simply a good time with a friend or relative, or of meeting them after a temporary separation due to travelling abroad or working away from home, or was due to the birth of a baby. Sadness resulted from the temporary or permanent loss of a friend or a parent. On the other hand, relationships gave rise to anger if the responsibility for an unsatisfactory meeting could clearly be attributed to a friend's or relative's inconsiderate behaviour or failure to behave in the expected way. This very particular concern with the intricacies of close relationships had its counterpart in the relative indifference or even hostility with which those outside the familiar circle were met. This familiar circle functioned like a protecting cocoon against an outside world which, when it could not be clearly made out, inspired fear (see the following section on the integrity of body and mind). If, however, the action of the outside world could be identified, the following reaction was rarely joy or sadness, but almost always anger. The outside world did not really seem to enter the students' minds, and if it did then mostly in a sudden and negative way. This was particularly pronounced in Paris, whence students reported significantly more anger incidences due to inconsiderate behaviour of strangers than those from Lyon.

The integrity of body and mind. Concern about the integrity of their body and to some extent of their mind was another important issue for the French students but a very different kind for it involved above all fear and uneasiness. One characteristic of fear is that the outcome of what is apprehended cannot be predicted. The threat is still a potential one, but nevertheless felt as real, be it the anticipation of traffic accident, aggression by others, a violent fall on a mountain, the effect of a thunderstorm or even the imponderable effect of something unknown. More frequently than subjects in other countries, the French students dreaded the potential death of loved ones. It is interesting to note that for the two samples of French students fear was only linked with potential harm to the body. Concern about the integrity of the body and mind (e.g. self-esteem) could also lead to other types of emotion. Harm done to moral integrity when the cause and the extent of the effect were identified, led to outright anger, for example in the context of an unfair accusation or behaviour of others, unexpected time loss, or bureaucracy. If, conversely, there was not harm but enhancement to be gained for the mind or body, for example from breathtaking scenery or an excellent meal, the outcome was inevitably happiness, joy or at least pleasure.

Success or failure. A student's life consists of a succession of examinations and tests, the outcome of which determines to not a small extent the rhythm of his life and the perspectives of his future. Therefore it is not surprising that success in examinations accounted for 14% of all joy experiences. However, only 3% of French students were sad following unsuccessful examinations, a lower proportion than for any of the other samples in the study.

The French students showed relatively little anxiety or fear in achievement situations. Their faith in their capacities is striking when compared to the 20% of British students who experienced anticipatory fear and the 17% of the German and Belgian students. Whereas the Belgians, Germans, and British felt fear, the French felt some fear (8%) and some anger (8%), as if the fact of potential failure was more likely due to some inconsiderate behaviour of the professor than something they had properly deserved.

A2.5 Control of emotional reactions

This was one of the few domains where the French students showed a marked difference to the general sample. For the emotion of joy in particular, the French subjects showed a significantly stronger degree of control (as established by *post-hoc* comparisons, see Chapter 9) than subjects in other countries. A sub-analysis between the Lyon and Paris samples showed that this effect was almost exclusively due to the Paris sample. The students here generally showed more control of physiological symptoms and particularly of verbalisation than did the students in Lyon. Given the generally low level of control of joy, this effect was particularly marked for this emotion. One possible explanation is that the somewhat *blasé* attitude of the inhabitants of the capital, the notion that one has to show a certain 'nonchalant' indifference to be considered a true, seasoned Parisian, is already visible in the student culture.

A2.6 Discussion

The very strong concern and feelings of the French student samples about private life and the integrity of the body – as opposed to the indifference to or even fear of the outside world – the intensity with which happiness or anger, and sadness or fear were felt, and the low amount of control exerted above all in joy, are quite in line with today's general tendency, outlined in the first section of this note to value feelings and emotions. It is, however, noteworthy and highly significant; that the importance given by the French students to personal experiences and the capacity for emotion did not totally obliterate the value of success and achievement. Thus, for the French students achievement considerations were woven into the tapestry of everyday experiences along with the trivial everyday events: quarrels, love, friendship, sickness and death. The French students tended to exclude from their lives, however, to some extent a concern for events beyond the familiar circle. Hence they reported little interest in world news, whether positive or negative (although the French students and particularly the Parisians, still cared more about it than most of the other samples).

For the French case, we had the unique opportunity, in the present study, to compare two regional sub-samples within a linguistically and culturally relatively uniform society. As was the case for the intercultural differences, the relatively few significant differences did form a rather consistent pattern. In spite of the fact that Lyon is the second biggest city in France with all the problems and advantages of a major urban centre, the students at Lyon University seemed to be part of a closely-knit social network, experiencing emotions often with familiar others and in small groups. The Parisian students, on the other hand, were more exposed to strangers (whose inconsiderateness often gave rise to anger) and tended to experience emotions more often alone or in smaller dyadic units. As cosmopolitans, they tended to get more emotionally involved in world news, both good and bad, than their colleagues from the province. At the same time, they kept their 'cool' at least in external appearance, by strongly controlling the manifestations of emotional arousal. It would be interesting to pursue these potential differences in emotionality between cosmo-politian capitals and provincial centres in future research to check whether this is a general pattern or one limited to the special Parisian 'flair'.

A3 The German case: personality correlates of emotional reactivity

Harald G. Wallbott and Heiner Ellgring

A3.1 Person characteristics and emotion: theoretical considerations

The discussions in the results chapters focussed mainly on the different characteristics of the emotional situations reported, such as antecedents, reactions, physiological symptoms, and control attempts, or configurations of these different aspects, either in terms of general differences between the emotions or in terms of differences between country samples. So far, the effects of personality traits have not been discussed in detail (with the exception of Chapter 10) since personality tests were not administered in all countries. Yet, the particular characteristics of the individual must be considered to be an important factor in shaping the nature of emotional experience.

The idea that the experience of emotional situations might be influenced by personality traits can be inferred from recent trends in personality research, for example from Mischel's (1979) cognitive social learning model of personality or from other theories which consider person-situation as a single system (Lewin, 1936; Murray, 1938; for an overview see Forgas, 1982). In particular, personality factors like extraversion and neuroticism, but also social desirability, seem to be significantly related to episode representations in 'social episode' research (see e.g. Forgas, 1979; Battistich & Thompson, 1980; Forgas, 1982).

For the German sample we had decided to include some personality measurements. Some major personality traits were assessed via questionnaire: we measured the personality dimensions of extraversion and neuroticism with the Eysenck Personality Inventory (Eysenck, 1956, in the German translation of Brengelmann & Brengelmann, 1960), and social desirability on the scale developed by Crowne & Marlowe (1960; German translation by Lück & Timaeus, 1969). Together with the information collected via the background questionnaire, these data provided a unique opportunity to test whether the situation descriptions for the different emotions were influenced by major personality traits.

A3.2 The effect of personality traits on emotional experience

Table A3.1 lists all the significant correlations between the personality traits measured and the coded characteristics of emotional situations separately for the four emotions studied. The correlations with the antecedent categories and the reaction/symptom categories were based on 0/1 data. Though some significant correlations were found, most of the relations between personality traits and situation codes were low and insignificant. We were not too surprised, however,

Table A3.1. *Significant correlations of personality traits with antecedent, control, and response characteristics (only significant correlations mentioned; West German sample, N = 90)*

	Emotion			
	Joy	Sadness	Fear	Anger
Neuroticism				
Intensity		0.24	0.30	
Duration			0.28	
Familiarity		−0.23		
Behave differently				0.32
Antecedent groups				
News				0.19
Permanent separation			0.25	
Response groups				
Voice reactions	0.21			
Hand movements	0.27			
Freezing	0.19			
Chest/breathing problems	−0.18		0.18	0.25
Changed face		0.25		
Laughing/smiling		0.20		
Normal movements of body parts		0.25		
Changed movements of body parts		−0.17		
General unrest			−0.18	
Perspiration			−0.28	
Blood pressure rise			−0.28	
Stomach sensations			0.21	
Crying				0.21
Unpleasant rest sensations				0.18
Extraversion				
Intensity	0.21			0.42
Amount of verbal behaviour		−0.19	0.21	
Familiarity			−0.22	
Control of reactions			−0.21	
Antecedent groups				
Achievement			0.20	
Response groups				
Hand movements	0.18			
Chest/breathing problems		−0.22		
Freezing			−0.18	
Muscle symptoms			−0.22	
Instrumental actions				0.18
Social desirability				
Duration	0.20	0.22		
How long ago?	0.25			
Behave differently	−0.29			
Antecedent groups				
News	0.23	−0.25		
Pleasure/pain			0.26	
Novel, unknown situations			0.18	
Social institutions				−0.17
Injustice				0.19
Response groups				
Changed speech quality	0.20	0.23		
Voice reactions	−0.18			−0.27
Chest/breathing problems	0.23			
Crying		0.18		
Speech reactions				0.18
Changed voice quality				−0.23
Freezing				0.19

because in reports we had found in the literature correlations between personality measures and behavioural measures also often only reached values of about 0.30 (Mischel, 1979). In general however, these results indicate that personality factors are less important for predicting reports on emotional situations than we expected (see Appendix A5, where similar results are reported for the Swiss sample).

In terms of neuroticism the correlations indicate that subjects high on this trait reported higher intensities for sadness and fear, but not for joy and anger. This implies that highly neurotic persons experienced the 'passive' negative emotions more intensely than subjects low on neuroticism. Furthermore, for these subjects fear was of longer duration and they seemed to experience sadness more often in the company of unfamiliar persons. The only antecedent that was important with respect to neuroticism was 'permanent separation' as an antecedent of fear. Highly neurotic subjects reported more incidents of this antecedent as a source of fear than did the other subjects. Another significant correlation indicates that highly neurotic subjects tended to react differently in similar situations when they experienced anger. These people seemed to be 'scrupulous' concerning their anger experiences and reactions. In terms of non-verbal reactions and physiological symptoms the correlations were usually relatively low and do not allow any conclusive argument with respect to differences between highly and less neurotic subjects. On the whole, the correlations we found do make some sense, because they indicate that highly neurotic subjects seemed to have different experiences from less neurotic subjects, especially for the negative emotions and especially in terms of intensity and duration.

Significant correlations with extraversion were also sparse. The most interesting finding seems to be that extraverted subjects reported stronger intensities for joy and anger than introverted subjects, that is for the 'active' emotions compared to the 'passive' emotions, sadness and fear, whose intensities were related to neuroticism. Furthermore, extraverts verbalised less when they were sad but more when experiencing fear compared to introverts. Extraverts also controlled their reactions less when experiencing fear and they experienced fear more often in situations with unfamiliar persons. In terms of antecedents, however, no significant differences indicating that extraverts and introverts experienced different situations were found. The only difference between extraverts and introverts in terms of antecedents was that extraverts reported more 'achievement situations' as sources of fear. Again, we will not discuss the correlations with reactions/symptoms here because the few significant results seem difficult to interpret. Thus, there were even fewer correlations between extraversion–introversion and situation characteristics than for neuroticism. The most interesting result seems to be that again intensity was related to this personality trait for joy and anger.

The data for social desirability were not very conclusive. Social desirability, that is the tendency to behave and describe oneself in a socially accepted manner, was associated with only a few situation characteristics, the larger number being for joy. For this emotion subjects with high social desirability described situations that were of longer duration and occurred further in the past than those described by subjects with low social desirability, and also said that they would not behave differently in such joy situations. For the negative emotions few important correlations could be observed in terms of social desirability, although one might have expected that, for instance, control of anger and other factors associated with anger and social norms might have been affected by this personality trait. The correlations with situation antecedents were also quite low. Subjects high in social desirability reported more news situations for joy, but fewer news situations for sadness than those low in social desirability. For fear, 'pain' situations and 'novel' experiences seemed to be more important for subjects high in social desirability than for those low in social desirability. For anger, high scorers reported more situations involving 'injustice', but fewer situations involving 'social insitutions' than low scorers. For non-verbal reactions and physiological symptoms high scorers reported a low number of reactions/symptoms, but only for the emotions joy and anger. This might be due to subjects high in social desirability not being willing to report on their reactions and symptoms in much detail, especially for joy and anger, probably because of their fear that such reports might be evaluated negatively. But again the correlations were too low to state any conclusive explanations for the findings (furthermore, most of the results reported here were not replicated with the Swiss sample; see Appendix A5).

Since these results for personality traits were not very impressive in terms of both the number of significant correlations found and the magnitude of these correlations, a last attempt was made to look at personality differences by using Eysenck's (Eysenck, 1956) personality model proposing the two independent dimensions of neuroticism and extraversion. With a median split technique groups of subjects who were high in both extraversion and neuroticism ('cholerics'), high in extraversion and low in neuroticism ('sanguinics'), low in extraversion and high in neuroticism ('melancholics'), and low in both extraversion and neuroticism ('phlegmatics') were distinguished. The 'old' and much discussed terminology stemming from the Greek physician Galen, who lived in the second century of our time (see Eysenck, 1956), was used here to highlight the results found.

Three significant effects emerged, indicating that Eysenck's proposed typology captures individual differences in emotional experience. All these results centred on the emotions fear and anger. For the duration of fear, phlegmatics and sanguinics obtained very low scores, while, on the other hand, cholerics and melancholics reported a significantly longer duration of fear. For the intensity of fear there was a marked difference between phlegmatics and the other three groups, indicating that phlegmatics reported a lower intensity of fear. Thus, phlegmatics in particular reported a shorter duration and lower intensity of fear, than the other groups, proving the common stereotype about this group of people being not very much affected by emotional, especially negative emotional situations. This was supported by the results for the intensity of anger. Again, a significant effect indicated that phlegmatics reported a lower intensity of anger than the other three groups. Thus, phlegmatics, as compared to the other groups, were affected to a lower degree by the negative emotions fear and anger, or at least they reported lower intensities and durations. Sanguinics, on the other hand, reported fear and anger situations of high emotional intensity but short duration. Thus, they reacted in a very 'impulsive' way, which is in fact often described as being a characteristic of this group of people. The significant effects for the personality groups are summarised in Figure A3.1.

A3.3 Conclusions

Even though the results reported at the end of section A3.2 provide some support for Eysenck's (1956) notion concerning personality differences, in general the

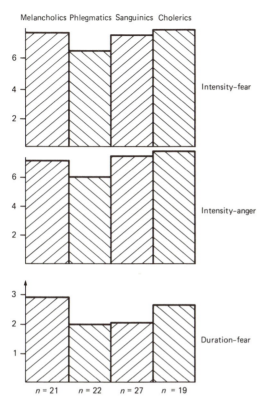

Figure A3.1 Significant relations between personality types and emotion characteristics (for the German sample)

pattern of results reported in this note does not support our assumption of the importance of personality traits and person characteristics as determinants of emotional experiences. While there are in fact some significant relations for some of the personality traits measured, on the whole these results are not very impressive. The personality characteristics discussed above do not seem to be very important predictors of emotional experiences. Subjects described more or less the same emotional situations irrespective of personality traits such as extraversion or neuroticism (see Appendix A5 for similar results).

Together with the finding that country differences seem to be less important for the experience of emotion than expected, this lends strong support to the hypothesis that the experience of emotion, in terms of the antecedents, the reactions, and the control attempts in a situation is a very general phenomenon, despite possible mediation by person factors. Situations in which subjects experienced joy, sadness, fear, or anger were more or less the same, irrespective of the background and personality factors of these people. This might imply that the 'universals' found for facial expressions (see Ekman, 1972) might find a parallel in terms of 'situation universals' and other 'reaction/symptom universals' besides facial expression. Although these results are limited, because only the German sample was analysed here and only a few personality measures were used, these findings seem to be important. Emotional experiences are affected to some degree by personality traits, like extraversion and neuroticism, but the role of 'emotional universals' seems to be much more prominent. If in fact the experience of emotions is not much affected by country and person differences but proves to be a general 'human characteristic', this would be an important finding for the theory of emotion.

A.4 The Italian case: a stereotype confirmed?

Dino Giovannini and Pio Ricci-Bitti
(Translated by Janet A. Oliver)

A4.1 Introduction: stereotypes about Italians

Common stereotypes represent the Italians, and Mediterraneans in general, as people who display great expressiveness and expansiveness in their social conduct. However, as is often the case with stereotypes, this generalisation does not necessarily correspond with the truth. The Italians are, naturally, a diverse race and, even in the area of expressive behaviour, one can pick out notable differences from region to region (Ricci-Bitti, 1976; Ricci-Bitti, Argyle, & Giovannini, 1978; Ricci-Bitti, Giovannini, Argyle, & Graham, 1980). A particularly striking example of this is the expressiveness of the Neapolitan people. Morris (1977) claims that the non-verbal communication of these people is so rich and expressive that they are able to convey any message whatsover without uttering a word.

The subjects who took part in our survey were all students attending Bologna University, but originating from various regions of Italy, including southern areas: our data cannot, however, be categorised so as to indicate the behaviour pattern of subjects of one particular region. In spite of these regional differences, we will explore in this note whether, compared to other European subjects considered in the survey, the Italians do in fact conform to the stereotype described above. One could hypothesise that the Italians experience a longer duration and stronger intensity of emotional experience, and display a wider range of expressive behaviour, a greater intensity of certain reactions, and a lesser degree of control over emotion-triggered verbal and non-verbal reactions. This note will consider these in turn.

A4.2 Italian–European comparison

First, let us examine the antecedent situations triggering the four emotions. The differences reported here are suggestive at most, since it is difficult to decide on the proper choice of *post-hoc* comparison tests even if there is a significant overall effect for country differences.

Relationship situations triggered joy and fear more frequently in Italian subjects than in other European subjects, and sadness and anger less frequently. The temporary meeting/separation category was, on the whole, mentioned less by Italian subjects and was a particularly infrequent cause of joy compared with the findings for European subjects (20% vs. 11%). The category birth/death was a less common antecedent for Italian subjects, with particular respect to joy (2% vs. 8%) and fear (2% vs. 7%). Relationships with strangers were a less frequent cause of fear (15% vs. 3%) and anger (20% vs. 5%) for European subjects.

Table A4.1. *Results for Italy and combined European countries on the intensity, verbal behaviour, and control characteristics of emotional reactions*

		Emotion			
Characteristic	Location	Joy	Sadness	Fear	Anger
Duration	Italy	2.8	3.3	2.1	2.5
	Europe	3.1	3.4	2.1	2.6
Intensity	Italy	7.6	7.9	7.1	6.9
	Europe	7.4	7.4	7.4	6.9
Verbal behaviour	Italy	2.6	2.0	1.9	2.5
	Europe	2.3	2.0	1.8	2.3
Control of verbal	Italy	1.9	3.8	3.6	3.7
behaviour	Europe	1.9	4.1	3.4	4.6
Control of reactions	Italy	1.4	3.4	3.5	3.0
	Europe	1.5	3.6	3.8	3.6

Success/achievement situations were, on the whole, more significant for Italians, while fear of failure was less so. Joy at success, sadness at failure, and anger at failure were more common for the Italians (17% vs. 13%; 12% vs. 7%; 10% vs. 6%, respectively).

As regards specific antecedents, Europeans seem to have had the greatest fear of risk (10% vs. 4%), while Italians experienced the greatest fear of the unknown/novelty situations (28% vs. 13%) and anger at misfortune (12% vs. 6%).

Second, in terms of response/reaction characteristics, there were several significant differences between the Italians and the Europeans (see Table A4.1). However, there were no significant differences relating to the duration of emotional experiences. If anything, for the Italians joy, sadness, and anger, contrary to expectation, lasted for a slightly shorter period than for the Europeans. While the Italians seemed to experience joy and sadness slightly more *intensively* and fear slightly less intensively than the other Europeans, these differences were not significant.

In terms of verbal conduct, the Italians produced somewhat greater verbalisation in joy, fear, and anger than the Europeans. The Italians exercised slightly less verbal control for sadness and anger and slightly more for fear. Again, these differences were generally not significant.

With respect to the other reactional patterns we again did not find strong differences (see Table A4.2). Joy produced a slightly greater incidence of pleasant sensations of wellbeing in the Italians. Similarly, the Italians experienced stronger unpleasant feelings of tension when they were sad. Consistently more frequent symptoms of all emotions in the Italians were 'feelings of warmth', 'rises in blood pressure', 'stomach upsets', and 'changes in voice quality'. Laughing and smiling on happy occasions, on the other hand, were more frequent for other Europeans. Muscular tension was typically an Italian reaction to joy and a reaction of other Europeans to fear.

Table A4.2. *Response/reaction characteristics; results for Italy and combined European countries on non-verbal behaviour, physiological symptoms, and general sensations (percentages)*[a]

| Characteristic | Location | Emotion | | | |
		Joy	Sadness	Fear	Anger
Non-verbal behaviour					
Changed facial expression	Italy	8	10		12
	Europe	10	10		10
Voice subjective quality changes	Italy	26	21	16	30
	Europe	11	12	9	25
Interpersonal movement	Italy	8			
	Europe	8			
Hand movements	Italy	16		8	12
	Europe	6		6	9
Physiological symptoms					
Coldness	Italy			9	
	Europe			9	
Warmth	Italy	11			13
	Europe	7			10
Blood pressure raise	Italy	33	17	46	28
	Europe	9	4	18	6
Muscle tension	Italy	16	20	31	17
	Europe	9	18	38	18
Stomach troubles	Italy		21	18	15
	Europe		13	17	9
General sensations					
Unpleasant rest	Italy		16		
	Europe		13		
Unpleasant arousal	Italy			14	15
	Europe			11	13
Pleasant rest	Italy	20			
	Europe	17			
Pleasant arousal	Italy	17			
	Europe	12			

[a] Values lower than 8% have not been reported in the table.

A4.3 Discussion

It is difficult to draw any conclusions from our data concerning the stereotype about 'Italians given the fact that scarcely any strong, statistically significant differences were found.

Generally speaking, many of the emotion-related behavioural characteristics would tend not to confirm the stereotype. For example, physiological symptoms of all the emotions – feelings of warmth, rises in blood pressure, gastric upsets – were more common for the Italian subjects than for the other Europeans, indicating a greater tendency to internalise rather than to externalise emotional reactions (see also Chapter 10). On the other hand, certain other patterns, while very weak, are in line with the stereotype, for example a greater incidence of verbal behaviour for three of the emotions (joy, fear, and anger). On the whole, however, there is little evidence for the pattern one might expect on the basis of the stereotype. It would appear that the most pronounced difference between Italian and European subjects might be not so much the types of reaction as the strategies used to control them. It is these which might well be largely responsible for the Italians' apparently more open affective behaviour. However, the present data provide very little substantive support for such speculation.

A final note. The Italian results appeared to bring to light some interesting facts regarding the differences between male and female subjects on the one hand, and between social sciences students and psychology students on the other.

These differences relate, above all, to coping strategies: in general, male subjects stated that they achieved, with the exception of anger, a higher level of control over behavioural reactions than did female subjects, although the emotions of the latter are more prolonged. The same trend, to a lesser extent, is also true for control of verbal behaviour. This difference can be explained by the different social constraints placed on the two sexes, which actually impose two differing sets of behavioural rules.

Finally, concerning the two groups of students considered (social sciences students and psychology students), a distinctively higher level of control was clearly exercised by psychology students in terms of both verbal and other behavioural reactions. This can be seen as a 'professional effect', if one recognises that psychology students, already in the course of their professional preparation, are acquiring a greater awareness of emotional experience and a tendency to 'control' their experiences with respect to social situations and the rules imposed by society.

A5 The Swiss case: down to earth

Eva Bänninger-Huber

A5.1 Introduction

The aim of this note is to present the Swiss data collected within the framework of the whole project. What is of particular interest here is the question of whether, and to what extent, Swiss people differ from non-Swiss people in their accounts of emotional experiences. The Swiss sample did not differ from the sample as a whole (on the basis of χ^2 tests) for most background variables. However, it is striking that significantly more of the Swiss subjects studied natural science (39% in the Swiss sample vs. 24% in the rest of the European sample) and fewer studied social science (14% vs. 24%). Furthermore, there were fewer really young students (18–20 year olds) in the Swiss sample compared to the rest of the total European sample (10% vs. 32%). This ties in with the Swiss education structure as secondary school education continues for longer than in other countries, and pupils are 19/20 before they leave school. Another difference between Swiss sample and the other samples is that most of the Swiss subjects had grown up in the country and fewer of them had grown up in large towns or cities.

A5.2 Antecedents

Joy. As in most of the other countries included in the study, the most important situations which produced joy in Switzerland were 'relationships with friends' and 'meeting friends'. The determinants of the individual events were, however, very varied. For a man, a cause of joy can be an exciting woman lying on the beach or a woman who presses her knee against his under the table or simply a woman who prepares a meal with loving care. For a woman, too, a meal may be a cause of joy...if cooked for her by someone else. But cosiness in relationships is also important for women, as the following example illustrates:

> 'I went to bed. My boyfriend was already asleep. Without making any noise, I lay down beside him in the dark. He opened his arms to me and we snuggled up to each other.'

Apart from contacts with other people, 'natural, non-cultural pleasures such as sex, good food, and experiences of nature and beautiful scenery were also determinants of joy; experiences of nature and beautiful scenery were mentioned most frequently. Here is an example:

> 'During Whitsuntide, I went hiking with a friend in the Swiss canton of Ticino for about five days. We didn't meet any tourists, but we saw

mountains, waterfalls, very beautiful villages, animals, and a lot of snow. The weather was good the whole time.'

Situations which understandably often give rise to joy are 'success experiences', for example success in an examination; this is, of course, of particular significance for students:

'I received the results of a language exam. My results were much better than I'd expected. I not only passed my exam, but I also had the best mark of all the candidates.'

Cultural pleasures which, in other contries, were occasionally a cause of joy were not reported by the Swiss subjects. Particularly typical of this was the lack of reports falling into the category 'new experiences'. This corresponds well with the stereotype of the conservative Swiss who sticks to his tried and tested ways.

Sadness. As for joy, problems with relationships played an important role in causing sadness, whether they were relationships with friends or relationships with relatives. In the category 'relationships with friends' it was mainly a case of situations where a partner, usually of the opposite sex, did not share positive feelings shown towards him/her, or even rejected them completely:

'A good friend of mine whom I thought a lot of slowly began to build a wall between us which I could do nothing about. I did not know what to do as he had certainly reciprocated my feelings earlier on.'

Similar feelings of rejection and lack of understanding of one's own problems also played a part in contact with relatives, for example:

'I wanted to talk to my mother about a very urgent problem, but she had hardly any time and I think that she underestimated the serious nature of my problem.'

Interestingly, blood relatives were often the cause of sadness but very seldom the cause of joy.

Broken relationships were likewise frequently the cause of sadness. These were often relationships with members of the opposite sex. Typical examples of this situation are:

'I thought I had found my partner for life, a human being with whom I did not experience any disharmonies. I had made big plans for our future, then one day she told me that she did not believe in our friendship and that she wanted to terminate this disastrous relationship (she did this on the advice of her mother).'

A 'classic' determinant of sadness is the death of someone close. Among the Swiss students this was often a friend, but sometimes it was a pet or even a withered plant.

'Sickness' was a further source of sadness. This is illustrated by the following example:

'My mother informed me over the telephone that she had had to have an operation and that her right hand was now in a cast, so she would not be able to run the house or even do her cooking.'

Generally speaking, as Izard stresses (1981, p. 322), separation seems to be one of the basic determinants of sadness, be it of a physical or a psychic nature. Contrary to the situation for joy, where there was always a specific determinant (the category 'happiness without reason' did not occur), a phenomenon which can be described as 'general depression' emerged. The trigger seemed to have no connection with a real situation, nor was any specific phantasy or idea which caused this emotional state described. Here is an example to show this:

> 'When I got up, I felt heavy and tired. All my movements were slower than usual and a deep sadness just rose inside me and I had the feeling of being paralysed. I started to cry.'

The end of a pleasurable experience did not seem to affect the Swiss too much. Also the separation from relatives did not make them sad and harming a stranger was not a cause for sadness. All these characteristics, however, do not distinguish them from other nationals. What has to be considered as typically Swiss, however, is the lack of sadness in connection with 'bad news'. This might be a consequence of the stable political and economic situation in Switzerland. World events did not seem to have an immediate impact on the individual and concern about news items was of relatively little significance to the Swiss students.

Fear. As in the other countries, the most frequent fear-inducing situations in Switzerland were connected with 'traffic'. Other important determinants were 'fear of the unknown', 'fear of failure in achievement-related situations', and physical aggression. Thus, the Swiss subjects described situations which consisted of a physical or psychic threat. A typical example of fear of traffic is:

> 'On the other side of the road a car broke out of the column in order to overtake another car. It came directly towards us. Only at the last moment did it swerve back to the right-hand side of the road.'

It was chiefly women who described 'physical aggression' as a determinant of fear (7% vs. 13%):

> 'It was already dark and I was on my way home when I noticed a man who was unfamiliar to me walking behind me. I began to walk faster and he also quickened his step. I ran into a back yard and rang the bell. The man remained at the entrance to his back yard. Finally, he went away and I ran home.'

'Fear of the unknown' contains determinants of fear which are of an unspecific nature, and this is illustrated in the following example:

> 'I had smoked hashish. Suddenly, I could no longer remember who, where and what I was. I had lost all control over reality. I felt as if I was in ten different worlds simultaneously and could not find reality any more.'

There were also situations which were felt to be threatening either because they were situations with which the subjects were unfamiliar, or because the stimulus was unfamiliar. The following example should illustrate this:

> 'I lay in my bed and was just about to fall asleep. The window was open

and the shutter was open, too. Thus, half asleep, I suddenly heard a kind of a loud hiss. It was a noise which I had never heard before and could therefore not explain. At first I thought it might be a wolf or tiger just about to jump in my room.'

'Fear of failure' applied particularly to situations connected with achievement requirements in studies. Two examples are:

'A paper written for a seminar was to be handed back to me, and I was really afraid that it would be marked as "unsatisfactory".'

and

'I had to give a speech which is something I do not like doing. I was very nervous at the beginning, especially when people entered the room and took their seats. In fact, I could hardly bear it.'

It is peculiar that the categories related to separation were hardly mentioned at all in connection with fear. This contradicts clinical experience insofar as the treatment of fears about separation is often of central significance in psychotherapy, a fact which allows the conclusion that fear of separation is a common phenomenon. We may therefore suppose that fear of separation is mostly unconscious and therefore not reported.

Supernatural events were not reported by the Swiss to cause fear, while no less than 4% of the total sample were afraid of witchcraft, seances, horror films, or the *Unheimliche*. This corresponds to the stereotype of the sober, down-to-earth Swiss who preferably deals with 'solid' matters, does not develop too much imagination and looks upon the inexplicable as belonging to fairyland.

Anger. Of all the emotions, the Swiss subjects differed least from the total sample for anger. The frequent antecedent categories for anger were 'failure of friends', 'failure of others', 'inappropriate rewards for oneself', and 'failure of blood relatives'. Anger was thus caused mainly by situations where other people did not behave as the subjects would have liked them to, or they did not behave as they were expected to behave. Typical examples of 'failure of friends' are:

'I had spent the afternoon cleaning up the flat and intended to go to the cinema in the evening. We had agreed that my friend and his brother would cook the dinner in time for this. However, they came back far too late. I felt they limited my freedom.'

'Failure of others' is illustrated by the following situations:

'We (my girlfriend and I) walked through town at night. A stranger passed us and tried to pinch my bottom.'

'I got out of the tram and was about to cross the street when a man passed me, turned round and said "You've got sagging breasts; you ought to fasten them a bit better".'

Typical situations for the category 'inappropriate rewards for self' are:

'Though my professor had spoken highly of my paper in a seminar only two months previously, three weeks ago he was not prepared to accept it, saying it was too superficial.'

'All the tenants in our house received information about an increase in the rent. I heard from a neighbour that the increase she would have to pay was much lower than my own.'

An example for the 'failure of blood relatives' is:

'I asked my parents to lend me their car because I wanted to go and spend the weekend with friends. My parents thought that I could take the train. However, I thought that this was asking too much; it would have meant travelling twice as long and walking a long way.'

Although on the basis of clinical experience one could expect that separation and death might often trigger aggressive feelings, the Swiss subjects did not report anger about separation and death. As a result of social norms the expression of such feelings is subject to strong taboo so that they are largely experienced unconsciously and therefore not a topic for description.

Discussion. It is striking that for the Swiss subjects group experiences were often connected with negative emotions. Group experiences comparatively often triggered anger and sadness and were therefore maybe more often feared. Are the Swiss bad mixers?

In order to evaluate to what extent the results reported are unique to the Swiss compared to the other nationalities, χ^2 tests were carried out for the individual antecedent categories, the combined antecedent categories (for the construction of the combined categories, see Chapter 4), and all the antecedent categories together; and the tests were carried out separately for all four emotions.

For joy and anger, there were really no significant differences between the Swiss sample and the rest with regard to the variables examined. For sadness, on the other hand, a significant difference was apparent for all the combined categories. This was due to significant differences in the reporting of the categories 'news', 'relationships', and 'permanent separation'. The Swiss reported that the category 'news' caused sadness with a lower frequency than the other subjects (2% Swiss vs. 11% rest). The opposite was the case for 'relationships' (38% Swiss vs. 26% rest) and 'permanent separation' (14% vs. 8% rest). For fear, the results of the χ^2 tests were highly significant, both with regard to the individual antecedent categories and throughout all the combined categories, but they cannot be readily interpreted because the cell frequencies are too small.

A5.3 Non-verbal behaviour and physiological symptoms

A statistical comparison showed that on average the Swiss subjects described significantly more reactions for sadness, fear, and anger (but not for joy) than the other subjects. When we compared the details submitted by the Swiss with those submitted by the other subjects about the individual variables it became obvious that particular variables were responsible for these differences.

For sadness, facial reactions occurred more often at the expense of voice reactions.

For fear, the Swiss subjects cited muscle symptoms more often than the other subjects. For anger, the variables voice reactions, hand movements, and muscle symptoms were more frequently cited than expected. For joy, pleasant rest and symptoms of warmth were mentioned significantly more frequently by the Swiss than by others, whereas voice reactions were mentioned significantly less frequently. It therefore seems to be the case that the Swiss specifically show more reactions with negative emotions than the other subjects. Moreover, for joy they described more physiological symptoms than did the other subjects. The former point hardly supports the stereotype image of the non-expressive Swiss. This stereotype is, however, backed up by the second finding: Swiss people do not enjoy themselves by coming out of their shell but enjoy pleasant rest and symptoms of warmth instead.

A5.4 Intensity and duration of emotions, control of verbal behaviour, and control of reactions

In terms of the major reaction variables intensity, duration, verbalisation, and control the Swiss sample showed a very similar pattern to the other countries combined. We comment briefly on the results for duration.

Joy and sadness were the longest lasting emotions, whereas anger and especially fear were usually described as being significantly shorter-lasting emotions. We have attempted to connect this finding with Roseman's approach (1979). Roseman maintains that every basic emotion influences behaviour because of characteristic 'emotivational goals' which are produced by specific cognition, that is that there are general strategies which serve to control the emotion-inducing situation (Roseman, 1979). In an analogous way we make the assumption that the duration of an emotion is connected with the corresponding 'emotivational goal'. Depending on the task which the control strategy has to fulfil, the emotion can last for a long or a short time. According to Roseman, the 'emotivational goal' of joy is 'sustain, extend'. This tendency seemed to be reflected relatively directly in the descriptions by the Swiss subjects. Sadness produces the strategy 'remedy, restore'. This function is also similarly conceptualised in the psychoanalytical concept of mourning (Freud, 1917). Seen from this functional perspective, it is plausible that the process of mourning is something which requires a certain amount of time. Fear, on the other hand, which is characterised by the strategies 'avoid, prevent', must be a short and effective mechanism seen from this aspect. The same is true for anger. With anger, the disturbing factors should be eliminated as soon as possible by 'avenge'.

After this rather general digression, we return to the more specific Swiss data. The Swiss subjects tended to experience shorter episodes of anger than the other subjects. As for the reasons, we can only speculate: we somewhat doubt ourselves that Swiss people regulate their anger differently from others. We are much more inclined to believe that norms specific to population have some influence here, that is in the sense that people do not like to admit to being angry for a long time for fear of admitting their own vulnerability.

With regard to control of verbal behaviour and control of reactions, joy was less strongly subjected to control than the three negative emotions. In this respect, the Swiss did not differ from the complete sample. It is, however, interesting to note that the Swiss subjects controlled their verbal utterances significantly less than the other subjects when they were happy. This result may also show that it is in the 'in thing' in the student and especially the psychological subculture to give vent to one's positive feelings.

For joy, sadness, and anger, there was a tendency in the Swiss sample to control verbal utterances more strongly than non-verbal behaviours. This was not the case for fear, however. The fact that verbal utterances were generally more strongly controlled than non-verbal ones can be explained by the negotiability (see Scherer, 1977a) of non-verbal behaviour. The reverse situation for fear was possibly due to the fact that one is often alone in fear situations, that is without a conversational partner, and so the attempts to control the reaction are shifted from the verbal level to the non-verbal level. This difference between the control of verbal behaviour and the control of non-verbal behaviour was particularly apparent for anger, and especially pronounced in the Swiss.

The Swiss subjects controlled their non-verbal reactions to a significantly lesser degree than the other subjects, whereas there was no significant difference between the groups for the control of verbal behaviour. Thus, it seems to be permitted for Swiss people to express their anger non-verbally as long as they keep their verbal behaviour under control.

A5.5 Personality traits

It can be assumed that, in addition to the biographical and sociographical characteristics of people personality traits also play a part in the experiencing and remembering of emotional components. We can make the supposition that this is particularly true for the antecedents of emotional reactions, as a cognitive assessment of the causative stimuli of an emotion always takes place, and this possibly covaries with certain personality traits.

In contrast to this hypothesis, which until the present day has hardly been investigated, investigation of the connection between personality traits and non-verbal expressional behaviour already has a long tradition. It is assumed that non-verbal behaviour is closely connected with personality traits and that it is expressed, for example, in a specific expressive way. Conversely, personality traits are attributed to a person particularly as a result of non-verbal behavioural characteristics.

We felt that it would be interesting to know whether such connections would become apparent in a questionnaire approach which is based on self-reports. The question also arises as to whether the regulation or control of emotions is also connected with certain personality traits.

In order that we might go some of the way towards finding an answer to this question, our subjects were given Eysenck's Personality Inventory (EPI), because it includes the main factors of non-cognitive personality aspects (Eysenck, 1973). Furthermore, Eysenck maintains that there are differences between extraverts and introverts or between high-level and low-level neurotics as regards the regulation of emotional behaviour (see e.g. Eysenck, 1973). The test was correlated with the following variables: antecedents, duration, intensity, verbal behaviour, control of verbal behaviour, control of reactions, group size, familiarity, all non-verbal and physiological reaction characteristics.

As a result of Eysenck's descriptions of personality types, we expected to be able to find a discriminating influence for the personality dimensions investigated (see Eysenck, 1973). In order to clarify whether extraverts and introverts and high-level neurotics and low-level neurotics differ with regard to the variables under consideration (the group division was made as a result of the median values), a χ^2 test was worked out separately for each variable for the individual emotions.

Analysis of the data revealed that, both for the dimension extraversion and for neuroticism, there were no significant differences for all but one of the variables investigated. With such a large number of variables under consideration, this one significant result must be interpreted as coincidental. There are several possible explanations for these results:

> There is actually no or only a loose connection between the personality dimensions postulated by Eysenck and the experiencing and remembering of emotional components.
>
> The personality dimensions of Eysenck are too global to allow the recording of such differences.
>
> The variables included in our study were not differentiated enough for the elucidation of this question.
>
> In general, our approach was not orientated specifically enough toward the investigation of this question.

These explanations are very global and do not affect all the variables that were considered to an equal extent. The question of which of these explanations is true and/or to what extent cannot be answered at this point, but has to be investigated in further studies.

A5.6 Final comments

In conclusion, we briefly comment on the applicability of our research approach in the field of clinical psychology.

For the clinical psychologist the question as to whether certain kinds of psychological disorders are connected with a specific type of emotional regulation is very important, particularly in terms of their diagnosis. How could we approach such a question using our questionnaire? Which difficulties were to be expected?

One approach in dealing with this matter would be to submit the questionnaire to subjects belonging to different clinical groups in order to study their specific ways of reporting emotional components. The main problem with this procedure is that the examination of just one single emotional situation is not very informative from the clinical point of view: in order to diagnose a psychological disorder it is not sufficient to consider the quality of one single emotion-eliciting situation; rather it is the frequency of occurrence of these situations which should be taken into account. In addition, the cognitive assessment of a situation is of major importance. Thus, according to several advocates of cognitive therapy (e.g. Beck, 1976; Hoffman, 1979), what is typical for a specific psychological disorder is not the eliciting situation itself but rather the type of cognitive assessment of the situation made by the person and the available coping strategies for dealing with the situation.

In order to take these considerations into account, it would be very important to hand out the questionnaires to the subjects not just once but repeatedly over a certain period of time. Moreover, it would be useful to change the questionnaires in such a way that the coping strategies used by the subjects could be recorded and analysed in a more differentiated manner.

Another problem in studying subjects with psychological disorders might be the fact that defence strategies are assumed to have much stronger effects on these subjects in terms of the remembering and reporting of emotional components than they have on healthy 'normal' subjects. Thus, it is quite probable that many emotions are not experienced consciously because of powerful defence mechanisms and can therefore not be recalled. However, it is precisely these 'omissions' that could be highly significant for the clinical group under investigation, and therefore very relevant for clinical research.

For this kind of investigation, it could be very interesting to look for relations between four emotional situations reported by each subject, on the basis of similarities of the reported contents. For this purpose, a structural analysis of the situational contents is required.

It would also be possible to use a more psychoanalytic approach. We could try to formulate equivalents on the level of relationship patterns in the different emotional situations. In other words, we could ask ourselves questions like the following: Has coping with the anxiety caused by the professor the same structure as coping with the anxiety experienced in the presence of one's father? All in all, we think that this approach provides many promising possibilities for studying questions that are important in the field of clinical psychology.

A6 The Belgian case: overt emotions in intimate contexts

Bernard Rimé

The Belgian sample was comparable to the global European sample in this study with respect to sex, the number of years spent at the University, marital status, and the number of brothers and sisters (see also Chapter 2). Some differences were revealed for the kind of environment in which subjects spent most of their life, as well as for social class. Indeed, subjects in the Belgian sample came from a much more rural environment than subjects in the general sample. Their families' socio-economic status also tended to be of a higher level. Because of these differences, we report the results mainly in a descriptive manner in this note, and simply consider any marked differences between the Belgian and European data in order to explore possible characteristics of the emotional life of people in this small country. Future studies using more systematic methods of inquiry will have to confirm the emerging picture. As a protection against overinterpretation in the comparisons reported, the data for the Belgian sample are always compared with the data recorded for the whole European sample including Belgium. Thus, any differences mentioned in the following pages will in fact be greater than they appear to be from the data.

A6.1 Social and environmental factors in emotion

In what sort of settings did the Belgian subjects experience emotion? As shown in Figure A6.1a, they preferred familar places. As compared to the European sample, they reported far fewer experiences of joy and of sadness having happened in unfamiliar places. The same trend was observed for anger, and still held for fear even though fear was generally the emotion most commonly associated with an unfamiliar environment. The question thus arose as to whether this difference in the physical environment of emotional experiences was reflected in the social one. Further explorations of the data yielded a clear positive answer. When we looked at the size of the group which was present at the moment of the reported emotion, it appeared that Belgian subjects systematically described emotional experiences that had occurred when they were alone or in dyads less often than their European counterparts and emotions that had occurred in the presence of a small group more often (see Figure A6.1b). While 31% of European subjects reported that they had experienced fear when alone, only 23% of Belgian ones did so, and while 8% of European subjects reported that they had experienced anger when alone, none of the Belgian subjects did. Thus, familiar environments and social surroundings seem to be more characteristic settings for the Belgian sample's emotions than for those of the total European sample. Since the social surroundings which are found in familiar environments are generally familiar people, it follows that the emotions

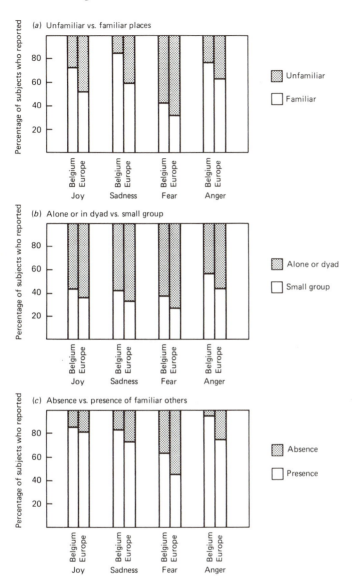

Figure A6.1 Environmental and social factors of emotional experiences as reported in the Belgian sample, and in the total European sample

described by this sample probably typically occurred in the presence of close relatives or friends. This was confirmed by data showing that the emotions remembered by subjects in the Belgian sample were much more often associated with the presence of familiar social support than was the case for the global European sample (see Figure A6.1c).

Do these data indicate that the Belgian subjects tended, more than the other Europeans, to share emotions with members of their familiar surroundings, and thus to be especially prone to empathic emotional experiences? For joy, 5% of European subjects reported such empathic experience, while 18% of them reported it for sadness, 5% for fear, and 5% for anger. In each of the corresponding cells of the Belgian data, a value of zero was obtained. It then became evident that while emotions in Belgium, as reported by this sample, had characteristically occurred in small, familiar, social and physical environments, they had always resulted from events which immediately affected the subject him- or herself. An examination of data concerned with the antecedents of emotions should reveal whether or not the sources of the emotions experienced by the Belgian subjects lay in their close familiar ties and relationships.

A6.2 Antecedents of emotions

There were two marked differences between the Belgian and the European subjects for the antecedents of joy. Firstly, as depicted in Figure A6.2 Belgian subjects reported far fewer experiences of joy associated with close relationships. Among European subjects, about a quarter of the reported experiences of joy were related to relationships with close friends, partners, or family members, but the figure was only slightly more than one-tenth for the Belgian subjects. Conversely, the latter subjects referred more often than the European ones to antecedents of joy which were scored in the category 'temporary meeting', that is to situations in which short contacts with friends or family members were re-established, as is the case for a dinner or a party. Thus, with respect to positive emotions, the Belgians seemed to experience them in the close circle of familiar persons, with joy often being felt on the re-establishing of contact with them, but much less often being felt in maintaining the contact in a more permanent way.

For sadness, the major difference which was observed in the Belgian–European comparison again confirmed the particular relevance of the intimate universe for the experiencing of emotions by Belgians as reported by the subjects in this study. Indeed, experiences of sadness were revealed as being much more often provoked by close relationships among the Belgian subjects than among the other European ones. Thus, those relationships which appeared to be less often a source of joy for Belgian subjects were also a particularly frequent source of sadness. Strikingly, two other trends emerged in this comparative analysis of the antecedents of sadness. Belgian subjects reported less often than European ones experiences of sadness induced by permanent separation and by death. Does this mean that the breaking, by fate or by circumstances, of the contentions permanent relationships they experienced with close friends or relatives, would leave them relatively unaffected?

There was no notable difference between the two groups for antecedents of fear, either for the common list of antecedents mentioned in Figure A6.2, or for the specific antecedents provided by the coding system for this particular emotion, except for achievement. This was more often reported as an antecedent of fear by the Belgian subjects than by the European ones. However, it should be recalled that the Belgian data were collected at the end of the academic year, just before the examination period, and memories of anxieties related to academic evaluations were

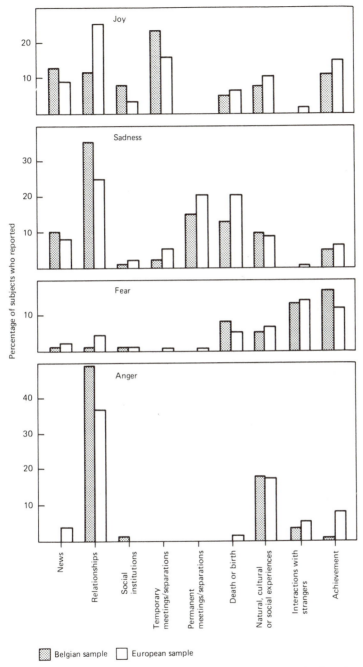

Belgian sample ☐ European sample

Figure A6.2 Frequency of antecedents of emotion reported by the Belgian and European samples for all four emotions

particularly often encountered among the subjects' descriptions of experiences of fear. Thus, the period of the year might well have been a source of bias which could explain the observed difference.

Finally, data which concerned experiences of anger were closely congruent with the preceding ones, as they again showed a clear-cut difference between the Belgian and European samples for antecedents categorised as 'relationships'. Those relationships which have already been noted as being poor sources of joy and rich sources of sadness for the Belgian subjects, were an equally rich source of anger. In fact, half of the experiences of anger reported by the Belgian sample were aroused by 'relationships', while this was the case for only one-third of the European sample.

We now go on to consider aspects of the emotional responses themselves: verbal and non-verbal behaviours, as well as physiological symptoms mentioned by the subjects in their answers to the open questions raised by the questionnaire for each described emotion. As in Belgium emotions were particularly frequently activated in the context of intimate relationships, one might expect to find abundant mention of strong expressive components among these subjects' descriptions of their emotional responses. Indeed, it is possible that intimate relationships generally preclude the attempt to control overt emotional displays as exerted by people in other countries where their emotions develop in less familiar social settings.

A6.3 Verbalisations

Verbal behaviour is highly sensitive to emotional states. Comparisons between the Belgian and the European samples revealed very strong and systematic differences. As is shown in Figure A6.3, in the case of each emotion, Belgian people reported verbalisations in the form of sentences much less frequently than other Europeans. This difference was especially marked for anger and for joy, but it also held for fear, and, to a lesser extent, for sadness. The reverse pattern was observed for exclamations. For all four emotions, Belgian subjects revealed themselves to be dramatically more prone to making exclamations than did European ones. The smallest difference recorded was for joy and amounted to 15%, while the greatest difference occurred for anger, amounting to nearly 40%. An exclamation is probably a rougher form of verbal response when one is under the influence of an emotion, and in this sense, these data confirm the expectation of strong expressive components in the emotional responses of Belgians.

A6.4 Non-verbal behaviours

The Belgian and European data for the major non-verbal variables of the coding system are summarised in Table A6.1. The data show that differences occurred between the two samples for all five groups of non-verbal variables. With the exception of the reported changes in the quality of the face, all notable differences suggest a higher frequency of non-verbal responses among Belgian subjects.

For joy, changes in the quality of the voice, as well as in the quality of body part movements were more frequently reported by the Belgians than by the Europeans. The reverse was true for changes in the quality of facial expressions. However, the detailed data for the face reveal a higher frequency of laughter and smiling among

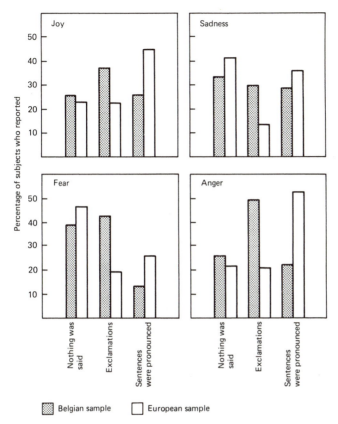

Belgian sample   European sample

Figure A6.3   Types of verbalisations made by the Belgian and European samples in the four emotional states

the Belgian subjects as compared to the European subjects. This precludes the hypothesis of a greater attempt by the Belgians to control their facial manifestations of joy. Similarly, for sadness, a facial display of their responses seemed quite characteristic of the sample under study in this chapter. The Belgian subjects reported crying in sadness twice as often as the European subjects. Practically one-half of their descriptions of sad experiences mentioned tears.

Few significant non-verbal responses were reported by the European sample in relation to fear. This was the case for the Belgian sample too, with one exception. The freezing response, rather rare among the Europeans, was important in Belgium. Finally, for anger, changes in the quality of speech and body part movements were reported more frequently by the Belgians than by the Europeans.

On the whole then, the data concerning non-verbal behaviours confirmed, as was already the case for verbalisation, the expectation of strong overt components in the emotional responses of Belgian subjects. It remains to be seen whether in the case of emotions with strong expressive components, physiological symptoms were also

Table A6.1. *Non-verbal behaviours reported by the Belgian and European samples (in %)*[a]

	Joy		Sadness		Fear		Anger	
	Belgium	Europe	Belgium	Europe	Belgium	Europe	Belgium	Europe
Speech								
Quality changes	8	—	—	—	—	—	16	6
Symptoms mentioned	—	—	—	—	—	—	—	—
Voice								
Quality changes	18	10	14	11	7	8	26	24
Symptoms mentioned	—	7	7	8	7	7	8	6
Face								
Quality changes	—	9	7	10	—	5	—	10
Laughter/smiling	43	33	—	—	—	—	—	—
Crying	5	—	47	25	—	—	7	—
Other symptoms	—	—	—	6	—	—	8	10
Body part movement								
Quality changes	10	—	5	—	—	—	25	8
Interpersonal movements	7	7	—	—	—	—	7	—
Instrumental action	—	—	—	—	—	—	—	—
General unrest	—	—	—	—	—	—	—	—
Hand symptoms	—	6	—	—	5	6	7	9
Whole body and posture								
Quality changes	—	—	—	—	—	—	—	—
Avoidance – distancing	—	—	—	—	—	—	5	—
Freezing	—	—	—	—	13	6	—	—
Expansive movements	5	5	—	—	—	—	—	—

[a] For clarity, all values of less than 5% have been omitted.

described with some particular frequency in these subjects' descriptions of their experiences.

A6.5 Physiological symptoms

Profiles of physiological symptoms by emotion (Figure A6.4) showed the Belgian sample to be very similar to the European one in their physiological responses to emotional experiences. Indeed, in the profiles for both samples, in peaks corresponded systematically. However, for each symptom the Belgian peak generally exceeded the European one. This was true for all four emotions. One might thus consider that

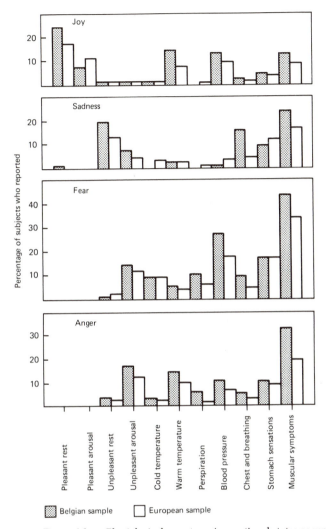

Figure A6.4   Physiological symptoms in emotional states as reported by the Belgian and European samples for all four emotions

the Belgian response pattern of physiological responses in emotional states as reported by subjects in this study is an accentuated form of the typical European response pattern of such responses.

In a further exploration of these data, the two samples' reported physiological symptoms were compared across the emotions. This was done by computing the number of subjects in each sample who mentioned a given symptom in at least one of the four described emotions. These results, which are reported in Table A6.2 clearly confirmed the higher incidence of physiological symptoms among Belgian subjects. Indeed, for 10 out of 11 symptoms in the coding list, the Belgian sample

Table A6.2. *Reported physiological symptoms across the emotions (Belgian and European data) (expressed as the percentage of subjects reporting each kind of symptom)*

	Belgian subjects	European subjects
Pleasant rest	25	17
Pleasant arousal	8	11
Unpleasant rest	23	17
Unpleasant arousal	31	25
Cold temperature	13	13
Warm temperature	30	18
Perspiration	16	10
Blood pressure rise	36	26
Chest and breathing problems	25	11
Stomach troubles	34	32
Muscular symptoms	70	55

presented a higher frequency as compared to the European one, the difference between the two samples often being marked. Thus, it might be concluded that among Belgian subjects in this study, emotional responses, which have been proven to have been particularly overt and expressive, were also heavily loaded in perceived physiological changes.

A6.6 Conclusions

This first overview of Belgian emotional experiences thus revealed a very characteristic pattern of overtly expressed intense emotional responses aroused particularly frequently by the subjects' intimate social milieu. This picture irresistibly evokes the memory of artistic representations of emotional life in northern Continental Europe. In the cloudy and humid countries of this area, people live predominantly in their own homes. There, they develop complex and contentious ties with those with whom they share their lives. Intimacy has been at the core of paintings by artists in Belgium as well as in the Netherlands. In Sweden, films by Ingmar Bergman have made famous the dramatic emotional outbursts which typically arise in the confined universe of intimate relationships. A very similar theme has been developed in Belgian films by Delvaux.

The first European project for the study of emotion, of which the present study is a part, did not include countries such as the Netherlands, Denmark, Norway, and Sweden. Thus, this chapter ends with a hypothesis to be tested: that the emotions depicted here as being typical of the Belgians are illustrative of the way in which people from northern continental countries experience such states.

A7 The Spanish case: the written expression of emotional routes

José M. F. Dols and Alfonso J. Fernandez

A7.1. Introduction: The script concept as a means for studying emotion

The cross-cultural study of behaviour teaches us that, before beginning an investigation we have to delimit clearly a dimension (e.g. Fridja & Jahoda, 1966; Carretero, 1982) that allows comparison. The definition of the 'emic' and 'etic' aspects of emotional behaviour necessitates, then, establishing whether the proposed task has the same meaning in every culture. We must therefore elucidate the basic elements of our analysis. The purpose of this note is to delimit some basic structures in the emotional situations reported by the Spanish subjects.

What we can assert is that the spoken or written reconstruction of emotional situations has a central role in the social control and representation of emotions.

To demonstrate that the symbolic expression (in this case written) of emotions has these important functions of representation and control of emotions two tasks must first be carried out. First, it is necessary to demonstrate that there are some basic structures that characterise the different social situations, which are seemingly heterogeneous. Second, once these structures have been detected, a process of decodification (vs. codification) similar to that of other means of emotional expression is possible (e.g. Salzen, 1981).

The purpose of our work was to determine which cognitive structures in emotional situations allow us to discriminate among the various emotions and which structures play a role in the regulation and social representation of emotions.

If we consider the emotional situation as a social situation, an obligatory point of departure for the search of these patterns is the work of Schank & Abelson (1977) on plans and understanding. The most popular contribution of Schank and Abelson to Social Psychology is the 'script' concept. A script (Abelson, 1981) is a cognitive structure that involves expectations about the occurrence of events and, in its stricter sense, about the order of sequence of the events.

According to Schank & Abelson (1977), understanding would be predictive in its nature. We are constantly involved in actions with a goal. Normally, the script lets us trace a route towards the goal and, in the remaining situations, we use plans. A plan is 'the repository for general information that will connect events' when there are no available scripts or standard causal chains.

Obviously, the script concept is as fertile as it is problematic (e.g. Langer, 1978; Bower *et al.*, 1979), and it is very important in social and cognitive psychology (e.g. Bartlett, 1932). But, while Abelson (1981) developed the concept, Schank (1982) built up a new theoretical framework centred on memory and learning.

The work of Schank (1982) changed the meaning of the script concept. According to him there is a more central concept, the 'scene', that is a set of simultaneous actions with the same goal and that can be defined by a setting, an instrumental goal, and some actions. Scripts are only specifications of scenes.

But let us return to our point of departure: the search for structures in emotions, that is in the expression of emotional situation. We may suppose that there will be different patterns of emotional-social behaviour and that these patterns will appear in the subjects' written accounts.

Thus, we can borrow some very general aspects from Schank's theory: there is a basic way of understanding and remembering situations in terms of *goals* and *related conditions* and there is a dynamic elaboration of memory in which *expectations are basic, especially the failure of implicit* and *explicit* expectations. For Schank, a developing memory needs failed expectations that imply new indices to memories for new generalisations and learning. Our opinion is that, if you ask people to remember emotional situations, their account will have an *implicit* ('non-initiated expectation of failure' according to Schank) or explicit goal. Therefore, according to the hypothesis of Schank, people do not remember familiar and near experiences; they remember situations that involve some broken expectations.

In our questionnaire study subjects did not remember emotional situations that had happened within a short period of time. The international survey questionnaire asked: 'describe for each emotion one event or situation which, in the last *few weeks*, has resulted in your experiencing the respective emotion' but subjects found it easier to look for more distant situations.

Emotional experiences are daily events, but many of the situations described did not fall within the time period demanded by the questionnaire and, moreover, we can suppose that a substantial number of the situations happened before the period referred to, especially if they were important for the person (this is 'forward telescoping', see Loftus, 1982).

A7.2. Definition of routes

We can maintain, for the moment, Schank's hypothesis applied to emotions but we need some analytical procedure for establishing the syntactic relationships between expectations and goals in given situations.

What kind of situations with failed expectations are we likely to find? Schank (1982) proposes a notation:

Given expectation Eo and X will happen; and Goal G that actor wants; and expectation E1 that X will lead to G and expectation E2 that G will make you happy and expectation E3 that no other goals will be satisfied if X happens. (Schank, 1982, p. 174)

There will be different outcomes if X happens or if X does not happen and if, in its place, another faction – Y – happens. Let us underline some of them:

$\underline{00}$	No	Eo	but	Y→G (unexpected success)
$\underline{01}$	No	Eo		No G (failure)
$\underline{02}$		Eo	but	X $\nrightarrow$ G (bad plan)
$\underline{03}$	No	Eo	but	G! (lucky success)
$\underline{04}$		Eo	and	G (success)

08		Eo	Eı	E2		E3! (more than G, unthinkable success)
09		Eo	Eı			No E2! (G does not satisfy me)
14	No	Eo		but		Y⇒G (Y is better than X).

The basic structure consists of a chain of expectations (see above) and a goal. So far we have seen eight different patterns. At first glance there is a difference among them; if you read the categories you can establish a clear distinction between 04 and the remaining categories: 00, 01, 02, 03, 08, 09 and 14 involve a break in the expectation, so we assume a greater uncertainty.

In some cases the categories that have been established give an intuitive idea of emotion. 'Unexpected success', 'lucky success', etc. immediately give us the label 'joy' or 'happiness'. A 'bad plan' is a frustration that suggests 'anger' or 'sadness'. Such an 'emotional tone' is undoubtedly determined by a semantic element being introduced into Schank's scheme. The aforesaid semantic element is an evaluative aspect in the patterns of expectations and goals.

Evaluation is essential, too, in any cognitive or social characterisation of emotion; it appears in all the work on emotional appraisal in psychology and also in sociological research on affective behaviour (see e.g. Kemper, 1978; Heise, 1979).

In order to apply the heuristic frame suggested by Schank to the study of emotional situations it is necessary to combine the goal-expectation structures with an affective component. How can we characterise this affective component? A solution offering guarantees is to use the characterisation developed by Osgood *et al.* (1957) in terms of a positive-evaluative pole and a negative-evaluative pole, which may be compared to the connotations of adjectives like 'good-bad', 'beautiful-ugly', etc. (e.g. Heise, 1979). As we know, the connotative dimensions proposed by Osgood have been contrasted in more than 30 countries of very different cultural contexts (e.g. Diaz-Guerrero & Salas, 1975).

The combination of goal-expectation structures with both poles of the affective continuum gives a cognitive-affective structure of the written expression of antecedent events that can be defined by different categories:

Route number code	Route	Definition and examples
00	|E+ Y→G	Unexpected success
		'I expected to take an exam about motivation but it was about perception; I was surprised I passed.'
01	|E+ (|G+)	Failure in positive expectation, goal is not explicit
		'Teacher promised to give us an exam about motivation but it was about perception.'
		'(Subject number: 1879, Emotion: Anger) Some girls were 'laughing at another, one who was with them, not with silly jokes but almost humiliating her.'

Route number code	Route	Definition and examples
02	E+ X↛G	**Bad plan**
		'As I expected the exam was about motivation but all the questions were only about the lesson that I did not study.'
		(Subject number: 1816, Emotion: Anger) 'I wanted to talk with a girl alone, and her friend did not leave us.'
03	|E+ G−G!	**Lucky Success**
		'When I went to take the exam a friend told me that I did not have to take it.'
		(Subject number: 1805, Emotion: Joy) 'I was studying in the library, some classmates arrived and on seeing me they all sat down around me as if I were part of their group. We talked and studied together with me not acting in a forced or artificial way.'
04	E+ →G	**Success**
		'As I expected the exam was about motivation. I got a good mark.'
		(Subject number: 1889, Emotion: Joy) 'A friend of mine had left home. After convincing her it was an error, I got her to forget the idea.'
05	|E− G−!	**Negative accident**
		'Yesterday a friend told me that I failed the exam.'
		(Subject number: 1855, Emotion: Fear) 'I was in the sea and the waves surrounded me.'
06	E− (? G−)	**Bad perspectives**
		'After I gave in the exam I remembered a stupid mistake.'
		(Subject number: 1840, Emotion: Fear) 'I had not attended English classes for one month and I was afraid I would not know what to say if the teacher asked me something.'
07	E− →G−	**Failure** 'I failed the exam but that is normal with this teacher.'

Route number code	Route	Definition and examples
		(Subject number: 1853, Emotion: Sadness) 'I felt distressed due to the change in the way of living when I came back after my holidays. People were different, I had to study and, in a way, I felt alone.'
08	$E0+,E1+,E2+,E3+!$	Unthinkable success 'I studied and I got a good mark in the exam. Moreover the teacher offered me a scholarship.'
09	$E0+,E1+,E2+!$	Unsatisfied 'I discovered that my brilliant academic curriculum does not mean anything to me.'
10	$|E+ (1G+)$	$= 01 + E+ XG \nrightarrow G = 02$
11	$|E+ (1G+)$	$= 01 + E- \rightarrow G- = 07$
12	$|E- G-!$	$= 05 + |E+ |G+ = 01$
13	$|E- G+!$	
14	$|E+ Y \Rightarrow X$	Unexpected and better success than expected 'The exam was not about motivation, but perception. It turned out to be a very easy subject and I got a good mark.'
15	$E- X \nrightarrow G-$	Bad perspectives without negative or positive consequences 'When I gave in the exam I remembered a stupid mistake. The teacher told me that the mistake was not substantial.' (Subject number: 1899, Emotion: Sadness) 'I was alone and began to feel even more lonely. I was waiting for someone to phone me to go for a walk. Nobody phoned. From a small problem I tried to make a real crisis.'

The analysis criteria these structures establish allow us to state the existence of certain 'routes' that configure a heuristic framework appropiate for the study of emotional appraisal, since this is considered to be a central or collateral factor to emotional phenomena.

We will call these structures 'emotional routes' in honour of the metaphor 'collective routes' from Maurice Halbwachs (1968), a pioneer in the study of relations among affect, social behaviour, and memory:

Or, c'est sur de telles routes, sur de tels sentier dérobés que nous retrouverions les souvenirs que son à nous, de meme qu'un voyageur peut considérer comme n'étant qu'à lui une source, un groupe de rochers, paysage qu'on n'atteint qu'à condition de sortir de la route, d'en rejoindre une autre par un chemin mal frayé et non fréquenté...(Halbwachs, 1968, pp. 31–2).

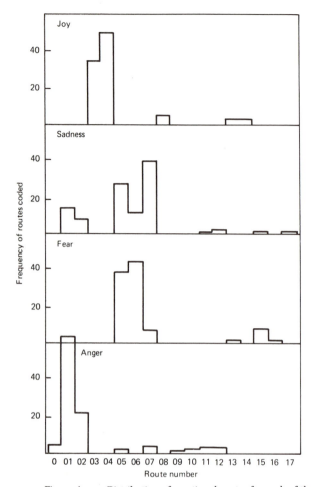

Figure A7.1   Distribution of emotional routes for each of the four emotions

A7.3 Empirical results

First experiment. The purpose of our first experiment was to test our first hypothesis: that there is an emotion-specific relationship between certain specific symbolic structures and antecedent events.

We established a set of 9 categories of expectation – goal patterns that were finally increased to 17. Two coders analysed the questionnaires first by a double blind method and then by observer consensus (Hollenbeck, 1978). The mean value for the reliability here was 70% agreement between coders.

Figure A7.1 gives the distribution of emotional routes for each of the four emotions according to the written expressions of emotion. As can be seen from the figure, there was a clear allocation of routes 05 and 06 to sadness and fear. Routes 03 and 04, of course, were exclusive to joy.

There were other clear correspondences: route 01 was particular to anger and sadness, route 07 to sadness, and route 15 to fear. It thus seems that our route categories could discriminate between different expressions of emotions but, obviously, it would be interesting to compare their characteristics for every emotional label.

If one observes the examples or the models in the definitions (see Section A7.2), it is easy to conclude that anger is, above all, a sociocultural emotion. Subjects were angry when their expectations, especially their expectations about the behaviour of other people, were not met. Anger was generally described in the accounts as a step in a routine towards social control (Averill, 1979).

It is very suggestive that there were 13 cases of route 01 in sadness; route 01 was, however, the most common route in anger. Other empirical studies will have to determine whether there are two different emotional responses to others' misbehaviours depending on character or social structures of dominance. However, the three most common routes in sadness were basically related to fear (05 and 06) or were independent (like 07); 07 route involves an inevitable negative event that, in a few cases, is characterised as a conflict or a depressive process and, in most cases, as some more or less important disagreeable situation.

The emotional status of joy is very clear from the data, as is the expression of joy. There was an arousing situation (03) and a routine of successful plans (04).

Finally, fear was depicted as routes with a negative surprise or an unknown not very promising conclusion.

Second experiment. According to our second hypothesis, the subject will be able to codify the symbolic expression of his/her emotional accounts in terms of the defined structures, but *he/she will also be able to decodify the emotional meaning of such structures.*

One hundred and twenty-eight subjects with the same characteristics as those forming the main sample in this study (see Chapters 2 and 3) were given a questionnaire in which were detailed, with no emotional referents, the most relevant cognitive-evaluative structures among those previously detected, that is those not including combinations or assumptions that might be difficult to understand.

The questionnaire format was as follows:

> In our everyday life we have expectations about the behaviour of others and objects surrounding us; they may be positive anticipations if we expect the event in question to have a happy ending; they may be negative anticipations if we expect the given event not to have a very happy ending. Sometimes we are right about our expectations and sometimes we aren't; similarly, sometimes such correct or incorrect guesses are accompanied by a characteristic emotion.
>
> Now we will put several situations to you and you must indicate what emotion they suggest to you; you must choose among the following alternatives:
>
> (a) No emotion
> (b) Joy or happiness
> (c) Anger or rage
> (d) Sadness or grief
> (e) Fear or fright
>
> 05   Our negative anticipations about others or surrounding objects are not fulfilled but what is happening leads to a bad final result.
>
> 03   Our positive anticipations about others or surrounding objects are not fulfilled but the final result is good.

13   Our negative anticipations about others or surrounding objects are not fulfilled but what is happening leads to a good final result.

02   Our positive anticipations about others or surrounding objects are fulfilled but the final result is bad.

06   Our negative anticipations about others or surrounding objects are fulfilled.

01   Our positive anticipations about others or surrounding objects are not fulfilled.

04   Our positive anticipations about others or surrounding objects are fulfilled and the final result is good.

15   Our negative anticipations about others or surrounding objects are fulfilled but the final result is not bad.

00   Our positive anticipations about others or surrounding objects are not fulfilled but what is happening leads to a good final result.

07   Our negative anticipations about others or surrounding objects are fulfilled and the final result is bad.

(The number points to the represented route; the order of presentation was randomised).

Table A7.1 shows the distribution of the routes coded in our first experiment (expression of emotional situations). On comparing this table with Figure A7.1 we found that the distributions of the routes for each emotion were similar in both experiments. Thus, subjects seemed to use the same structures both to codify emotional situations and to decodify them.

It is evident from the data that structures are more easily perceived in emotional situations of joy than in emotional situations of fear. Further research will be needed to define the differences.

Third experiment. We have tried to demonstrate up to this point the descriptive utility and discriminative power of molecular analyses on the basis of cognitive-evaluative routes. But what is the social function of these routes? According to our point of view, the routes play an important role in the regulation and representation of emotional situations. The context of this survey does not permit an exhaustive verification of the functional characteristics of the routes. We can, however, at least check the relationships between routes and learning. This is obviously the first step to establishing the adaptative value of these cognitive-evaluative devices in the process of socialisation.

We chose two other indexes in the elicitation questionnaire: the responses to the question 'What would you do differently, if you found yourself in such a situation again?' and the responses to the question 'How long ago was it?'

If we accept Schank's (1982) proposition, routes are stored in a dynamic memory and if you remember them it is because there will be some interesting point in them. Their interest will be a function of their value as a learning feature. So, the situations remembered during a longer period of time should be those that confronted the subject with an unresolved threat or a dangerous failure. On the other hand, there should be a larger number of new plans of behaviour in response to the question: ('What would you do differently?') associated with failures or unresolved problems.

The only modification we made to the international coding for the purposes of this experiment was to set up new criteria in coding the answer to 'What would you do differently ...?'

Table A7.1. *Emotion attributions for route descriptions in Experiment 2*[a]

Emotion	Route Number									
	00	01	02	03	04	05	06	07	13	15
Joy	89	7	3	91	112	2	13	5	98	38
Sadness	9	55	53	11	2	69	54	62	3	27
Fear	1	2	4	3	0	6	7	11	3	2
Anger	2	48	51	3	1	26	14	20	5	4
Nothing	22	15	11	13	10	23	40	27	18	51

[a] The figures are the number of route descriptions decoded as pertaining to that particular emotion.

Coders established a finer set of categories with different possibilities to the old alternative 'there will be changes vs. no changes'. Thus, there were two codes for 'no changes': $S+$, comprising future plans that do not modify the original strategies (e.g. 'I would shout even more', and S, comprising responses such as 'I would do the same' or 'I would do nothing'. In addition, a code D was established for responses that implied qualitative changes, and there was an intermediate code $S-$ which involved ambiguous and tautological arguments that, in fact, did not refute the actual behaviour in the situation (e.g. 'I would have less fear'). There was also a code N for blank and 'I don't know' responses. In summary, then, we used the codes $S+$ (more of the same thing); S (the same); $S-$ (less of the same); D (different strategies); and N (blank and don't know).

With regard to the responses to the question 'How long ago was it?', we used the original categories of the cross-cultural study: 'today'; 'yesterday'; 'up to a week ago'; 'up to a month ago'; 'several months ago'; 'several years ago'.

If measures of association among routes, time, and emotion are considered, it is possible to establish the number of 'memorable routes'. We can then propose a hypermnesia index (see e.g. Loftus, 1982, for the concept of hypermnesia). This was computed by dividing the number of times that a situation had happened at a particular time in the past (e.g. several months or years ago) according to the subjects' responses by the total frequency of this route across all the sample. The results are shown in Table A7.2.

The results agree with our hypothesis: threatening routes (05, 06, and 15) were the best remembered, and the worst remembered route was bad plans (02). The most plausible explanation for this distribution is that failures are indexed in memory if they involve some negative-affective component that threatens the subjects' adaptation. The irregular values of the remembering index of bad plans (02) across the emotions point to this: bad plans that involve sadness are well remembered (0.28), but failures of plans that involve anger are forgotten (0.04).

It should be noticed that except for bad plans, the hypermnesia index is independent of the emotions, that is, its values for a route are very similar across all the emotions.

The responses concerning the number of new coping plans associated with emotional situations are summarised in Table A7.3. Two additional scores were

Table A7.2. *Hypermnesia Index[a] for different routes and emotions*

Route number	Emotion				
	Joy	Sadness	Fear	Anger	Mean
01		0.23		0.20	0.21
02		0.28		0.04	0.10
03	0.24				0.24
04	0.23				0.23
05		0.64	0.44		0.52
06		0.50	0.45		0.46
07		0.32	0.33		0.32
15			0.50		0.50

[a] Index = Route (frequency) in time (categories 05 and 06)/Route in time (total frequency).

Table A7.3. *Number of strategies by emotion[a]*

Emotion	Codes					
	S	S−	D	N	S+N	(S+N)/D
Joy	81	1	7	14	95	13.5
Sadness	50	7	21	21	71	3.4
Fear	44	11	29	15	59	2.0
Anger	49	8	36	10	59	1.6

[a] S = The same and more of the same; S− = less of the same; D = different; N = nothing (no answer).

established for each emotion by computing the ratio of the number of responses of 'more of the same thing' (S+) plus 'the same' (S) plus 'I don't know' (N) divided by the number of responses of 'different strategies' (D). The responses of 'less of the same' (S−) were not included in this calculation as this category occurred with a very low frequency (see Table A7.3).

If one looks at the distribution of these frequencies by emotion (see Table A7.3), one can see that there were no differences in the direction of the strategies adopted; in all cases the subjects adopted conservative strategies.

The panorama changes, however, if we consider emotional routes. Table A7.4 shows the dichotomic frequency of S+ plus S plus N responses. If you divide this frequency by the number of D, the result will be an index of strategy election. If D < S, the index will be above 1; if S < D, the index will be below 1.

Again, the results point to our hypothesis; where the index had a low value, that is of 0.9 it was for 'bad plans'; if you had a bad plan you would change coping strategies. Furthermore, the other lower value of the index was associated with

Table A7.4. *Computation of Strategy Election Index for different routes*

Route	Number of 'same' strategies					Divided by	Total number of 'different' strategies D					Index
	$\underline{S+}$	+	$\underline{S}$	+	$\underline{N}$							
01			7	+	39	/	4	+	1	+	18 =	2.0
02			4	+	9	/	3	+	12		=	0.9
03					31	/	1				=	31.0
04					53	/	6				=	8.8
05	19	+	30	+	1	/	5	+	6	+	1 =	4.2
06			7	+	20	/	2	+	17		=	1.4
07	33	+	5	+	3	/	4	+	1	+	1 =	6.8

another potential source of failures: the unsure situation of route 06 (threat in suspense).

Route 01 came out with quite a low value on the index too. Perhaps its value was not lower because failure situations are not the responsibility of the subject (see above) (see D-AGENCY in Schank & Abelson, 1977). The high values on the index were associated with routes that gave satisfaction.

It is important to note that there was a problem in analysing the data frequencies for this index because the subjects' responses did not always refer to the situation-frame but instead to some non-substantial antecedents or outcomes. However, the general pattern of strategies by route was so clear that the uniform distribution across the emotions did not cast doubt on the main results.

There is a last point to note: the low number of alternative actions reported in two 'bad' situations – 05 and 07 – which have high values on the Hypermnesia Index is surprising. This does not mean, however, that there is any failure in these routes; there are, on the contrary, unexpected or unavoidable 'bad goals'. Are these routes of helplessness (Seligman, 1975)?

A7.4 Discussion

In the context of cross-cultural work, the aim of our study was to obtain precise characterisation of one of the considered dimensions: the emotional situation ('what happened?').

The proposed cognitive-evaluative structure is not a new theoretical hypothesis in the overcrowded world of models explaining emotion. It is, first of all, a heuristic model that permits the accurate establishment of the characteristics of emotional appraisal.

The results from our sample allow the postulation of an index of routes that delineates the relations between expectations and goals in any emotional-social situation.

We have observed that these routes play a role in the expression and impression of the symbolic representation of emotions. In terms of the function of the structures a tentative model could be built in a cartesian space with two dimensions (hypermnesia and strategic choice), where the zero point is occupied by the medians of each

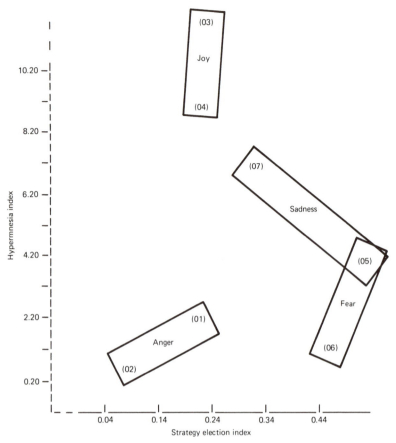

Figure A7.2   Location of emotions in the two-dimensional space of the Hypermnesia and Strategy Election Indexes

dimension. This model is shown in Figure A7.2. Some routes are well remembered but the subject has no alternatives for acting differently, others have a high value on the Hypermnesia Index but there are more possible alternatives reported; finally, there are no salient situations with high values on the Hypermnesia Index and either very low or very high values on the Strategy Election Index. There is, however, a clear correspondence between emotional labels (joy, sadness, fear, and anger) and quadrants.

The fact that we are working with a basic repertory of discrete emotions and that our data are adjusted to such a repertory is encouraging: taking into account the point of view of authors such as Kemper (1978) or Lazarus (1968), our opinion is that the cognitive characterisation of emotion is perhaps not as unspecific as the plurality of human contexts suggests.

A discriminative point of view of cognitive-evaluative structures would permit us to connect the social aspect of Lazarus' (1968) 'emotional drama' with the study of emotion in terms of 'specific programs genetically inherited' (see Tomkins, 1962, 1963; Ekman, 1972; Izard, 1977).

It is obvious that the study of the psychology of emotion needs integrative models but a more solid descriptive basis is also necessary. The questionnaire supplied us with information that is compatible with the observation of emotional behaviour; Ericsson & Simon (1980) have convincingly shown that, if an adequate selection of questions, centred on information that the subject heeds, is used, there is no contradiction between verbal and behavioural data.

In this area, empirical work such as that of Bartlett & Izard (1972) point to a basic similarity in subjects' emotion profiles in both real and imagined emotional situations, and theoretical models such as Leventhal's (1979) integrate in a polemical but stimulating way motor, perceptual, and cognitive patterns based on data from very different methodologies.

A8 The Israeli case: minority status and politics

Elisha Y. Babad

A8.1 Introduction

'Etic' and 'emic' are basic concepts in cross-cultural psychology (see e.g. Segall, 1979). Taken from linguistics ('phonetics' and 'phonemics'), they describe the search for universal generalisations that hold true for all cultures, as contrasted with the search for culture-unique phenomena and cross-cultural differences. From a simplistic point of view, it would seem that emic and etic are opposites: one searches either for universal similarities or for cross-cultural differences. And indeed some of the cross-cultural psychological literature seems to reinforce this polarisation. However, etic and emic can, and should, be viewed as complementary rather than contradictory. With this view, researchers then try to discover which aspects of a given phenomenon are universal and which are culture-specific, and what determines the etic or emic nature of particular aspects. One such example of an etic–emic integration was reported by Babad, Alexander & Babad (1983) in their cross-cultural investigation of the tendency of children to return the smile of a friendly stranger.

In this note, I compare the responses of the Israeli subjects in this study to those of the European subjects. The question as to whether Israel is a 'European' country cannot be resolved, but the resemblance between Israelis' and Europeans' experience of emotions can be analysed and discussed. In addition, the questionnaire was administered to 40 Arab students at the Hebrew University, making it possible to compare 'mainstream Israelis' to a unique minority group that has to cope with very special conditions for their social adjustment.

A8.2 The uniqueness of Israeli culture

Geographers 'know' that Israel is in Asia, and therefore it is not a 'European' country. But socio-political realities do not follow geographic laws anymore. The 'distance' from Tel Aviv to Rome and Paris is 'shorter' than the 'distance' from Tel Aviv to Damascus or Amman. Israel twice won the Eurovision song contest, and Maccabee Tel Aviv were twice the European champions in basketball. Israel is a 'member' of a particular definition in the European Common Market (but so are countries like Morocco). And yet in soccer, Israel competes nowadays in the Oceania region, together with Australia and New Zealand. The population of Israel is extremely mixed – Jews, Moslems, and Christians; Jews from Europe, America, Asia, and Africa – and yet several generations ago the land was virtually empty of people.

The Jewish people have a very long history, dating back to ancient times, and yet the State of Israel has a very short history, dating back only to 1948. Israel is a country of immigration, and many groups still maintain their own customs and guard their boundaries; only now is a distinct 'Israeli culture' beginning to emerge.

Israelis have to live through, and cope with events and situations that might be viewed by outsiders as ranging from 'difficult' to 'traumatic': long periods of military service till age 55 (for the men, less for the women); painful and costly wars with many dead and wounded; continuous terrorism and Arab-Jewish tension; a failing economy with three-digit inflation; and a sense of isolation in the light of world-wide criticism of Israel. But Ephraim Kishon, the Israeli humorist, once observed that although Israel is the only country under constant threat of survival, one gets ulcers because of the neighbour upstairs or downstairs in one's apartment building!

At the beginning of the study I asked myself the following questions: how would all this be reflected in the subjective reports of the experience of emotions? Would Israelis differ from Europeans in their reports? Would Israelis of different cultural origins differ from each other? Would students in different countries differ at all from each other, or is 'studentdom' a universal identity?

Prior to the analysis of the data I felt that I did not have sufficient grounds for formulating specific hypotheses and predictions. My only hunch was that 'antecedent events', that is, the situations in which the various emotional experiences were evoked, would play the major role in differentiating between Israeli and European responses to the questionnaire.

A8.3 Arabs and Jews in Israel

In addition to the Jewish/Israeli sample, the questionnaire was administered to a group of 40 Arab students at the Hebrew University of Jerusalem. This made it possible to add Jewish-Arab comparisons to the Israeli-European comparisons. These students were all 'Israeli Arabs', that is, Arabs whose families lived in Israel before 1948, who are Israeli citizens, and who are educated in the Israeli educational system (which has elementary and high school 'Arab' sectors). This group is distinguished from Arabs in the West Bank and the Gaza Strip, who came under Israeli control in 1967. The latter (with the exception of the citizens of Jerusalem) are not Israeli citizens, and they do not attend 'Israeli' schools.

Arab society is less technological and less progressive than the Israeli and the Western European societies. Israeli Arabs reside mostly in rural areas. They are more affluent and more highly educated than other Arab populations, but they also suffer more internal conflict with regard to being 'Arab' and 'Israeli' at the same time. Despite their relative affluence and increasing educational level, the gaps between Israeli Jews and Israeli Arabs are quite noticeable. The Arabs are of lower status and often perceive themselves to be second-rate citizens. They cannot serve in the Israeli armed forces, and their job opportunities in Israeli society-at-large are limited. Despite their ambitions, many Arab students find it more difficult to succeed at university.

The picture of the Israeli-Arab society is of a society in cultural transition, a minority group facing a more advantaged majority group. The animosity between Israel and the Arab states, and the natural tendency of many Israeli-Arab youngsters to assert their 'Palestinian' identity adds to Jewish-Arab tensions on the university campus.

Female Arab students must cope with another source of tension. Norms and behavioural codes with regard to women are extremely traditional in Arab society, and therefore the gap between the Jewish women and the Arab women on campus is particularly wide. I therefore expected to find greater male–female differences among the Arab respondents than among the Jewish respondents.

A8.4 Procedures and samples

The questionnaire was administered to the Israeli samples in Spring 1983, about 9 months after the beginning of the Israeli military involvement in the Lebanon. The Jewish-Israeli sample (hereafter 'Israeli sample' consisted of 157 students, and the Arab-Israeli sample (hereafter 'Arab sample') consisted of 40 students (this Israeli sample is larger than the Israeli sample described in the main chapters of this book – in this note the full Israeli sample is utilised, while in the main chapters subjects who had not lived in Israel all their lives were eliminated).

Most of the analyses in this note compare the Israeli results with the combined results of all European countries. This is done to make the presentation more concise and pointed. Comparisons with particular countries are made at times, when the findings are of particular interest.

The equivalence between the Israeli sample and the combined European sample is indicated by the fact that for none of the variables used to describe the samples was there a significant difference between Israel and Europe. The unique characteristic of the Israeli sample was that 58% of the subjects had served in the Israeli Defence Forces, and 16% of the subjects actually had participated in battlefield activity. Another characteristic distinguishing the Israeli sample from the other European samples was the broad distribution of country of origin of parents: many of the subjects' parents had emigrated to Israel from European, American, Asian, and African countries.

The Arab sample had a higher proportion of males (58%), a higher number of brothers and sisters, a higher proportion of villagers, more students of blue collar background, and a younger average age (due to the fact that they do not serve in the army) than the Israeli sample. In effect, the Arab sample was not exactly equivalent to the Jewish sample or to the combined European sample.

Due to the immense size of this study, hundreds of comparisons between Israel and Europe were made, and a sizable proportion of them yielded statistically significant differences. To simplify the presentation and focus the reader's attention on what I consider are the most meaningful differences, I chose to ignore or to mention briefly in passing numerous variables in these comparisons. Most analyses were based on simple frequency tables, and the level of significance was determined through χ^2 tests. Because of the different sample sizes used for Israel for this particular aspect of the study, proportions and means reported here sometimes differ somewhat from those reported in the main chapters.

A8.5 Results of the Israeli-European comparison

Major differences were found between Israel and Europe in the characteristics of the antecedent situations that elicited emotions. For each of the four emotions, the Israeli distribution of all antecedent events differed significantly from the European

Table A8.1. *Antecedent events: comparison between Israeli (N = 157) and combined European (N = 677) results[a] (expressed as the percentage of subjects reporting)*

Antecedent event	Location	Emotion			
		Joy	Sadness	Fear	Anger
News	Israel	$13^{b,c}$	$15^{b,c}$	$7^{b,c}$	7
	Europe	8	7	1	4
Relationships	Israel	$11^{b,d}$	$8^{b,d}$	$1^{b,d}$	$13^{b,d}$
	Europe	27	29	5	40
Social institutions	Israel	3	5	1	3
	Europe	3	2	1	1
Temporary meeting/separation	Israel	13	3^{d}	0	
	Europe	17	6	1	
Permanent separation	Israel		10	0	
	Europe		8	1	
Birth/death	Israel	$11^{b,c}$	$27^{b,c}$	5	1
	Europe	6	19	5	1
Body/mind centred	Israel	8	6	8	1
	Europe	11	9	6	2
Interaction with strangers	Israel	1	$5^{b,c}$	19^{b}	$22^{b,c}$
	Europe	2	0	13	17
Achievement	Israel	$22^{b,c}$	5	7^{b}	4
	Europe	13	7	12	6
Supernatural	Israel			1	
	Europe			4	
Traffic	Israel			7^{b}	
	Europe			21	
Risk-taking/natural forces	Israel			11	
	Europe			10	
Fear of the unknown	Israel			17	
	Europe			13	
Injustice	Israel				$24^{b,c}$
	Europe				17
Inconvenience	Israel				8
	Europe				6

[a] Vertical proportions do not sum up to 100% due to missing data and uncodable responses.
[b] χ^2 value significant at the 0.05 level or better.
[c] Israeli result higher than the result of each and every European country.
[d] Israeli result lower than the result of each and every European country.

distribution (see also Chapter 4). For 15 of the 41 specific comparisons (of each particular antecedent for a particular emotion) the Israeli result was the most extreme – either the highest or the lowest – compared to the result for each individual European country. Table A8.1 presents the summary of the Israeli-European comparisons for each antecedent and each emotion.

'News' played a greater role for the Israeli subjects than for the European subjects in evoking each of the four emotions, while 'relationships' played a smaller role for the Israeli subjects than for the European ones. For sadness, 'Death', 'Rituals' (mostly funerals), and interactions with strangers were more frequent antecedents in Israel than in Europe. For joy, there was a large difference in frequency for 'Achievement'; joy over achievement was more common in Israel than in any of the other countries. There was less fear of failure among the Israelis than among the Europeans. Israelis showed more frequent fear of strangers and less frequent fear of traffic (despite the frightening objective statistics on traffic fatalities in Israel). As for anger, Israelis showed more anger directed at strangers and more anger related to 'injustice'.

The data in Table A8.1 show a major difference between Israel and 'Europe' in the structure of antecedents. In Europe, about one-third of the antecedents were of an interpersonal nature (relationships, temporary and permanent meetings and separations, etc.), while in Israel only about one-seventh of the antecedents were interpersonally related. On the other hand, the Israelis reported a much higher proportion of emotional experiences caused by news, political events, and society-at-large situations. Emotions related to death were sometimes focussed on an acquaintance or a relative, but were more often focussed on military casualties or victims of political terrorism. The Israelis also showed a higher achievement orientation, reflected in more frequent joy over achievement and less frequent fear of failure. And finally, the Israelis reported more anger at injustice. Thus, it can be summarised that the European experience of emotions tends to be influenced more by interpersonal antecedents, while the Israeli experience of emotions is more impersonal and more strongly related to global social and political forces that affect society-at-large.

Other characteristics of a situation are related to its social nature. Israeli subjects showed a tendency to experience emotions more often than Europeans with familiar persons; this variable reached statistical significance for sadness and anger. As to group size, the only significant finding was a lower preference for dyad and higher preference for small groups in sadness situations. Thus, for the emotion of sadness – with its emphasis on death-related situations – Israelis showed a clear preference for a more 'social' experience.

A second set of data relate to response/reaction characteristics, that is to the ways in which the emotions were experienced, and how they were controlled. The Israeli subjects reported a lower intensity of emotion than the Europeans for joy and anger, and also lower amounts of verbalisation for these emotions. They reported having exercised more control over their verbalisations for joy, fear, and anger, and more control over their joy and sadness reactions/symptoms.

On analysis of the various groups of reaction characteristics, two patterns emerged: one pattern showed no difference between the Israelis and the Europeans; the other showed Israelis reporting particular behaviours/symptoms less frequently (or less intensely) than the Europeans. The first pattern – no noticeable Israeli-European differences – was found for facial expressions, gaze variables, speech variables, and whole body movements. The second pattern was found for the other groups of variables; general and vegetative sensations, body part movements, and voice variables. Generally, the Europeans mentioned symptoms/reactions in these categories about twice as frequently, proportionally, as the Israelis. For vegetative sensations, the European-Israeli difference was significant for all four emotions, with

Europeans reporting more muscle symptoms for all the emotions, more stomach symptoms for the negative emotions, and slightly more symptoms of warmth and coldness, blood pressure, chest and breathing problems. For joy and anger, the Europeans reported more pleasant/unpleasant rest and arousal sensations than the Israelis. As to body part movements, the Europeans reported more hand movements and changed movements of body parts than the Israelis for joy and anger, while there were no differences for instrumental behaviour, interpersonal behaviour, and general unrest. Thus, the Europeans reported more body gestures than the Israelis, whose reports thus portray them as being more reserved. This pattern was repeated for voice changes, where the Europeans reported more changes than the Israelis for sadness and anger, with a tendency in the same direction for joy as well.

The picture that emerged from this set of data is one of Israeli subjects who portrayed themselves as more reserved and inhibited than the Europeans: their emotions were of lower intensity, and they reported more control, fewer and less intense visceral symptoms, and fewer body gestures and voice changes.

It is not easy to interpret this pattern. The image of the Israeli-born 'Sabra' contains elements of reservation and covering up of emotions sometimes, but stereotypes of Israel as a Mediterranean country include noisiness, intense expressivity, and expansiveness in body gestures. As Wallbott and I argue in Chapter 11 (on social interaction), it is possible to explain findings both consonant and dissonant with existing stereotypes as confirming these stereotypes. Among the present findings, the differences observed for vegetative symptoms are the hardest to understand, since these symptoms are probably the most universal, with stronger etic than emic elements. A possible explanation is that the observed European–Israeli differences might reflect a differential style of reporting rather than (or at least, in addition to) 'true' differences in the experiences of emotions. The Israelis would then appear as more shy and less willing than the Europeans to report in writing about their visceral reactions, voice changes, etc. Such inhibition is in line with the image of the 'Sabra', who is 'thorny on the outside but sweet and feeling inside'. Stated more strongly, this interpretation views the observed differences in symptoms/reactions as artefacts of the measurement method and of the questionnaire employed, when no 'real' differences in visceral symptoms, voice changes, or body gestures may actually exist between the two populations.

This hypothesis cannot be fully confirmed or disconfirmed. If the patterns of Israeli and European reactions are very similar, and the gap represents a constant difference, this might support the writing-style artefact hypothesis. On the other hand, if the Israeli and European patterns of the structure of the symptoms/reactions are dissimilar, it will be more reasonable to view the observed differences as representing real differences in the internal experience of these emotions.

To test this hypothesis, correlation coefficients were computed between the frequencies of the different reaction/symptom categories in Israel and in Europe. The correlations between the frequencies of all 34 reaction/symptom variables for each emotion ranged from 0.73 for anger to 0.90–0.92 for the other three emotions. The 11 variables measuring visceral reactions only (general and vegetative symptoms) were then singled out, and correlations between Israeli and European frequencies were computed. These correlations ranged from 0.89 to 0.97. Thus, the uniformity (or universality) of the underlying structure was demonstrated, particularly for the visceral sensations, where large European–Israeli differences in frequencies were observed. This supported, although it could not 'prove', the 'writing artefact' hypothesis, strengthening my inclination to take a conservative approach in interpreting the European–Israeli differences in reactions/symptoms. (It is interesting to note that a similar set of correlations for the 11 variables describing body movements and gestures ranged from 0.54 to 0.71, in line with the view that body gestures have stronger emic elements, compared to the more etic nature of physiological reactions in emotions.)

Since the correlations between the structures of variables in Europe and Israel influenced, and changed, the interpretation of the previously reported differences, I felt compelled to compute similar correlations for the antecedents listed in Table A8.1, in order to examine whether uniformity of underlying structure existed for antecedents as well. The emerging correlations (0.43 for sadness; 0.48 for joy; 0.61 for anger; and 0.64 for fear) were sufficiently low to reject the notion of identical structure, leaving intact the previous interpretation of a differential structure of antecedents in Europe and Israel.

A8.6 Results of the Arab-Jewish comparison

Although the Jewish and the Arab samples were not equivalent in terms of their demographic characteristics, both samples consisted of students at the same university who were studying on the same campus and attending the same departments.

Arab respondents did not show a different preference from Jewish subjects for familiar or unfamiliar persons, nor did group size differ from the Jewish distribution. The Arabs mentioned fewer future situations for fear and anger; described more emphatic situations for sadness, fear, and anger; and reported a higher amount of verbalisation for joy and sadness. In terms of antecedent events, there were considerable differences between the Jewish and Arab distributions. Table A8.2 presents a summary of the results on antecedents.

The Arab students mentioned more achievement situations than did the Jewish students. This difference was significant for joy, sadness, and anger. They also reported more anger over interpersonal relationships, more fear of death, less joy with new friends, more sadness about illness, less fear of the unknown, less anger about injustice and inconvenience, and more joy for the 'social institutions' category. This joy was almost exclusively joy over the success of Arab candidates in the elections for the student council.

The pattern of antecedents observed for the Arab students was more similar to that of Jewish students than to that of European students, but the differences between the Jews and Arabs were quite noticeable. In general the Arabs presented more personal antecedents – more concern about relationships and illness, a strong concern over achievement, and less concern about news and injustice. It is to be expected that members of a minority group who are struggling to 'make it' in the prestigious university of the majority group would manifest a high level of achievement-orientation. At the same time, the Arabs showed political awareness in mentioning frequently the elections to the student body as an antecedent event for their emotions.

Turning to the actual experience of the emotions, we again find some Jewish–Arab differences, although the groups did not differ from each other on most variables.

Table A8.2. *Antecedent events: comparison between Jewish (N = 157) and Arab (N = 40) subjects (expressed as the percentage of subjects reporting)*[a]

		Emotion			
Antecedent event	Group	Joy	Sadness	Fear	Anger
News	Jews	13	15	7	7
	Arabs	7	10	2	2
Relationships	Jews	11	8	1	13[b]
	Arabs	5	2	0	35[b]
Social institutions	Jews	3[b]	5	1	3
	Arabs	15[b]	5	7	7
Temporary meeting/separation	Jews	13	3	0	
	Arabs	15	5	2	
Permanent separation	Jews		10		1
	Arabs		5		0
Birth/death	Jews	11[b]	27	5	1
	Arabs	0[b]	27	18	0
Body/mind centred	Jews	8	6[b]	8	1
	Arabs	0	20[b]	10	2
Interaction with strangers	Jews	1	5	19	22
	Arabs	0	2	15	18
Achievement	Jews	22[b]	5[b]	7	4[b]
	Arabs	35[b]	13[b]	10	18[b]
Supernatural	Jews			1	
	Arabs			5	
Traffic	Jews			7	
	Arabs			8	
Risk-taking/natural forces	Jews			11	
	Arabs			13	
Fear of the unknown	Jews			17[b]	
	Arabs			0[b]	
Injustice	Jews				24[b]
	Arabs				15[b]
Inconvenience	Jews				8[b]
	Arabs				00[b]

[a] Vertical proportions for each group do not sum up to 100% due to missing data and uncodable responses.
[b] χ^2 value significant at the 0.05 level or better.

For all emotions, the Arabs reported a higher intensity of the emotional experience, and for almost all variables where significant differences were found, the frequencies for the Arab students were higher than those for the Jewish students. For joy, the Arab students reported more voice changes (23% vs. 5%), more changes in facial expression (30% vs. 6%), less laughter (20% vs. 38%), and more crying (8% vs. 1%). For sadness, the Arab students reported more changes in facial expression (30% vs. 11%). For anger, they reported higher frequencies of muscle symptoms (45%

vs. 23%), stomach troubles (13% vs. 3%), and changes in blood pressure (10% vs. 3%). Thus, the Arab students were more expressive than the Jewish students in describing their internal reactions and symptoms and their non-verbal behaviours in the open-ended questionnaire. It seemed pointless to compute correlations between the frequencies observed for each of the reactions/symptoms variables for Arabs and Jews, since the size of the Arab sample was very small, and the frequencies for most variables were extremely low. Finally, although the Arab students reported higher intensities of emotion and described several more symptoms than the Jewish students, there were no differences in the control of either symptoms or verbalisations.

I hypothesised earlier that another Jewish-Arab difference might be a greater male–female difference in the Arab population than in the Jewish population, due to the traditionalism among the Arab population with regard to women even if the latter are allowed to attend the Jewish university. For each of the 41 antecedent variables, the difference between the proportion of males and females was calculated for both samples. Greater sex differences were indeed found for the Arab sample. The male–female difference was larger in the Arab sample in 26 of the 41 variables, and the t-test between the two distributions of differences was statistically significant (mean male–female difference of 7.68% in the Arab sample, 2.73% in the Jewish sample; $t(40) = 3.59$; effect size, $d = 1.14$). Similar differences were found for other variables, such as intensity, group size, familiarity, control of symptoms, and control of verbalisations.

Owing to the small size of the Arab sample, and particularly the small number of women ($n = 13$), no significance tests were carried out on these male–female differences within the Arab sample. However, a glance at the distributions reveals the following trends: Arab women experienced more news-related joy and sadness than Arab men; more joy and less anger over relationships; less joy and anger over social institutions; more joy and sadness over temporary meetings and separations; less death-related sadness and fear; more sadness over illness; much more fear and anger at strangers; and less achievement-oriented joy and sadness. The equivalent examination of male–female comparison in the Jewish sample yielded very few differences: Jewish women showed more fear of strangers; more anger at injustice; more joy over temporary meetings; less relationships-oriented anger; and less achievement-oriented joy.

A8.7 Discussion

As for other analyses discussed in this book, the findings discussed here revealed both similarities and differences in the cross-cultural comparison. Many components of the experience of emotion are universal, with few qualitative differences between cultures (or at least, few differences among students in various cultures, since 'studentdom' might be a subculture that transcends national boundaries). Cross-cultural differences in the style of responding and writing in this type of questionnaire were evident, but similarity of pattern could be readily examined even when differences in frequency or intensity existed. It seems that when a particular emotion is experienced, this experience is rather universal. The cross-cultural similarities, or 'etic' elements, were observed mainly in the characteristics of the actual experience of the emotional state, and the immediate sensations, symptoms, and non-verbal reactions.

On the other hand, the Israeli-European and Jewish-Arab comparisons showed that the unique characteristics of given culture influence the structure of the antecedent situations in which particular emotions are evoked. Here the differences were substantial and the patterns quite dissimilar. Given that a great deal of the universality of antecedent situations is trivial and *a priori* – people are not joyful in sad or frightening situations nor angry or afraid on happy occasions – the observed differences are doubly meaningful. Particular antecedents that are unique to a given culture or subculture gain salience and the power to evoke emotions in the members of that particular group. In the cases discussed here, these antecedents included powerful public events that took place recently (elections to the student body, a political murder during a demonstration), as well as more global and continuous characteristics such as war situations, military service, and minority status. Beyond these, characteristics of 'national character' (achievement orientation, talkativeness, social orientation, etc.) can also determine the salience of particular antecedents, although in this project, findings did not necessarily follow commonly held stereotypes.

In tl analysis of antecedent events, I found a marked difference in the relative salience of antecedents in Israel and Europe. The antecedents concerned included reactions to news, death, and joining of new members, social relationships, achievement orientation, reactions to strangers, and attitudes toward injustice. Within Israel, Arabs differed from Jews in achievement orientation, reactions to death and illness, and social relationships.

Appendix B
English version of the emotion questionnaire

Note: The questionnaire covered four emotions, 'joy or happiness', 'sadness or grief', 'fear or fright', and 'anger or rage'; the questions for only one of them, 'anger or rage', are reproduced here.

A study of emotional reactions

The present study is concerned with the investigation of events and situations that provoke emotional reactions. We shall ask you to describe situations and events that have led to emotional reactions on your part. On the following pages you will find four emotions each illustrated with two different words. Please describe for each emotion one event or situation which, in the last few weeks, has resulted in your experiencing the respective emotion more or less intensely.

We should like you to give the following information for each event:

Where did it happen?	Please describe the place where the event occurred. Did it happen in your living room, in a restaurant, in a public place, etc.?
How long ago was it?	
Who was involved?	Please indicate who else was involved in the situation and your relationship to these people.
What happened?	Please describe the nature, cause and development of the event.
How long did it last?	Did the feeling continue for some minutes, hours or days?

We shall also be asking you some questions about what you said and how you otherwise reacted. Furthermore we shall ask a series of questions about your feelings and your behaviour during the event.
You should not try to specify only extreme situations, in which your emotional reactions were very strong and very obvious. It is equally important to recall those events in which you reacted emotionally without anybody noticing it.
Perhaps you will have difficulties in recalling one event for each emotion right away. Try then, to recall the events that have happened during the last few weeks and try to think of an appropriate situation.

Think of a situation in which you experienced

| ANGER or RAGE |

Description of the situation
>
> Where did the situation occur?
>
> ———————————————————————
>
> How long ago was it?
>
> ———————————————————————
>
> Who was involved?
>
> ———————————————————————
>
> What exactly happened?
>
> ———————————————————————
>
> How long did the feeling last? Was it some minutes, hours, days?
>
> ———————————————————————
>
> In what way did the situation end?
>
> ———————————————————————

Description of your emotional reaction
>
> In your opinion, what words would best describe your emotion?
>
> ———————————————————————
>
> How strongly did you feel this emotion? (Please circle the appropriate number)

| not at all   0   1   2   3   4   5   6   7   8   9   very much |

> What did you say?
>
> ———————————————————————
>
> What were your bodily reactions (for example trembling or a churning stomach) and your non-verbal reactions (for example specific facial expressions, voice qualities or gestures)?
>
> ———————————————————————

Control of emotion
>
> How strongly did you try to control what you said?

| not at all   0   1   2   3   4   5   6   7   8   9   very much |

> What did you do?
>
> ———————————————————————
>
> How strongly did you try to control your non-verbal reactions?

| not at all   0   1   2   3   4   5   6   7   8   9   very much |

> How did you do that?
>
> ———————————————————————
>
> What would you do differently, if you found yourself again in such a situation?
>
> ———————————————————————

PERSONAL INFORMATION

Sex: male   female
Age: years
Number of brothers and sisters:————————————————————
Marital status: ————————————————————————————
Number of children: ——————————————————————————
Nationality:———————————————————————————————
Nationality of parents: ————————————————————————
Number of years spent at university: ——————————————————
Where did you spend most of your life?
        In a country district: ———————   a town: ————————   a city: ————————
In which country/nation?————————————————————————
Where do you now live permanently (present place of residence)?
        In a country district: ———————   a town: ————————   a city: ————————
In which country/nation?————————————————————————
Languages spoken:
        mother language (specify):————————————————————
        other languages (specify): —————————————————————
        ——————————————————————————————————————
        ——————————————————————————————————————

Occupation:————————————————————————————————
If you are a student, please indicate field of study: ——————————————
Father's occupation:————————————————————————————
Mother's occupation: ——————————————————————————

Appendix C
Antecedent and reaction codes

In this appendix all codes that have been developed (see Chapter 3) and used to code the questionnaires are reported. As for some analyses antecedent categories and symptom/reaction categories were combined into broader categories, the combination rules are also given.

1. Codes for background questionnaire

Country (COUN)
   1 = Great Britain
   2 = France
   3 = West Germany
   4 = Italy
   5 = Switzerland
   6 = Belgium
   7 = Spain
   8 = Israel

City (CITY)
   10 = London
   20 = Paris
   21 = Lyon
   30 = Giessen
   31 = Munich
   40 = Bologna
   50 = Zürich
   60 = Louvain-la-Neuve
   70 = Madrid
   80 = Jerusalem

Sex (SEX)   1 = male
           2 = female

Age (AGE) (in years)

Number of brothers and sisters
   (NBS) (code 9 if 9 and more)

Number of children (NCHILD)
   (code 9 if 9 and more)

Marital status (MARIT)
   1 = single
   2 = living with
   3 = married
   4 = divorced
   5 = widowed

Subject's nationality (see country
   code)

Parents' nationality (see country
   code)

Years spent at university
   (YUNI) (code 9 if 9 and more)

Mother tongue (see language code)

1st other language (see language
   code)
2nd other language

Where spent most of one's life (place of upbringing) (MLI) and present place of residence (PLI)
   1 = rural area   3 = city
   2 = town   4 = suburb/conurbation/agglomeration

What country? (see country code)

Father's occupation (FOCCUP) and Mother's occupation (MOCCUP)

1 = housewife/houseman
2 = unemployed
3 = retired
4 = blue collar worker

5 = white collar worker
6 = self-employed
7 = student

Field of study (faculty) (STUDF)

1 = psychology
2 = social sciences
3 = philosophy, literature, languages
4 = fine arts, architecture

5 = law, political sciences
6 = natural sciences
7 = computer sciences, engineering
8 = medical studies

(language and country codes are not reported here because of space limitations)

2. Codes for characteristics of the reported emotion

Which emotion? (EMOT)
1 = joy
2 = sadness
3 = fear
4 = anger

Where did the event happen? (location) (WHERE)
1 = inside, familiar place
2 = inside, unfamiliar place
3 = outside
4 = transport

How long ago was it? (PAST)
1 = today
2 = yesterday
3 = up to a week ago
4 = up to a month ago
5 = several months ago
6 = several years ago

Who was involved? (WHO)
1 = alone
2 = one other person known
3 = one other person unknown
4 = several persons known
5 = several persons unknown
6 = one person known & one unknown
7 = one person known & sev. unknown
8 = persons known & unknown

Time (TIME)
1 = past or present (still going on)
2 = future

Reality (REAL)
1 = realistic, actually perceived or anticipated (cognitive)
2 = imagined or dreamt, unrealistic fantasies

Immediacy (IMM)
1 = own experience (event happened to subject)
2 = empathic experience (event happened to other person, subject empathises)

How long did it last? (DUR)
1 = under 5 minutes
2 = 5 minutes to 1 hour
3 = 1 to 24 hours
4 = several days and longer

End of situation
(information not used)

Intensity (INTEN)
0–9

Handle the situation differently?
(HANDL)
1 = the same
2 = something different

Control of verbal behaviour
(CVERB) 0–9

Control of symptoms/reactions
(CSYMP) 0–9

Description of situation (ANTS)
(compare antecedent codes)

Verbal behaviour (VERB)
1 = says nothing
2 = 'inner' talk
3 = exclamation, affect word, humming
4 = sentences, complete expressions, discussion

Type of control attempt
(information not used)

Type of control attempt
(information not used)

3. Antecedent codes

JOY = 1

00 = uncodable
01 = GOOD NEWS (immediate social context). *Example*: an unexpected job offer
02 = GOOD NEWS (mass media). *Example*: cheering news in newspapers or on TV
03 = CONTINUING RELATIONSHIPS WITH FRIENDS AND PERMANENT PARTNERS. *Example*: pleasure from contact with friends
04 = CONTINUING RELATIONSHIPS WITH BLOOD RELATIVES AND IN-LAWS (see 03)
05 = IDENTIFICATION WITH GROUPS (actual and reference). *Examples*: pleasure in belonging to a club; returning to your own country after a holiday
06 = MEETING FRIENDS, ANIMALS, PLANTS. *Examples*: seeing one's dog again; meeting one's friend for dinner
07 = MEETING BLOOD RELATIVES OR IN-LAWS (see 06)
10 = ACQUIRING NEW FRIENDS
11 = ACQUIRING NEW FAMILY MEMBERS. *Examples*: birth of a baby; marriage of one's brother
12 = PLEASURE IN MEETING STRANGERS (short-term chance encounters). *Example*: talking to a stranger on a train
13 = PLEASURE IN SOLITUDE. *Example*: being left alone with one's own thoughts
14 = NEW EXPERIENCES. *Examples*: adventures; planning a holiday
15 = SUCCESS EXPERIENCES IN ACHIEVEMENT SITUATIONS. *Example*: passing an examination
16 = ACQUIRING SOME MATERIAL FOR SELF OR OTHER (buying or receiving). *Examples*: presents from others; buying something nice for oneself or others
18 = RITUAL. *Examples*: religious, academic ceremonies, festivals, birthdays
19 = NATURAL, ALSO REFINED, NON-CULTURAL PLEASURES. *Examples*: sex, food, nature, landscape
21 = CULTURAL PLEASURES. *Examples*: art, music, ballet, etc.

22 = ACQUIRING NON-MATERIAL BENEFITS (emotional support, altruism). *Example*: helping an old lady cross the road

23 = HAPPINESS WITHOUT REASON

31 = 'SCHADENFREUDE'. *Example*: malicious pleasure in another person's misfortune

SADNESS = 2

00 = uncodable

01 = BAD NEWS (immediate social context). *Example*: not selected for a job

02 = BAD NEWS (mass media). *Example*: bad news in newspapers or on TV

03 = PROBLEMS WITH FRIENDS, ANIMALS, PLANTS. *Examples*: quarrels, disappointments, estrangement, rejection

04 = PROBLEMS WITH BLOOD RELATIVES AND IN-LAWS (see 03)

05 = PROBLEMS WITH GROUPS (actual and reference). *Examples*: feeling rejected, an outsider, etc.

06 = TEMPORARY SEPARATION FROM LOVED FRIENDS, ANIMALS, PLANTS (indication that they will come back)

07 = TEMPORARY SEPARATION FROM LOVED BLOOD RELATIVES AND IN-LAWS (indication that the relative or in-law will come back)

08 = PERMANENT SEPARATION FROM LOVED FRIENDS, ANIMALS, PLANTS

09 = PERMANENT SEPARATION FROM LOVED BLOOD RELATIVES AND IN-LAWS

10 = DEATH OF FRIENDS, ANIMALS, PLANTS

11 = DEATH OF BLOOD RELATIVES AND IN-LAWS

12 = HARMING A STRANGER OR STRANGERS. *Example*: running over their dog with one's car

13 = UNEXPECTED OR UNWISHED FOR SOLITUDE. *Examples*: having to spend a holiday on one's own; having little social contact; having not made new acquaintances yet when living in a new place

14 = END OF PLEASURABLE EXPERIENCE. *Examples*: end of holiday; end of nice evening with friends

15 = FAILURE TO ACHIEVE WHAT WAS HOPED FOR IN AN ACHIEVEMENT-RELATED ENTERPRISE (frustration). *Example*: failure to pass an examination

16 = OBJECT LOSS (selling, theft, loss). *Examples*: loss of a piece of jewelry; selling one's car

18 = SADNESS ABOUT RITUALS. *Example*: the anniversary of one's mother's death

19 = SICKNESS OF CLOSE ORGANISMS IMPORTANT TO SUBJECT AND OF SELF. *Examples*: sickness of one's dog; friend has heart attack

23 = GENERAL DEPRESSION, ALIENATION (for no specific reason)

FEAR = 3

00 = uncodable

01 = BAD NEWS (immediate social context). *Example*: anticipation of losing one's job

02 = BAD NEWS (mass media). *Example*: anticipation of bad news in newspapers or on TV

03 = FEAR OF PROBLEMS IN RELATIONSHIPS WITH FRIENDS AND PERMANENT PARTNERS, ANIMALS AND PLANTS. *Example*: fear of quarrels, estrangement, etc.

04 = FEAR OF PROBLEMS IN RELATIONSHIPS WITH BLOOD RELATIVES AND IN-LAWS (see 03)

05 = FEAR OF PROBLEMS WITH GROUPS (actual and reference). *Example*: anticipation of problems with the members of one's football team

06 = FEAR OF TEMPORARY SEPARATION FROM FRIENDS AND PERMANENT PARTNERS, ANIMALS AND PLANTS (indication that the person will come back)

07 = FEAR OF TEMPORARY SEPARATION FROM BLOOD RELATIVES AND IN-LAWS (indication that the person will come back)

08 = FEAR OF PERMANENT SEPARATION FROM FRIENDS, ANIMALS AND PLANTS

09 = FEAR OF PERMANENT SEPARATION FROM BLOOD RELATIVES AND IN-LAWS

10 = FEAR OF DEATH OF FRIENDS AND PERMANENT PARTNERS, ANIMALS AND PLANTS

11 = FEAR OF DEATH OF BLOOD RELATIVES AND IN-LAWS

12 = FEAR OF PHYSICAL AGGRESSION BY OTHERS. *Examples*: sexual assault, robbery, attack by hooligans

13 = FEAR OF SOLITUDE

14 = FEAR OF THE UNKNOWN (something unspecified)

15 = FEAR OF FAILURE IN ACHIEVEMENT-RELATED SITUATIONS

16 = FEAR OF LOSS OR DAMAGE OF OBJECT OR MONEY. *Example*: burglary

17 = FEAR OF TRAFFIC (accidents). *Examples*: driving too fast; being endangered by others

18 = FEAR OF RITUALS AND ANNIVERSARIES. *Example*: fear of the anniversary of a loved one's death

19 = FEAR OF OWN SICKNESS (illness, tests or treatments) *Example*: believing one is seriously ill or in danger of death

20 = FEAR OF PAIN

23 = FREE-FLOATING ANXIETY

24 = FEAR OF SUPERNATURAL EVENTS, AND THE 'UNHEIMLICHE'. *Examples*: horror films, seances, witchcraft, weird situations

25 = CONSCIOUS RISK-TAKING. *Example*: rock climbing

26 = PHOBIA (situations such as fear of closed spaces, animals, high altitudes, going out)

27 = FEAR OF ADVERSE EFFECTS FROM EXTERNAL FORCES. *Examples*: thunderstorms, bad weather at sea, dangerous machine not functioning

ANGER = 4

00 = uncodable

01 = BAD NEWS (immediate social context). *Example*: your sister having been humiliated by her boss

02 = BAD NEWS (mass media)

03 = ANGER AT FAILURE OF FRIENDS, ANIMALS, PLANTS TO CONFORM TO SOCIAL NORMS, TO BE CONSIDERATE ABOUT PERSONS AND PROPERTY

04 = ANGER AT FAILURE OF BLOOD RELATIVES AND IN-LAWS TO CONFORM TO SOCIAL NORMS, TO BE CONSIDERATE ABOUT PERSONS AND PROPERTY

05 = ANGER AT GROUPS (actual or reference). *Example*: one's club behaves badly during an outing

06 = ANGER ABOUT TEMPORARY SEPARATION FROM FRIENDS, ANIMALS, PLANTS (indication that person will come back)

07 = ANGER ABOUT TEMPORARY SEPARATION FROM BLOOD RELATIVES AND IN-LAWS (indication that person will come back)

08 = ANGER ABOUT PERMANENT SEPARATION FROM FRIENDS, ANIMALS, PLANTS

09 = ANGER ABOUT PERMANENT SEPARATION FROM BLOOD RELATIVES AND IN-LAWS

10 = ANGER ABOUT DEATH OF FRIENDS, ANIMALS AND PLANTS

11 = ANGER ABOUT DEATH OF BLOOD RELATIVES AND IN-LAWS

12 = ANGER AT FAILURE OF OTHERS TO CONFORM TO SOCIAL NORMS AND TO BE CONSIDERATE ABOUT PERSONS AND PROPERTY

15 = FAILURE TO REACH GOALS OR TO ACHIEVE AN OBJECTIVE. *Example*: anger about failing an examination

16 = DAMAGE TO PERSONAL PROPERTY BY OTHERS AND ONESELF. *Example*: anger about losing money

17 = ANGER IN TRAFFIC (about inconsiderate, norm-violating behaviour by others)

18 = ANGER ABOUT RITUALS AND ANNIVERSARIES. *Example*: anger about having to attend an aunt's birthday party

20 = ANGER ABOUT A PHYSICAL HURT. *Example*: an assault

23 = FREE-FLOATING ANGER (bad mood for no specific reason)

28 = ANGER ABOUT INAPPROPRIATE REWARDS FOR SELF (feeling unjustly treated). *Examples*: failure to get a deserved reward; being the object of unfair accusation

29 = ANGER AT DAMAGE TO COMMON PROPERTY. *Examples*: damage to public buildings; vandalism

30 = UNEXPECTED, UNNECESSARY INCONVENIENCE, TIME LOSS. *Example*: time loss caused by failure of machines to work properly

4. Codes for non-verbal and physiological concomitants of emotions

Experienced subjective quality (ESQ)

XX1	Normal	Code ESQ only if mentioned explicitly by subject! Check other more specific codes first!
XX2	Aroused positive	
XX3	Aroused negative ('tight, nervous, tense')	
XX4	Increase (Fast/Much/ Strong)	In case of uncertainty: Aroused positive/negative dominates

XX5   Decrease (Slow/Little/   increase
      Weak
XX6   Controlled
XX7   Changed (unspecified)

Associated emotions

XX1   Happiness
XX2   Sadness   Code Associated emotions only if
XX3   Fear   mentioned explicitly by subject!
XX4   Anger
XX5   Surprise
XX6   Disgust
XX7   Contempt

4.1 Speech

101   Silence, Say nothing

11X   Experience subjective   12X   Associated emotions (see
      quality (ESQ, see above)   above)

181   Hesitant   100   Not specified
182   Change in articulation   109   Other
183   Change in rhythm

4.2 Voice

21X   ESQ (see above)   If possible code ESQ for:
                                      23X   Loudness

22X   Associated emotions (see   ·
      above)   ·   (1 to 7)
                                      24X   Pitch
                                      ·
                                      ·   (1 to 7)

281   Tense, choked   285   Warm
282   Harsh
283   Trembling   200   Not specified
284   Whistling   209   Other

4.3 Facial expression

331   Laugh   334   No smile
332   Smile   335   Cry
333   Painful smile

31X   ESQ (see above)   32X   Associated emotions (see
                                            above)

381   Pressing, biting lips   385   Other action in lower face
382   Clenched teeth   386   Action around nose
383   Pulling lip corners down   (wrinkle etc.)

384 Mouth open	387 Action around forehead
	388 Other muscular action
300 Not specified	309 Other

4.4 Gaze

431 Stared	434 Closed one's eyes
432 Sought eye contact	435 Looked at objects
433 Avoided eye contact	
41X ESQ (see above)	42X Associated emotions (see above)
400 Not specified	
409 Other	

4.5 Movements and posture of bodily parts

Behaviours of head, arms, feet, trunk; person staying in one place (for movement of whole body see 4.6):

531   Turning towards other (head or trunk)
532   Turning away from other (head or trunk)
533   Touching positive (to hug, caress, also to kiss)
534   Touching negative (to hit, beat)
535   Instrumental action positive (putting away something carefully, etc.)
536   Instrumental action negative (throwing, also kicking objects, slamming door, etc.)
537   Rest, relaxing, lean back
538   Unrest, not to be able to sit quietly, move back and forth
539   Tense, attending movements (lean forward, etc.)

51X ESQ (see above)	52X Associated emotions (see above)
551 Eating, drinking	500 Not specified
552 Sleeping	509 Other

If necessary, specify further:

Head	Arms, hands, gestures
561 Head down	571 Adaptors (Manipulation of body or objects)
562 Head up	
569 Head other	572 Illustrators (Speech-related gestures of head, hands, arms)
Feet, legs	573 Emblems (Head shaking, clenched fist, gesture of kicking, etc.)
581 Legs pulled up	
582 Stamp one's foot	
589 Feet, legs, other	574 Hands in pockets, arms crossed
	575 Arms, hands, other
	591 Trunk movements, other

4.6 Body movement, displacement, and posture
(When walking, taking a chair, posture related to *whole* body; for bodily parts, see 4.5):

631	Approaching, turning towards somebody to contact (walking, not only 531!)	641	Collapsed posture
		642	Freezing
		643	Sitting down
		644	Erect posture, attending, tense
632	Distancing, turning away from somebody (walking, not only 532!)	645	Walking up and down
		646	Jumping, dancing around
633	Leaving the situation, slow to normal	600	Not specified
		609	Other
634	Running away		
61X	ESQ (see above)	62X	Associated emotions (see above)

4.7 Behavioural tendencies
(not actually done but rather 'feel like to . . .' or 'need for . . .' or 'have a desire to . . .'):

Bodily parts (see 4.5)
731 Turning towards other (head or trunk)
732 Turning away from other (head or trunk)
733 Touching positive (to hug, caress, also to kiss)
734 Touching negative (to hit, beat)
735 Instrumental action positive (putting away something carefully, etc.)
736 Instrumental action negative (throwing, also kicking objects, slamming door, etc.)
737 Rest, relaxing, leaning back
738 Unrest, not to be able to sit quietly, move back and forth
739 Tense, attending movements (lean forward, etc.)

751	Eating, drinking	700	Not specified
752	Sleeping	709	Other

Whole body (see 4.6)

781	Approaching, turning towards somebody to contact (walking, not only 731!)	791	Collapsed posture
		792	Freezing
		793	Sitting down
782	Distancing, turning away from somebody (walking, not only 732!)	794	Erect posture, attending, tense
		795	Walking up and down
783	Leaving the situation, slow to normal	796	Jumping, dancing around
784	Running away		

4.8 General sensations
831 Pleasant – Rest
Harmony, ease, complete absorption, feeling delight, relaxed, rest, satisfaction, to feel well

841   Pleasant – Arousal
       Refreshed, lighthearted, 'winged', watchfulness, full of energy, animated,
       boiling over with happiness, pleasant arousal of the whole body
851   Unpleasant – Rest
       Feeling tired, drowsiness, feeling heavy, weakness, laxity, slackness, decreasing
       readiness to react, dejected, disappointed
861   Unpleasant – Arousal
       Tense, restless, not concentrated, being nervous, to feel like exploding,
       impatience

800   Not specified   809   Other

4.9 Vegetative sensations and symptoms
General

931   Pleasant
932   Unpleasant (slight pain, etc.)
933   Severe pain   900   Not specified
934   Headaches   909   Other

Body temperature and skin
sensations   Chest and heart

941   Pleasant   961   Pleasant
942   Unpleasant   962   Unpleasant
943   Cold (coldness, to feel cold,   963   Rising blood pressure, heart
       to be pale)   beats faster
944   Warm (heat, raising of body   964   Heart beats slower
       temperature, rush of blood   965   Chest (chest pain, sense of
       to the brain, head feels hot)   weight, anguish, feeling
945   Blushing   squeezed)
946   Perspiration, sweaty palms   966   Difficulty in breathing,
949   Other (Goose pimples, pins   breath stops
       and needles in the arm)   967   Deep breathing
                                        969   Other

Mouth   Muscles

951   Pleasant   981   Pleasant
952   Unpleasant (dry mouth, etc.)   982   Unpleasant
959   Other   983   Trembling, weak knees
                                        984   Tension of the muscles,
                                               muscle cramps
Stomach   985   Other

971   Pleasant
972   Unpleasant or other odd feelings
973   'Butterflies in the stomach'
974   Pressure on the stomach
975   Churning stomach, feeling sick in the stomach
976   Hunger, thirst
979   Other

5. Combined non-verbal and physiological symptoms/reactions

As the symptom/reaction codes consisted of a multitude of categories, most of which were reported with low frequency, it was necessary to combine the categories into larger symptom/reaction groups. Some categories, for example all 'behavioural tendency' codes, were not used in these combinations because of generally very low frequencies. The symptom/reaction groups that were finally used are specified in the following table and the relevant categories are indicated by their respective code numbers (see Section 4).

Variable Code	Name of variable	Codes combined
Speech		
SPEEQN	Speech subjective quality normal	111, 116
SPEEQC	Speech subjective quality changed	112–115, 117
SPEESY	Speech reactions mentioned	181–183, 100, 109
Voice		
VOIQN	Voice subjective quality normal	211, 216, 231, 236
VOIQC	Voice subjective quality changed	212–215, 217, 232–235, 237
VOISY	Voice reactions mentioned	281–285, 200, 209
Facial expression		
FACQN	Face subjective quality normal	311, 316
FACQC	Face subjective quality changed	312–315, 317
LAFSMI	Laughing/smiling	331, 332
CRY	Crying	335
FACSY	Face reactions mentioned	381–388, 300, 309
Gaze		
GAZESY	Gaze reactions mentioned	431–435
Body part movements		
MOVQN	Normal movements of body parts	511, 516
MOVQC	Changed movements of body parts	512–515, 517
PERSMOV	Interpersonal movement	531–534
INSTACT	Instrumental action	535–536
UNREST	General unrest	538–539
HANDSY	Hand movements mentioned	571–575
Whole body movements and postures		
BODYQN	Normal body movements	611, 616
BODYQC	Changed body movements	612–615, 617
AVOID	Avoidance/distancing	632–634
FREEZ	Freezing	642, 644
EXPAN	Expansive movements	645, 646

Sensations

PLEARES	Pleasant rest sensations	831
PLEAROU	Pleasant arousal sensations	841
UNPLRES	Unpleasant rest sensations	851
UNPLROU	Unpleasant arousal sensations	861

Vegetative symptoms

COLDTEM	Symptoms of coldness	943, 949
WARMTEM	Symptoms of warmth	944, 945
PERSPIR	Perspiration	946
BLOPRES	Blood pressure rise	963
CHESBRE	Chest/breathing problems	965, 966
STOTROU	Stomach symptoms	972–975
MUSCLSY	Muscle symptoms	983, 984

6. Combined antecedent codes – antecedent groups

As for the symptom/reaction codes, for statistical purposes some of the antecedent codes were combined into larger groups for some analyses. These combinations were based on frequencies of occurrence and on content of categories and are presented in the following table together with the categories included in each group. Most of the groups were used for all four emotions, but some were emotion specific.

Variable code	Antecedent	Categories included
NEWS	News	01, 02
RELA	Relationships	03, 04
INST	Social institutions	05, 18
TEMP	Temporary meeting/separation	06, 07
PERM	Permanent separation	08, 09
ALPH	Birth/death	10, 11
BODY	Pleasure/pain	19, 20, 21
STRANG	Interactions with strangers	12
ACHI	Achievement	15
only for fear:		
SUPER	Supernatural	24
RISKI	Risk-taking/External forces	25, 26, 27
TRAF	Traffic	17
NOVEL	Novelty	14
only for anger:		
JUST	Injustice	28
INCON	Inconvenience	30

7. Miscellaneous code combinations and variables

For some statistical analyses (ANOVAs) other variables were grouped. These are listed in the following table. For categories combined in each case, please refer to the categories described above.

Grouped variables	Codes combined

Social class (CLASS), grouped from 'Father's occupation':
1   blue collar   (1, 2, 3, 4)
2   white collar   (5, 6, 7)

Field of study/faculty (FISTU), grouped from 'Field of study':
1   psychology   (1)
2   social sciences   (2, 3, 4, 5)
3   natural sciences   (6, 7, 8)

Age (AGEG):
1   18–20 years
2   21–23 years
3   24–35 years

Number of brothers and sisters (NBSG):
1   none
2   1–2 brothers/sisters
3   more than 2 brothers/sisters

Years spent at the university (YUNIG):
1   up to 1 year
2   2–4 years
3   more than 4 years

Group size (GRPSZ), grouped from 'Who was involved':
1   alone   (1)
2   dyad   (2, 3)
3   small group   (4, 5, 6)
4   large group   (7, 8)

Familiarity with persons involved (SOSUP), grouped from 'Who was involved':
1   unfamiliar   (3, 5, 8)
2   familiar   (2, 4, 6, 7)

How long ago (PASTG):
1   up to a week ago   (1, 2, 3)
2   longer than a week ago   (4, 5, 6)

Duration (DURG):
1   short   (1, 2)
2   medium   (3)
3   long   (4, 5)

Intensity (INTG):
1   low   (0–5)
2   medium   (6, 7)
3   high   (8, 9)

Control of verbal behaviour (CVERBG) and
Control of symptoms/reactions (CSYMPG):
1   low   (0, 1)
2   medium   (2–5)
3   high   (6–9)

Appendix D
Statistical analyses

In the chapters of this book the significance data of statistical comparisons are usually not mentioned. Thus, for the interested reader in this appendix all the significant statistical comparisons are listed in tabular form by chapter, including the type of analysis computed (for example ANOVA), the dependent and independent variables tested, the degrees of freedom, etc. Furthermore, the effect size 'd' was computed for ANOVA- and t-test results, providing an index for the magnitude of the statistical differences as a proportion of the standard deviations. In some chapters the data are discussed only in a descriptive way, so, for these chapters no results are listed in this appendix. Means and standard deviations of data are not reported here because of space limitations. The interested reader may obtain these directly from the author(s) of the respective chapter. The abbreviations for variables listed in this appendix are explained in detail in Appendix C.

Statistical test	Dependent variable	Independent variable(s)	F/t/chi2	df	p <	Effect size d
Chapter 5						
chi2	RELA	EMOT	24.64	2	0.001	
chi2	ALPH	EMOT	24.95	2	0.001	
chi2	STRANG	EMOT	28.32	2	0.001	
chi2	BODY	EMOT	8.25	2	0.05	
chi2	TEMP	EMOT	33.21	2	0.001	
chi2	NEWS	EMOT	6.93	2	0.05	
chi2	JUST	EMOT	63.00	2	0.001	
chi2	TRAF	EMOT	60.00	2	0.001	
chi2	NOVEL	EMOT	45.00	2	0.001	
chi2	RISKI	EMOT	33.00	2	0.001	
chi2	PERM	EMOT	22.80	2	0.001	
chi2	INCON	EMOT	27.00	2	0.001	
chi2	SUPER	EMOT	12.00	2	0.01	
ANOVA	PAST	EMOT	18.51	3029/3	0.001	0.16
ANOVA	IMM	EMOT	41.44	3075/3	0.001	0.23
ANOVA	GRPSZ	EMOT	29.45	3073/3	0.001	0.20
ANOVA	SOSUP	EMOT	96.69	3073/3	0.001	0.36
ANOVA	REAL	EMOT	62.49	3080/3	0.001	0.29
ANOVA	REAL-sad	COUN	3.48	758/7	0.01	0.14
ANOVA	REAL-fear	COUN	5.16	761/7	0.001	0.17
ANOVA	REAL	COUN	6.48	760/7	0.001	0.18
ANOVA	IMM-joy	COUN	8.83	764/7	0.001	0.26
ANOVA	IMM-sad	COUN	14.65	759/7	0.001	0.28
ANOVA	IMM-ang	COUN	5.56	764/7	0.001	0.17
ANOVA	IMM	COUN	10.69	750/1	0.001	0.24
ANOVA	GRPSZ	COUN	2.29	771/7	0.05	0.11
ANOVA	SOSUP	COUN	6.57	771/7	0.001	0.19

Statistical test	Dependent variable	Independent variable(s)	F/t/chi2	df	p <	Effect size d
chi2	RELA-joy	COUN	46.28	7	0.001	
chi2	TEMP-joy	COUN	24.49	7	0.001	
chi2	BODY-joy	COUN	30.30	7	0.001	
chi2	ACHI-joy	COUN	14.31	7	0.05	
chi2	ALPH-joy	COUN	15.70	7	0.05	
chi2	STRANG-joy	COUN	17.00	7	0.01	
chi2	RELA-sad	COUN	26.98	7	0.001	
chi2	ALPH-sad	COUN	16.04	7	0.05	
chi2	NEWS-sad	COUN	30.95	7	0.001	
chi2	PERM-sad	COUN	13.26	7	0.05	
chi2	ACHI-sad	COUN	13.60	7	0.05	
chi2	TEMP-sad	COUN	16.56	7	0.05	
chi2	INST-sad	COUN	15.82	7	0.05	
chi2	STRANG-fear	COUN	15.09	7	0.05	
chi2	NOVEL-fear	COUN	32.79	7	0.001	
chi2	SUPER-fear	COUN	30.47	7	0.001	
chi2	BODY-fear	COUN	17.22	7	0.01	
chi2	RELA-fear	COUN	20.11	7	0.01	
chi2	NEWS-fear	COUN	19.00	7	0.01	
chi2	INST-fear	COUN	14.57	7	0.05	
chi2	RELA-ang	COUN	34.86	7	0.001	
chi2	STRANG-ang	COUN	25.70	7	0.001	
chi2	BODY-ang	COUN	41.32	7	0.001	
chi2	INCON-ang	COUN	14.34	7	0.05	
chi2	ACHI-ang	COUN	18.67	7	0.01	
ANOVA	IMM-joy	ANTS	14.99	578/4	0.001	0.32
ANOVA	GRPSZ-joy	ANTS	2.79	580/4	0.05	0.14
ANOVA	SOSUP-joy	ANTS	27.42	580/4	0.001	0.44
ANOVA	PAST-joy	ANTS	7.11	571/4	0.001	0.22
ANOVA	IMM-sad	ANTS	34.75	359/1	0.001	0.62
ANOVA	SOSUP-sad	ANTS	18.40	354/1	0.001	0.46
ANOVA	PAST-sad	ANTS	77.64	352/1	0.001	0.94
ANOVA	REAL-fear	ANTS	7.56	525/4	0.001	0.24
ANOVA	IMM-fear	ANTS	3.74	524/4	0.01	0.17
ANOVA	GRPSZ-fear	ANTS	4.58	524/4	0.01	0.19
ANOVA	SOSUP-fear	ANTS	8.48	524/4	0.001	0.25
ANOVA	PAST-fear	ANTS	4.82	509/4	0.001	0.20
ANOVA	GRPSZ-ang	ANTS	14.44	556/2	0.001	0.32
ANOVA	SOSUP-ang	ANTS	49.64	556/2	0.001	0.60

Chapter 6

Statistical test	Dependent variable	Independent variable(s)	F/t/chi2	df	p <	Effect size d
chi2	PLEARES-joy	NORSOU	19.74	1	0.001	
chi2	WARMTEM-joy	NORSOU	5.43	1	0.05	
chi2	BLOPRES-joy	NORSOU	8.47	1	0.01	
chi2	STOTROU-joy	NORSOU	4.43	1	0.05	
chi2	UNPLROU-sad	NORSOU	4.26	1	0.05	
chi2	BLOPRES-sad	NORSOU	7.60	1	0.01	
chi2	CHESBRE-sad	NORSOU	10.06	1	0.01	
chi2	STOTROU-fear	NORSOU	15.72	1	0.001	
chi2	BLOPRES-ang	NORSOU	6.36	1	0.05	
chi2	MUSCLSY-ang	NORSOU	7.57	1	0.01	
PEARSON r	No. SYMPTOMS	NBS	−0.09	770	0.01	
PEARSON r	No. SYMPTOMS	SOSUP-joy	0.07	777	0.05	
PEARSON r	No. SYMPTOMS	SOSUP-sad	0.10	761	0.01	
PEARSON r	No. SYMPTOMS	SOSUP-fear	0.09	766	0.01	
PEARSON r	No. SYMPTOMS	SOSUP-ang	0.07	773	0.05	

Statistical test	Dependent variable	Independent variable(s)	F/t/chi2	df	p <	Effect size d
Chapter 7						
ANOVA	CSYMP	EMOT	81.44	29229/3	0.001	0.33
ANOVA	CSYMP-joy	COUN	4.64	637/7	0.001	0.17
ANOVA	CSYMP-sad	COUN	2.16	637/7	0.05	0.12
ANOVA	CSYMP-ang	COUN	2.87	613/7	0.05	0.14
ANOVA	CSYMP-fear	SEX	4.50	613/1	0.05	0.17
Chapter 8						
chi2	SPEECH	EMOT	65.20	15	0.001	
chi2	SPEECH-joy	COUN	96.48	14	0.001	
chi2	SPEECH-sad	COUN	87.70	14	0.001	
chi2	SPEECH-fear	COUN	104.77	14	0.001	
chi2	SPEECH-ang	COUN	115.14	14	0.001	
ANOVA	SPEECH	SOSUP	1.90	92/1	0.01	0.29
chi2	CVERB	EMOT	30.90	6	0.001	
chi2	CVERB-joy	COUN	37.38	14	0.01	
chi2	CVERB-sad	COUN	29.96	14	0.001	
chi2	CVERB-fear	COUN	27.04	14	0.05	
chi2	CVERB-ang	COUN	27.53	14	0.05	
ANOVA	No. WORDS (1st question)	COUN	8.08	413/4	0.001	0.28
ANOVA	No. WORDS (2nd question)	COUN	5.70	381/4	0.001	0.25
ANOVA	No. WORDS (2nd question)	EMOT	2.53	381/3	0.06	0.16
Chapter 9						
ANOVA	DUR-joy	ANTS	5.71	618/5	0.001	0.19
ANOVA	DUR-sad	ANTS	5.56	582/5	0.001	0.20
ANOVA	DUR-fear	ANTS	12.59	598/6	0.001	0.29
ANOVA	DUR-ang	ANTS	2.14	633/4	0.08	0.12
ANOVA	CVERB-joy	ANTS	3.45	599/5	0.01	0.15
ANOVA	CVERB-sad	ANTS	2.05	546/5	0.07	0.12
ANOVA	CVERB-fear	ANTS	3.51	533/6	0.05	0.16
ANOVA	CVERB-ang	ANTS	3.60	625/4	0.01	0.15
ANOVA	CSYMP-joy	ANTS	2.44	599/5	0.05	0.13
ANOVA	CSYMP-sad	ANTS	2.38	571/5	0.05	0.13
ANOVA	CSYMP-fear	ANTS	5.10	575/6	0.001	0.19
ANOVA	CSYMP-ang	ANTS	2.62	617/4	0.05	0.13
ANOVA	INTEN-sad	ANTS	2.11	569/5	0.07	0.12
ANOVA	VERB-sad	ANTS	2.49	538/5	0.05	0.14
ANOVA	VERB-fear	ANTS	2.40	565/6	0.05	0.13
ANOVA	VERB-ang	ANTS	2.18	615/4	0.07	0.12
ANOVA	INTEN	EMOT	9.65	2944/3	0.001	0.12
ANOVA	DUR	EMOT	182.21	3023/3	0.001	0.30
ANOVA	VERB	EMOT	66.31	2839/3	0.001	0.31
ANOVA	VERB-joy	COUN	4.46	771/7	0.001	0.15
ANOVA	CVERB	EMOT	90.31	2844/3	0.001	0.36
ANOVA	CSYMP	EMOT	81.44	2929/3	0.001	0.33
ANOVA	PAST	EMOT	9.99	3030/3	0.001	0.12
ANOVA	DUR-sad	WHERE	5.29	657/2	0.01	0.18
ANOVA	DUR-fear	WHERE	23.77	701/2	0.001	0.37
ANOVA	DUR-ang	WHERE	3.84	710/2	0.05	0.15
(for ANOVA results with GRPSZ and SOSUP see results for chapter 11)						
ANOVA	CVERB	INTG	3.58	2707/2	0.05	0.08
ANOVA	CVERB	DURG	14.05	2707/2	0.001	0.14
ANOVA	CSYMP	INTG	11.36	2791/2	0.001	0.13

Statistical test	Dependent variable	Independent variable(s)	F/t/chi2	df	p <	Effect size d
ANOVA	CSYMP	EMOT/INTG	2.06	2791/6	0.06	0.11
ANOVA	CSYMP	INTG/DURG	3.32	2791/4	0.01	0.07
ANOVA	CVERB	VERB	16.46	2677/2	0.001	0.16
ANOVA	CVERB	EMOT/VERB	7.10	2677/6	0.001	0.10
chi2	PERSMOV	ANTS-joy	17.35	6	0.01	
chi2	HANDSY	ANTS-joy	11.39	6	0.08	
chi2	EXPAN	ANTS-joy	19.67	6	0.01	
chi2	PLEARES	ANTS-joy	34.32	6	0.001	
chi2	BLOPRES	ANTS-joy	11.86	6	0.07	
chi2	CRY	ANTS-sad	47.74	6	0.001	
chi2	HANDSY	ANTS-fear	22.54	7	0.01	
chi2	FREEZ	ANTS-fear	17.06	7	0.05	
chi2	PERSPIR	ANTS-fear	13.53	7	0.06	
chi2	MUSCLSY	ANTS-fear	21.69	7	0.01	
chi2	VOIQC	ANTS-ang	15.63	5	0.01	

Chapter 10

Statistical test	Dependent variable	Independent variable(s)	F/t/chi2	df	p <	Effect size d
chi2	SENS	COUN	81.90	7	0.01	
ANOVA	SENS	COUN	17.20	777/7	0.01	0.30
chi2	SENS	NORSOU	4.30	1	0.05	
t-test	SENS	NORSOU	2.40	777	0.05	0.15
chi2	SENS	MLI	9.80	2	0.01	
ANOVA	SENS	MLI	5.80	777/2	0.01	0.17
chi2	SENS	FISTU	9.00	2	0.05	
ANOVA	SENS	FISTU	8.10	777/2	0.01	0.21
chi2	SENS	SEX	10.60	1	0.01	
t-test	SENS	SEX	4.30	774	0.01	0.31
chi2	INTER	COUN	80.60	7	0.01	
ANOVA	INTER	COUN	22.10	777/7	0.01	0.34
chi2	INTER	MLI	13.20	2	0.01	
ANOVA	INTER	MLI	10.20	2	0.01	0.23
ANOVA	INTER	FISTU	5.20	777/2	0.01	0.17
t-test	INTER	SEX	2.70	774	0.01	0.19
chi2	EXTER	COUN	19.30	7	0.01	
ANOVA	EXTER	COUN	3.50	777/7	0.01	0.13
chi2	EXTER	SEX	14.00	1	0.01	
t-test	EXTER	SEX	5.40	774	0.01	0.39
t-test	EXTER	NORSOU	2.20	777	0.05	0.16
chi2	BODREAC	COUN	19.50	7	0.01	
t-test	BODREAC	COUN	4.00	7	0.01	0.14
chi2	BODREAC	NORSOU	4.90	1	0.05	
t-test	BODREAC	NORSOU	2.40	777	0.05	0.17
chi2	BODREAC	SEX	24.80	1	0.01	
t-test	BODREAC	SEX	5.20	774	0.01	0.37
t-test	INTEN	SENS	3.60	221	0.01	0.48
t-test	CSYMP	SENS	2.20	212	0.05	0.30
t-test	CVERB	SENS	2.30	216	0.05	0.31
t-test	HANDL	SENS	5.00	210	0.01	0.69
t-test	INTEN	INTER	5.80	202	0.01	0.82
t-test	CSYMP	INTER	2.20	201	0.05	0.31
t-test	CVERB	INTER	2.40	200	0.05	0.34
t-test	HANDL	INTER	3.90	196	0.01	0.56
t-test	HANDL	EXTER	2.20	210	0.05	0.31

Chapter 11

Statistical test	Dependent variable	Independent variable(s)	F/t/chi2	df	p <	Effect size d
ANOVA	DUR-sad	ALONE/SOC.	19.37	761/1	0.001	0.32
ANOVA	DUR-sad	SOSUP	17.41	754/1	0.001	0.30
ANOVA	DUR-sad	GRPSZ	3.12	752/3	0.05	0.13
ANOVA	INTEN-sad	GRPSZ	2.34	730/3	0.08	0.11

Statistical test	Dependent variable	Independent variable(s)	F/t/chi2	df	p <	Effect size d
ANOVA	INTEN-sad	GRPSZ	5.50	732/1	0.05	0.17
ANOVA	INTEN-sad	ALONE/SOC.	11.54	739/1	0.001	0.25
ANOVA	VERB-joy	GRPSZ	17.26	700/3	0.001	0.31
ANOVA	VERB-joy	SOSUP	34.59	702/1	0.001	0.44
ANOVA	VERB-sad	GRPSZ	10.78	699/3	0.001	0.25
ANOVA	VERB-sad	SOSUP	42.48	701/1	0.001	0.49
ANOVA	VERB-fear	GRPSZ	23.92	710/3	0.001	0.37
ANOVA	VERB-fear	SOSUP	45.46	712/1	0.001	0.51
ANOVA	VERB-ang	GRPSZ	6.59	736/3	0.001	0.19
ANOVA	VERB-ang	SOSUP	2.87	738/1	0.10	0.13
ANOVA	CVERB-joy	GRPSZ	3.10	741/3	0.05	0.13
ANOVA	CVERB-sad	GRPSZ	8.23	696/3	0.001	0.22
ANOVA	CVERB-fear	GRPSZ	4.89	666/3	0.01	0.17
ANOVA	CVERB-ang	GRPSZ	5.90	745/3	0.001	0.18
ANOVA	CVERB-joy	SOSUP	9.70	743/1	0.01	0.23
ANOVA	CVERB-sad	SOSUP	9.64	698/1	0.01	0.24
ANOVA	CVERB-ang	SOSUP	17.66	747/1	0.001	0.31
ANOVA	CSYMP-sad	GRPSZ	4.21	29/3	0.01	0.15
ANOVA	CSYMP-sad	SOSUP	3.71	731/1	0.06	0.14
ANOVA	INTEN-joy	SOC/NONSOC	8.18	746/1	0.01	0.21
ANOVA	INTEN-sad	SOC/NONSOC	4.87	732/1	0.05	0.16
ANOVA	DUR-sad	SOC/NONSOC	9.13	754/1	0.01	0.22
ANOVA	DUR-fear	SOC/NONSOC	2.66	753/1	0.11	0.12
ANOVA	VERB-joy	SOC/NONSOC	46.90	702/1	0.001	0.52
ANOVA	VERB-sad	SOC/NONSOC	27.96	701/1	0.001	0.40
ANOVA	VERB-fear	SOC/NONSOC	39.25	712/1	0.001	0.47
ANOVA	VERB-ang	SOC/NONSOC	5.80	738/1	0.05	0.18
ANOVA	CVERB-sad	SOC/NONSOC	15.65	698/1	0.001	0.30
ANOVA	CSYMP-sad	SOC/NONSOC	7.49	731/1	0.01	0.20
ANOVA	CVERB-ang	SOC/NONSOC	10.80	747/1	0.001	0.24
ANOVA	SEX	IND.DIFF.	9.83	773/2	0.001	0.23
ANOVA	DUR	IND.DIFF.	3.53	776/2	0.05	0.14
ANOVA	INTEN	IND.DIFF.	4.69	776/2	0.01	0.16
ANOVA	VERB	IND.DIFF.	9.78	776/2	0.001	0.23
ANOVA	CVERB	IND.DIFF.	3.04	776/2	0.05	0.13
ANOVA	IND.DIFF.	COUN	4.72	771/7	0.001	0.16

Appendix A2

chi2	STUDF	PARIS-LYON	11.24	4	0.05	
chi2	PAST-joy	PARIS-LYON	12.52	4	0.05	
chi2	GRPSZ-joy	PARIS-LYON	14.43	3	0.01	
chi2	SOSUP-sad	PARIS-LYON	8.69	1	0.01	
chi2	NEWS-joy	PARIS-LYON	5.28	1	0.05	
chi2	NEWS-sad	PARIS-LYON	4.98	1	0.05	
chi2	STRANG-ang	PARIS-LYON	5.38	1	0.05	

Appendix A3

ANOVA	DUR-fear	EXT/NEUR	3.39	83/3	0.05	0.40
ANOVA	INTEN-fear	EXT/NEUR	3.94	84/3	0.05	0.43
ANOVA	INTEN-ang	EXT/NEUR	7.07	85/3	0.001	0.58

Appendix A4

ANOVA	INTEN-joy	ITAL/TOTAL	6.15	877/1	0.05	0.17
ANOVA	INTEN-sad	ITAL/TOTAL	11.75	877/1	0.001	0.23
ANOVA	VERB-joy	ITAL/TOTAL	3.91	877/1	0.05	0.13
ANOVA	CVERB-ang	ITAL/TOTAL	2.76	877/1	0.10	0.11
chi2	TEMP-joy	ITAL/TOTAL	2.91	1	0.10	
chi2	STRANG-fear	ITAL/TOTAL	2.97	1	0.10	

Statistical test	Dependent variable	Independent variable(s)	F/t/chi2	df	p <	Effect size d
chi2	RISKI-fear	ITAL/TOTAL	2.97	I	0.10	
chi2	NOVEL-fear	ITAL/TOTAL	12.69	I	0.001	
chi2	STRANG-ang	ITAL/TOTAL	10.53	I	0.01	
chi2	INCON-ang	ITAL/TOTAL	3.76	I	0.05	
chi2	BLOPRES	ITAL/TOTAL	47.10	I	0.001	
chi2	STOTROU	ITAL/TOTAL	5.25	I	0.05	
chi2	VOIQC	ITAL/TOTAL	18.74	I	0.001	
chi2	LAFSMI	ITAL/TOTAL	5.98	I	0.05	
chi2	MUSCLSY-joy	ITAL/TOTAL	4.17	I	0.05	

Appendix A5

Statistical test	Dependent variable	Independent variable(s)	F/t/chi2	df	p <	Effect size d
chi2	STUDF	SWISS/TOTAL	9.59	2	0.01	
chi2	AGE	SWISS/TOTAL	20.65	2	0.001	
chi2	MLI	SWISS/TOTAL	15.38	2	0.001	
chi2	ANTS-sad	SWISS/TOTAL	23.64	9	0.01	
chi2	NEWS-sad	SWISS/TOTAL	6.39	I	0.05	
chi2	RELA-sad	SWISS/TOTAL	6.58	I	0.01	
chi2	PERM-sad	SWISS/TOTAL	3.99	I	0.05	
chi2	ANTS-fear	SWISS/TOTAL	32.59	13	0.01	
t-test	No. REACTIONS-sad	SWISS/TOTAL	2.89	106.9	0.01	0.56
t-test	No. REACTIONS-fear	SWISS/TOTAL	2.76	777.0	0.01	0.20
t-test	No. REACTIONS-anger	SWISS/TOTAL	3.20	107.6	0.01	0.62
chi2	FACSY-sad	SWISS/TOTAL	10.99	I	0.001	
chi2	MUSCLSY-fear	SWISS/TOTAL	9.95	I	0.01	
chi2	VOISY-ang	SWISS/TOTAL	8.79	I	0.01	
chi2	HANDSY-ang	SWISS/TOTAL	7.42	I	0.01	
chi2	MUSCLSY-ang	SWISS/TOTAL	9.31	I	0.01	
chi2	PLEARES-joy	SWISS/TOTAL	24.80	I	0.001	
chi2	WARMTEM-joy	SWISS/TOTAL	5.60	I	0.05	
chi2	VOISY-joy	SWISS/TOTAL	27.36	I	0.001	

Appendix A8

Statistical test	Dependent variable	Independent variable(s)	F/t/chi2	df	p <	Effect size d
chi2	ANTS-joy	ISRAEL/TOTAL	26.50	8	0.01	
chi2	ANTS-sad	ISRAEL/TOTAL	56.12	9	0.01	
chi2	ANTS-fear	ISRAEL/TOTAL	43.37	13	0.01	
chi2	ANTS-ang	ISRAEL/TOTAL	33.17	11	0.01	
chi2	NEWS-joy	ISRAEL/TOTAL	8.98	I	0.01	
chi2	RELA-joy	ISRAEL/TOTAL	7.17	I	0.01	
chi2	BIRTH-joy	ISRAEL/TOTAL	9.41	I	0.01	
chi2	ACHI-joy	ISRAEL/TOTAL	5.53	I	0.05	
chi2	NEWS-sad	ISRAEL/TOTAL	18.22	I	0.01	
chi2	RELA-sad	ISRAEL/TOTAL	21.11	I	0.01	
chi2	DEATH-sad	ISRAEL/TOTAL	6.33	I	0.05	
chi2	STRANG-sad	ISRAEL/TOTAL	39.50	I	0.01	
chi2	NEWS-fear	ISRAEL/TOTAL	11.85	I	0.01	
chi2	RELA-fear	ISRAEL/TOTAL	4.55	I	0.05	
chi2	TRAF-fear	ISRAEL/TOTAL	4.42	I	0.05	
chi2	RELA-ang	ISRAEL/TOTAL	20.56	I	0.01	
chi2	STRANG-fear	ISRAEL/TOTAL	7.37	I	0.01	
chi2	JUST-ang	ISRAEL/TOTAL	7.03	I	0.01	
chi2	SOSUP-sad	ISRAEL/TOTAL	10.37	I	0.01	
chi2	SOSUP-ang	ISRAEL/TOTAL	5.97	I	0.05	
chi2	GRPSZ-sad	ISRAEL/TOTAL	12.27	3	0.01	
chi2	INTG-joy	ISRAEL/TOTAL	10.59	2	0.01	
chi2	INTG-ang	ISRAEL/TOTAL	14.63	2	0.01	
chi2	VERB-joy	ISRAEL/TOTAL	8.53	2	0.01	

Statistical test	Dependent variable	Independent variable(s)	F/t/chi2	df	p <	Effect size d
chi2	VERB-ang	ISRAEL/TOTAL	8.84	2	0.01	
chi2	CVERBG-joy	ISRAEL/TOTAL	4.82	2	0.10	
chi2	CVERBG-fear	ISRAEL/TOTAL	8.60	2	0.05	
chi2	CVERBG-ang	ISRAEL/TOTAL	5.77	2	0.10	
chi2	CSYMPG-joy	ISRAEL/TOTAL	6.79	2	0.05	
chi2	CSYMPG-sad	ISRAEL/TOTAL	10.36	2	0.01	
chi2	SENSAT-joy	ISRAEL/TOTAL	22.04	5	0.01	
chi2	SYMPT-joy	ISRAEL/TOTAL	30.00	7	0.01	
chi2	SENSAT-ang	ISRAEL/TOTAL	19.78	5	0.01	
chi2	IMM-sad	ARAB/JEW	6.10	1	0.05	
chi2	IMM-fear	ARAB/JEW	32.74	1	0.01	
chi2	IMM-ang	ARAB/JEW	16.59	1	0.01	
chi2	VERB-joy	ARAB/JEW	11.46	2	0.01	
chi2	VERB-sad	ARAB/JEW	10.86	2	0.01	
chi2	INST-joy	ARAB/JEW	6.28	1	0.05	
chi2	BIRTH-joy	ARAB/JEW	3.80	1	0.10	
chi2	BODY-sad	ARAB/JEW	6.47	1	0.05	
chi2	DEATH-fear	ARAB/JEW	5.26	1	0.05	
chi2	RELA-ang	ARAB/JEW	8.67	1	0.01	
chi2	ACHI-ang	ARAB/JEW	6.30	1	0.05	
chi2	INTG-joy	ARAB/JEW	16.43	2	0.01	
chi2	INTG-sad	ARAB/JEW	7.30	2	0.05	
chi2	INTG-fear	ARAB/JEW	9.62	2	0.01	
chi2	INTG-ang	ARAB/JEW	17.50	2	0.01	
chi2	IMM-joy	ARAB/JEW	3.75	1	0.10	
chi2	SYMPT-fear	ARAB/JEW	16.90	6	0.01	

References

Abelson, R. P. (1981). Psychological status of the script concept. *American Psychologist*, **36**, 715–29.

Aristotle (1941). Ethica Nicomachea. In *The basic works of Aristoteles*, ed. R. McKeon. New York: Random House.

Arnold, M. B. (1960). *Emotion and personality*. (Vol. 1). *Psychological aspects*. New York: Columbia University Press.

Arnold, M. B. (1960). *Emotion and personality*. (Vol. 2). *Neurological and physiological aspects*. New York: Columbia University Press.

Asendorpf, J. & Scherer, K. R. (1983). The discrepant repressor: Differentiation betwen low anxiety, high anxiety, and repression of anxiety by autonomic–facial–verbal patterns of behaviour. *Journal of Personality and Social Psychology*, **45**, 1334–46.

Asendorpf, J., Wallbott, H. G. & Scherer, K. R. (1983). Der verflixte Represser: Ein empirisch begründeter Vorschlag zu einer zweidimensionalen Operationalisierung von Repression-Sensitization. *Zeitschrift für Differentielle und Diagnostische Psychologie*, **4**, 113–28.

Averill, J. R. (1968). Grief: Its nature and significance. *Psychological Bulletin*, **70**, 721–48.

Averill, J. R. (1979). Anger. In R. Dienstbier (Ed.), *Nebraska Symposium on Motivation, 1978*, pp. 1–80. Lincoln: University of Nebraska Press.

Averill, J. R. (1980). A constructivist view of emotion. In R. Plutchik & H. Kellerman (Eds.), *Emotion. Theory, research, and experience. Vol. 1: Theories of emotion*, pp. 305–339. New York: Academic Press.

Averill, J. R. (1982). *Anger and aggression: An essay on emotion*. New York: Springer.

Ax, A. F. (1953). The physiological differentiation between fear and anger in humans. *Psychosomatic Medicine*, **15**, 433–42.

Babad, E. Y., Alexander, I. E. & Babad, B. Y. (1983). *Returning the smile of the stranger: Developmental patterns and socialization factors. Monographs of the Society for Social Child Development*, **48**, No. 5.

Babad, E. Y., Birnbaum, M. & Benne, K. D. (1983). *The social self: Group influences on individual identity*. Beverly Hills, Ca.: Sage Publications.

Barker, R. G. (1960). Ecology and motivation. In M. R. Jones (Ed.), *Nebraska Symposium on Motivation*, pp. 1–49. Lincoln: University of Nebraska Press.

Barker, R. G. (1968). *Ecological psychology*. Palo Alto, Ca.: Stanford University Press.

Barker, R. G. *et al.* (1978). *Habitats, environment and human behaviour: Studies in ecological psychology and eco-behavioural science from the Midwest Psychological Field Station 1947–1972*. San Francisco, Ca.: Jossey-Bass.

Barron, F. (1955). Threshold for the perception of human movement in inkblots. *Journal of Consulting Psychology*, **19**, 33–8.

Bartlett, E. S. & Izard, C. E. (1972). A dimensional and discrete emotions investigation of the subjective experience of emotion. In C. E. Izard (Ed.), *Patterns of emotions: A new analysis of anxiety and depression*, pp. 129–73. New York: Academic Press.

Bartlett, F. C. (1932). *Remembering: A study in experimental and social psychology*. New York: MacMillan.

Battistich, V. A. & Thompson, E. G. (1980). Student's perception of the college milieu. *Personality and Social Psychology Bulletin*, **6**, 74–82.

Beck, A. T. (1976). *Cognitive therapy and the emotional disorders*. New York: International Universities Press.

Berger, P. & Luckmann, T. (1969). *Die gesellschaftliche Konstruktion der Wirklichkeit*. Frankfurt: Fischer.

Bernstein, D. A. & Allen, G. J. (1969). Fear Survey Schedule II: Normative data and factor analysis based upon a large college sample. *Behavior Therapy and Research*, **7**, 403–7.

Birdwhistell, R. L. (1970). *Kinesics and context*. Philadelphia, Pa.: University of Pennsylvania Press.

Blanck, P. D., Rosenthal, R., Snodgrass, S. E., DePaulo, B. M. & Zuckerman, M. (1981). Sex differences in eavesdropping on non-verbal cues: Developmental changes. *Journal of Personality and Social Psychology*, **41**, 391–6.

Boucher, J. D. (1983). Antecedents to emotions across cultures. In S. H. Irvine, & J. W. Berry (Eds.), *Human assessment and culture factors*, pp. 407–20. New York: Plenum Press.

Boucher, J. D. & Brandt, M. E. (1981). Judgment of emotion: American and Malay antecedents. *Journal of Cross-Cultural Psychology*, **12**, 272–83.

Bower, G. H., Black, J. B. & Tunner, T. J. (1979). Script in memory for text. *Cognitive Psychology*, **11**, 177–220.

Bowers, K. S. (1973). Situations in psychology: An analysis and a critique. *Psychological Review*, **80**, 307–36.

Bradburn, N. M. (1969). *The structure of psychological well-being*. Chicago: Aldine.

Brandstätter, H. (1983). Emotional responses to other persons in everyday life situations. *Journal of Personality and Social Psychology*, **45**, 871–83.

Brengelmann, J. C. & Brengelmann, L. (1960). Deutsche Validierung von Fragebogen der Extraversion, neurotischen Tendenz und Rigidität. *Zeitschrift für Experimentelle und Angewandte Psychologie*, **7**, 291–331.

Breuer, J. & Freud, S. (1895). *Studien über Hysterie*. Leipzig: Deuticke.

Buck, R. W., Miller, R. E. & Caul, W. F. (1974). Sex, personality, and physiological variables in the communication of affect via facial expression. *Journal of Personality and Social Psychology*, **30**, 587–90.

Buck, R. W., Savin, V. J., Miller, R. E., & Caul, W. F. (1972). Communication of affect through facial expressions in humans. *Journal of Personality and Social Psychology*, **3**, 362–71.

Buss, D. M. & Craik, K. H. (1983). The act frequency approach to personality. *Psychological Review*, **90**, 105–26.

Byrne, D. (1964). Repression-sensitization as a dimension of personality. In B. Maher (Ed.), *Progress in Experimental Personality Research, Vol. 1*, pp. 169–219. New York: Academic Press.

Byrne, D., Barry, J. & Nelson, D. (1963). Relation of the revised Repression-Sensitization-Scale to measures of self-description. *Psychological Reports*, 13, 323–34.

Cacioppo, J. T. & Petty, R. E. (1981). Lateral asymmetry in the expression of cognition and emotion. *Journal of Experimental Psychology: Human Perception and Performance*, 7, 333–41.

Cacioppo, J. T. & Petty, R. E. (Eds.) (1982). *Perspectives in cardiovascular psychophysiology*. New York: Guilford.

Carretero, M. (1982). El desarrollo de los procesos cognitivos: Investigaciones trasculturales. *Estudios de Psicologia*, 9, 50–70.

Cohen, J. (1977). *Statistical power analysis for the behavioral sciences*. New York: Academic Press.

Cotton, J. L. (1981). A review of research on Schachter's theory of emotion and the misattribution of arousal. *European Journal of Social Psychology*, 11, 303–97.

Crowne, D. P. & Marlowe, D. (1960). A new scale of social desirability independent of psychopathology. *Journal of Consulting Psychology*, 66, 547–55.

Darwin, C. (1872). *The expression of the emotions in man and animals*. London: Murray. (Reprinted, Chicago: University of Chicago Press, 1965).

Deutsch, M. (1983). Current social psychological perspectives on justice. *European Journal of Social Psychology*, 13, 305–19.

Diaz-Guerrero, R. & Salas, M. (1975). *El diferencial semantico del idioma espanol*. Mexico: Trillas.

Dohrenwend, B. S. & Dohrenwend, B. P. (1974). *Stressful life events: Their nature and effects*. New York: Wiley.

Duffy E. (1941). An explanation of 'emotional' phenomena without the use of the concept 'emotion'. *Journal of General Psychology*, 25, 283–93.

Eastwood, M. R. & Stiasny, S. (1978). Monthly variation of suicides and undetermined death compared. *British Journal of Psychiatry*, 132, 275–8.

Egerton, M. Emotion representations and emotion rules. Unpublished manuscript, University of Oxford.

Eggert, D. (1983), Eysenck-Persönlichkeits-Inventar E-P-I. *Handanweisung für die Durchführung und Auswertung*. Göttingen: Hogrefe.

Ekehammar, B. (1974). Interactionism in personality from a historical perspective. *Psychological Bulletin*, 81, 1026–48.

Ekman, P. (1972). Universals and cultural differences in facial expression of emotion. In J. R. Cole (Ed.), *Nebraska Symposium on Motivation*, pp. 207–83. Lincoln: University of Nebraska Press.

Ekman, P. (1973). Darwin and cross-cultural studies of facial expression. In P. Ekman (Ed.), *Darwin and facial expression*, pp. 1–83. New York: Academic Press.

Ekman, P. (1977). Biological and cultural contributions to body and facial movement. In J. Blacking (Ed.), *Anthropology of the body*, pp. 39–84. London: Academic Press.

Ekman, P. (1982). Methods of measuring facial action. In K. R. Scherer & P. Ekman (Eds.), *Handbook of methods in nonverbal behavior research*, pp. 45–90. Cambridge: Cambridge University Press.

Ekman, P. (1984). Expression and the nature of emotion. In K. R. Scherer & P. Ekman (Eds.), *Approaches to emotion*, pp. 319–344. Hillsdale, N.J.: Erlbaum.

Ekman, P. & Friesen, W. V. (1969a). Nonverbal leakage and clues to deception. *Psychiatry*, **32**, 88–106.

Ekman, P. & Friesen, W. V. (1969b). The repertoire of nonverbal behavior: Categories, origins, usage, and coding. *Semiotica*, **1**, 49–98.

Ekman, P. & Friesen, W. V. (1971). Constants across cultures in the face and emotion. *Journal of Personality and Social Psychology*, **17**, 124–9.

Ekman, P. & Friesen, W. V. (1975). *Unmasking the face*. Englewood Cliffs, N.J.: Prentice Hall.

Ekman, P. & Friesen, W. V. (1978). *Manual for the facial action coding system*. Palo Alto, Ca.: Consulting Psychologists Press.

Ekman, P. & Scherer, K. R. (1984). Questions about emotion: An introduction. In K. R. Scherer & P. Ekman (Eds.), *Approaches to emotion*, pp. 1–12. Hillsdale, N.J.: Erlbaum.

Ekman, P., Friesen, W. V. & Ancoli, S. (1980). Facial signs of emotional experience. *Journal of Personality and Social Psychology*, **39**, 1125–34.

Ekman, P., Levenson, R. W. & Friesen, W. V. (1983). Autonomic nervous system activity distinguishes between emotions. *Science*, **221**, 1208–10.

Ekman, P., Sorenson, E. R. & Friesen, W. V. (1969). Pan-cultural elements in facial displays of emotion. *Science*, **164**, 86–8.

Elias, N. (1977). *The civilizing process*. New York: Urizen.

Endler, N. S. & Magnusson, D. (1974). Interactionism, trait psychology, and situationism. Reports from the Department of Psychology 418, University of Stockholm.

Endler, N. S. & Magnusson, D. (Eds.) (1976). *Interactional psychology and personality*. Washington: Hemisphere Publications.

Erdmann, G. & Janke, W. (1978). Interaction between physiological and cognitive determinants of emotions: Experimental studies on Schachter's theory of emotions. *Biological Psychology*, **6**, 61–74.

Ericsson, K. A. & Simon, H. A. (1980). Verbal reports as data. *Psychological Review*, **87**, 215–51.

Eysenck, H. J. (1956). *The structure of human personality*. London: Methuen.

Eysenck, H. J. & Rachmann, S. (1973). *Neurosen – Ursachen und Heilmethoden*. Berlin: Deutscher Verlag der Wissenschaften.

Fernandez Dols, J. M. & Ortega. J. E. (1984). Los niveles de analisis de la emocion: James cien afinos depues. *Estudios de Psicologia*.

Forgas, J. P. (1979). *Social episodes: The study of interaction routines*. London: Academic Press.

Forgas, J. P. (1982). Episode cognition: Internal representations of interaction routines. In L. Berkowitz (Ed.), *Advances in experimental social psychology*. Vol. 15, pp. 59–103. New York: Academic Press.

Fraisse, P. (1963). Les emotions. In J. Nuttin, P. Fraisse & R. Meili (Eds.), *Traite de psychologie experimentale. Vol. V. Motivation, emotion et personalité*, pp. 83–154. Paris: Presses Universitairés de France.

Freud, S. (1917). *Trauer und Melancholie. Gesammelte Werke*, Bd. X. Frankfurt: Fischer.

Freyberger, H. (Ed.) (1972). *Topics of psychosomatic research*. Basel: Karger.

Frijda, N. H. (in press). *The emotions*. New York: Cambridge University Press.

Frijda, N. H. & Jahoda, G. (1966). On the scope and methods of cross-cultural research. *International Journal of Psychology*, 1, 110–27.

Funkenstein, D. H., King, S. H. & Drolette, M. (1954). The direction of anger during a laboratory stress-inducing situation. *Psychosomatic Medicine*, 16, 404–13.

Geer, J. H. (1965). The development of a scale to measure fear. *Behavior Research and Therapy*, 3, 45–53.

Giovannini, D. & Ricci-Bitti, P. (1981). Culture and sex effect in recognizing emotions by facial and gestural cues. *Italian Journal of Psychology*, 8, 95–102.

Graham, J. A., Ricci-Bitti, P. & Argyle, M. (1975). A cross-cultural study of the communication of extra-verbal meaning by gestures. *International Journal of Psychology*, 10, 57–67.

Green, S. (1975). Variation of vocal pattern with social situation in the Japanese monkey (*Macaca fuscata*): a field study. In L. A. Rosenblum (Ed.), *Primate behavior*, pp. 1–102. New York: Academic Press.

Halbwachs, M. (1968). *Le memoire collective*. Paris: P.U.F. (originally published, 1925).

Hall, G. S. (1899). A study of anger. *American Journal of Psychology*, 10, 516–91.

Hall, J. A. (1978). Gender effects in decoding nonverbal cues. *Psychological Bulletin*, 85, 845–57.

Harper, R. G., Wiens, A. N., & Matarazzo, T. (1978). *Nonverbal communication: The state of the art*. New York: Wiley.

Heise, D. R. (1979). *Understanding events: Affect and the construction of social action*. Cambridge: Cambridge University Press.

Hinde, R. A. (1974). *Biological bases of human social behavior*. New York: McGraw-Hill.

Hinde, R. A. (1979). *Towards understanding relationships*. London: Academic Press.

Hochschild, A. R. (1979). Emotion work, feeling rules, and social structure. *American Journal of Sociology*, 3, 551–75.

Hochschild, A. R. (1983). *A managed heart*. Berkeley, Ca.: University of California Press.

Hoffmann, N. (1979). Einstellungsänderungen und kognitive Therapie. In N. Hoffmann (Ed.), *Grundlagen kognitiver Therapie*, pp. 67–90. Bern: Huber.

Hollenbeck, A. R. (1978). Problems of reliability in observational research. In G. P. Sackett (Ed.), *Observing behavior, Vol. II. Data collection and analysis methods*, pp. 78–98. Baltimore, Md.: University Park Press.

Hupka, R. B. (1981). Cultural determinants of jealousy. *Alternative Lifestyles*, 4, 311–56.

Izard, C. E. (1968). Cross-cultural findings on development and recognition of facial behavior. Paper presented at the Symposium 'Universality of the Emotions' of the American Psychological Association.

Izard, C. E. (1970). The emotions and emotion constructs in personality and culture research. In R. B. Cattell (Ed.), *Handbook of modern personality theory*. Chicago: Aldine.

Izard, C. E. (1971). *The face of emotion*. New York: Appleton-Century-Crofts.

Izard, C. E. (1977). *Human emotions*. New York: Plenum.

Izard, C. E. (1981). *Die Emotionen des Menschen*. Weinheim: Beltz.

James, W. (1884). What is an emotion? *Mind*, 9, 188–205.

James, W. (1890). *Principles of psychology.* New York: Dover.

Jones, H. E. (1935). The galvanic skin reflex as related to overt emotional expression. *American Journal of Psychology,* **47**, 241–51.

Jourard, S. M. (1966). An exploratory study of body-accessibility. *British Journal of Social and Clinical Psychology.* **5**, 221–31.

Karlins, M., Coffman, T. L. & Walters, G. (1969). On the fading of social stereotypes: Studies in three generations of college students. *Journal of Personality and Social psychology,* **13**, 1–16.

Katz, D. & Braly, K. (1932). Racial stereotypes in one hundred college students. *Journal of Abnormal and Social Psychology,* **28**, 280–90.

Kemper, T. K. (1978). *A social interactional theory of emotions.* New York: Wiley.

Kessler, R. C. & McLeod, J. D. (1984). Sex differences in vulnerability to undesirable life events. *American Sociological Review,* **49**, 620–31.

Koffka, K. (1935). *Principles of gestalt psychology.* New York: Harcourt-Brace-Janovich.

La Barre, W. (1947). The cultural basis of emotions and gestures. *Journal of Personality,* **16**, 49–68.

Lacey, J. I. & Lacey, B. C. (1958). Verification and extension of the principle of autonomic response-stereotypy. *American Journal of Psychology,* **71**, 50–73.

Landis, C. (1924). Studies of emotional reactions: II. General behavior and facial expression. *Journal of Comparative Psychology,* **4**, 447–509.

Landis, C. (1926). Studies of emotional reactions: V. Severe emotional upset. *Journal of Comparative Psychology,* **6**, 221–42.

Lange, C. (1885). *Om Sinsbevaegelser.* Kopenhagen: Rasmussen (German: Über Gemütsbewegungen. Leipzig: Thomas, 1887).

Langer, E. J. (1978). Rethinking the role of thought in social interaction. In J. Harvey, W. Ickes & R. Kidd (Eds.), *New directions in attribution research, Vol. 2,* pp. 36–58. Hillsdale, N.J.: Erlbaum.

Lazarus, R. S. (1966). *Psychological stress and the coping process.* New York: McGraw-Hill.

Lazarus, R. S. (1968). Emotions and adaptation: Conceptual and empirical relations. In W. J. Arnold (Ed.), *Nebraska Symposium on Motivation (Vol. 16),* pp. 175–270. Lincoln, Ne.: University of Nebraska Press.

Lazarus, R. S. & Launier, R. (1978). Stress-related transactions between person and environment. In L. A. Pervin & M. Lewis (Eds.), *Perspectives in interactional psychology,* pp. 287–327. New York: Plenum.

Le Bon, G. (1896). *Psychologie des foules,* 2nd edn. Paris: Alcan.

Lester, D. (1971). Seasonal variation in suicidal deaths. *British Journal of Psychiatry,* **118**, 627–8.

Leventhal, H. (1979). A perceptual-motor processing model of emotion. In P. Pliner, K. Blankstein & I. M. Spigel (Eds.), *Advances in the study of communication and affect; Perception and emotion in self and others,* pp. 263-99. New York: Plenum Press.

Levine, S. (1960). Stimulation in infancy. *Scientific American,* **202**, 80–6.

Lewin, K. (1936). *Principles of topological psychology.* New York: McGraw-Hill.

Lewin, K. (1951). *Field theory in social science. Selected theoretical papers.* New York: Harper.

Lewy, A. J. (1983). Effects of light on melatonin secretion and the circadian system of man. In T. W. Wehr & F. K. Goodwin (Eds.), *Biological rhythms and psychiatry*. Pacific Grove, Ca.: Boxwood Press.

Lewy, A. J., Kern, H. A., Rosenthal, N. E. & Wehr, T. A. (1982). Bright artificial light treatment of a manic-depressive patient. *American Journal of Psychiatry*, **139**, 1496–8.

Leyhausen, P. (1967). Biologie von Ausdruck und Eindruck (Teil 1). *Psychologische Forschung*, **31**, 113–76.

Loftus, E. F. (1982). Memory and its distortions. In A. G. Kraut (Ed.), *The G. Stanley Hall Lecture Series, Vol. 2*. Washington, DC: A.P.A.

Lück, H. E. & Timaeus, E. (1969). Skalen zur Messung Manifester Angst (MAS) und sozialer Wünschbarkeit (SDS-E und SDS-SM). *Diagnostica*, **15**, 134–41.

McDougall, W. (1920). *The group mind: A sketch of the principles of collective psychology with some attempt to apply them to the interpretation of national life and character*. Cambridge: Cambridge University Press.

McGrath, J. E. (1982). Methodological problems in research on stress. In H. W. Krohne & L. Laux (Eds.), *Achievement, stress, and anxiety*, pp. 19–50. Washington: Hemisphere.

McHugh, P. (1968). *Defining the situation: Organization of meaning in social interaction*. Indianapolis: Bobbs-Merrill.

Magnusson, D. (1981). *Toward a psychology of situations: An interactional perspective*. Hillsdale, NJ: Erlbaum.

Magnusson, D. & Stattin, H. (1981). Situation-outcome contingencies: A conceptual and empirical analysis of threatening situations. Reports from the Department of Psychology, **571**, University of Stockholm.

Mandler, G. (1975). *Mind and emotions*. New York: Wiley.

Mandler, G. (1980). The generation of emotion: A psychological theory. In R. Plutchik & H. Kellerman (Eds.), *Emotion: Theory, research and experiences, Vol. I*, pp. 219–44. New York: Academic Press.

Mandler, G. (1984). *Mind, emotion, and cognition*. New York: Praeger.

Marshall, G. D. & Zimbardo, P. G. (1979). Affective consequences of inadequately explained physiological arousal. *Journal of Personality and Social Psychology*, **37**, 970–88.

Marty, P., de M'Uzan, M. & David, C. (1963). *L'investigation psychosomatique*. Paris: Presse Universitaire de France.

Maslach, C. (1979a). The emotional consequences of arousal without reason. In C. E. Izard (Ed.), *Emotions in personality and psychopathology*, pp. 565–90. New York: Plenum, Press.

Maslach, C. (1979b). Negative emotional biasing of unexplained arousal. *Journal of Personality and Social Psychology*, **37**, 953–69.

Meares, R., Mendelsohn, F. A. D. & Milgrom-Friedman, L. (1981). A sex difference in the seasonal variation of suicide-rate: A single cycle for men, two cycles for women. *British Journal of Psychiatry*, **138**, 321–5.

Milgram, S. (1970). The experience of living in cities. *Science*, **167**, 1461–8.

Milgram, S. (1977). *The individual in a social world*. Reading, Mass.: Addison-Wesley.

Mischel, W. (1979). On the interface of cognition and personality. *American Psychologist*, **34**, 740–54.

Morris, D. (1977). *Manwatching*. Oxford: Elsevier.

Murray, H. A. (1938). *Explorations in personality*. New York: Oxford University Press.

Murray, H. A. (1951). Toward a classification of interaction. In T. Parsons & E. A. Skils (Eds.), *Toward a general theory of action*, Cambridge, Mass.: Harvard University Press, 434–64.

Myers, D. H. & Davies, P. (1978). The seasonal incidence of mania and its relationship to climatic variables. *Psychological Medicine*, **8**, 433–40.

Newman, J. & McCauley, C. (1977). Eye contact with strangers in city, suburban, and small town. *Environment and Behavior*, **9**, 547–58.

Notarius, C. I. & Levenson, R. W. (1979). Expressive tendencies and physiological responses to stress. *Journal of Personality and Social Psychology*, **37**, 1204–10.

Notarius, C. I., Kemple, C., Ingraham, L. J., Burns, T. J. & Kollar, E. (1982). Multichannel responses to an interpersonal stressor: Interrelationships among facial display, heart rate, self-report of emotion, and threat appraisal. *Journal of Personality and Social Psychology*, **43**, 400–8.

Orne, M. T. (1962). On the social psychology of the psychological experiment. *American Psychologist*, **17**, 776–83.

Osgood, C. E. (1966). Dimensionality of the semantic space for communication via facial expressions. *Scandinavian Journal of Psychology*, **7**, 1–30.

Osgood, C. E., Suci, G. J. & Tannenbaum, P. H. (1957). *The measurement of meaning*. Urbana: University of Illinois.

Oster, H. (1978). Facial expression and affect development. In M. Lewis & L. A. Rosenblum (Eds.), *The development of affect*, pp. 43–75. New York: Plenum Press.

Parker, G. & Walters, S. D. (1982). Seasonal variation in depressive disorders and suicidal deaths in New South Wales. *British Journal of Psychiatry*, **140**, 626–32.

Pennebaker, J. W. (1981). Stimulus characteristics influencing estimation of heart rate. *Psychophysiology*, **18**, 540–8.

Pennebaker, J. W. (1982). *The psychology of physiological symptoms*. New York: Springer.

Pennebaker, J. W. & Epstein, D. (1983). Implicit psychophysiology: Effects of common beliefs and idiosyncratic physiological responses on symptom reporting. *Journal of Personality*, **51**, 468–96.

Plutchik, R. (1962). *The emotions: Facts, theories, and a new model*. New York: Random House.

Plutchik, R. (1980). *Emotion: A psychobioevolutionary synthesis*. New York: Harper & Row.

Plutchik, R. & Kellerman, H. (Eds.). (1980). *Emotion. Theory, research, and experience. Vol 1: Theories of emotion*. New York: Academic Press.

Reich, W. (1942). *The function of the orgasm*. New York: Orgone Institute Press.

Reisenszein, R. (1983). The Schachter theory of emotion: Two decades later. *Psychological Bulletin*, **94**, 239–64.

Ricci-Bitti, P. E. (1976). Communication by gestures in South and North Italians. *Italian Journal of Psychology*, **2**, 77–83.

Ricci-Bitti, P. E., Argyle, M. & Giovannini, D. (1978). Emotional arousal and gestures. *Italian Journal of Psychology*, **5**, 59–67.

Ricci-Bitti, P. E., Giovannini, D., Argyle, M. & Graham, J. (1980). La communicazione delle emozioni attraverso indici facciali e corporei. *Giornale Italiano di Psicologia*, 1, 85–94.

Riskind, J. H. (1983). Feedback effects of physical posture appropriateness: Or, when people 'slump to conquer'. Paper presented at Nags Head Conference on 'Stress, conflict, and emotion'. Kill Devil Hills, USA.

Rose, R. J. & Ditto, W. B. (1983). A developmental-genetic analysis of common fears from early adolescence to early adulthood. *Child Development*, 54, 361–8.

Roseman, I. (1979). Cognitive aspects of emotion and emotional behavior. Paper read at the 87th Annual Convention of the American Psychological Association in New York City.

Rosenthal, R. (1966). *Experimenter effects in behavioral research*. New York: Appleton-Century-Crofts.

Salzen E. (1981). Perception of emotion in faces. In G. Davies, H. Ellis & J. Shepherd (Eds.), *Perceiving and remembering faces*, London: Academic Press.

Sarbin, T. R. & Hardyck, C. R. (1955). Conformance in role perception as a personality variable. *Journal of Consulting Psychology*, 19, 109–11.

Schachter, J. (1957). Pain, fear, and anger in hypertensives and normotensives. *Psychosomatic Medicine*, 19, 17–29.

Schachter, S. (1959). *The psychology of affiliation*. Stanford: Stanford University Press.

Schachter, S. (1964). The interaction of cognitive and physiological determinants of emotional state. In L. Berkowitz (Ed.), *Advances in experimental social psychology*, Vol. 1, pp. 49–81. New York: Academic Press.

Schachter, S. & Singer, J. E. (1962). Cognitive, social, and physiological determinants of emotional states. *Psychological Review*, 69, 379–99.

Schank, R. C. & Abelson, R. P. (1977). *Scripts, plans, goals, and understanding*. Hillsdale, NJ: Erlbaum.

Schank, R. G. (1982). *Dynamic memory: A theory of reminding and learning in computers and people*. Cambridge University Press.

Scherer, K. R. (1977a). Kommunikation. In T. Herrmann, P. R. Hofstätter, H. P. Huber & F. E. Weinert (Eds.), *Handbuch psychologischer Grundbegriffe*, pp. 228–39. München: Kösel. (Reprinted in K. R. Scherer & H. G. Wallbott (Eds.) (1979) *Nonverbale Kommunikation*, pp. 14–24; Weinheim: Beltz.

Scherer, K. R. (1977b). Affektlaute und vokale Embleme. In R. Posner & H. P. Reinecke (Eds.), *Zeichenprozesse – Semiotische Forschung in den Einzelwissenschaften*, pp. 199–214. Wiesbaden: Athenaion.

Scherer, K. R. (1981a). Speech and emotional states. In J. Darby (Ed.), *Speech evaluation in psychiatry*, pp. 189–220. New York: Grune & Stratton.

Scherer, K. R. (1981b). Wider die Vernachlässigung der Emotion in der Psychologie. In W. Michaelis (Ed.), *Bericht über den 32. Kongress der Deutschen Gesellschaft für Psychologie in Zürich*, pp. 304–17. Göttingen: Hogrefe.

Scherer, K. R. (1982). Methods of research on vocal communication: Paradigms and parameters. In K. R. Scherer & P. Ekman (Eds.), *Handbook of methods in nonverbal behavior research*, pp. 136–98. Cambridge: Cambridge University Press.

Scherer, K. R. (1983). Prolegomina zu einer Taxonomie affektiver Zustände: Ein Komponenten-Prozess-Modell. In G. Lüer (Ed.), *Bericht über den 33. Kongress der Deutschen Gesellschaft für Psychologie in Mainz*, pp. 415–23. Göttingen: Hogrefe.

Scherer, K. R. (1984). On the nature and function of emotion: A component process approach. In K. R. Scherer & P. Ekman (Eds.), *Approaches to emotion*, pp. 243–318. Hillsdale, NJ: Erlbaum.

Scherer, K. R. (1986). Vocal affect expression: A review and a model for future research. *Psychological Bulletin*, **99**, 143–65.

Scherer, K. R. (1985). Stress und Emotion: Ein Ausblick. In K. R. Scherer, H. G. Wallbott, F. Tolkmitt & G. Bergmann (Eds.), *Die Stressreaktion: Physiologie und Verhalten*, pp. 195–205. Göttingen: Hogrefe.

Scherer, K. R. & Ekman, P. (Eds.) (1982). *Handbook of methods in nonverbal behavior research*. Cambridge: Cambridge University Press.

Scherer, K. R., Summerfield, A. B., & Wallbott, H. G. (1983). Cross-national research on antecedents and components of emotion: A progress report. *Social Science Information*, **22**, 355–85.

Scherer, K. R., Wallbott, H. G., Tolkmitt, F. & Bergmann, G. (1985). *Die Stressreaktion: Physiologie und Verhalten*. Göttingen: Hogrefe.

Schwartz, G. E. (1982). Psychophysiological patterning and emotion revisited: A systems perspective. In C. Izard (Ed.), *Measuring emotions in infants and children*, pp. 67–93. Cambridge: Cambridge University Press.

Schwartz, G. E. & Weinberger, D. A. (1980). Patterns of emotional responses to affective situations: Relations among happiness, sadness, anger, fear, depression, and anxiety. *Motivation and Emotion*, **4**, 175–91.

Schwartz, G. E., Weinberger, D. A. & Singer, J. A. (1981). Cardiovascular differentiation of happiness, sadness, anger, and fear following imagery and exercise. *Psychosomatic Medicine*, **43**, 343–64.

Segall, M. H. (1979). *Cross-cultural psychology*. Monterey, Ca.: Brooks/Cole.

Seligman, M. E. P. (1975). *Helplessness: On depression, development and death*. San Francisco: W. H. Freeman.

Sells, S. B. (1970). On the nature of stress. In J. E. McGrath (Ed.), *Social and psychological factors in stress*. New York: Holt, Rinehart & Winston.

Shields, S. A. (1984). Reports of bodily change in anxiety, sadness, and anger. *Motivation and Emotion*, **8**, 1–21.

Shott, S. (1979). Emotion and social life: A symbolic interactionist analysis. *American Journal of Sociology*, **84**, 1317–334.

Smith, C. A. & Ellsworth, P. C. (1985). Patterns of cognitive appraisal in emotion. *Journal of Personality and Social Psychology*, **48**, 813–38.

Stattin, H. & Magnusson, D. (1983). Outcome classes of anxiety-provoking situations. Report from the Department of Psychology, 597, University of Stockholm.

Swinscow, D. (1951). Some suicide statistics. *British Medical Journal*, i, 1417–25.

Tarde, G. (1900). *Les lois de l'imitation*, 3rd edn. Paris: Alcan.

Tembrock, G. (1977). *Tierstimmenforschung. Eine Einführung in die Bioakustik*, 2. Aufl. Wittenberg: A. Ziemsen.

Thomas, W. I. (1928). Situational analysis: The behavior pattern and the situation. (Reprinted in: M. Janowitz (Ed.), (1966), W.I. *Thomas on social organization and social personality*, pp. 154–67. Chicago: University of Chicago Press.

Tomkins, S. S. (1962). *Affect, imagery, consciousness. Vol. 1. The positive affects*. New York: Springer.

Tomkins, S. S. (1963). *Affect, imagery, consciousness. Vol. 2. The negative affects*. New York: Springer.

Tomkins, S. S. (1980). Affect as amplification: Some modifications in theory. In R. Plutchik & H. Kellerman (Eds.), *Emotion theory, research and experience*, pp. 141–64. New York: Academic Press.

Vohwinckel, G. (1983). *Von politischen Köpfen und schönen Seelen. Ein soziologischer Versuch über die Zivilisation der Affekte und ihres Ausdrucks*. München: Juventa.

Wainer, H. & Thissen, D. (1981). Graphical data analysis. *Annual Review of Psychology*, **32**, 191–224.

Wallbott, H. G. (1982a). *Bewegungsstil und Bewegungsqualität: Untersuchungen zum Ausdruck und Eindruck gestischen Verhaltens*. Weinheim: Beltz.

Wallbott, H. G. (1982b). Audiovisual recording: procedures, equipment and trouble-shooting. In K. R. Scherer & P. Ekman (Eds.), *Handbook of methods in nonverbal behavior research*, pp. 542–79. Cambridge: Cambridge University Press.

Wallon, H. (1949). *Les origines du caractere chez l'enfant*. Paris: PUF.

Warr, P. & Payne, R. (1982). Experiences of strain and pleasure among British adults. *Social Science and Medicine*, **16**, 1691–7.

Weinberger, D. A., Schwartz, G. E. & Davidson, R. J. (1979). Low-anxious, high-anxious, and repressive coping styles: Psychometric patterns and behavioral and physiological responses to stress. *Journal of Abnormal Psychology*, **88**, 369–80.

Weisfeld, G. E. & Beresford, J. M. (1982). Erectness of posture as an indicator of dominance or success in humans. *Motivation and Emotion*, **6**, 113–31.

Whitton, J. L., Kramer, P. & Eastwood, R. (1982). Weather and rhythms in self-reports of health, sleep and mood measures. *Journal of Psychosomatic Research*, **26**, 231–5.

Wicker, F. W., Payne, G. C. & Morgan, R. D. (1983). Participant descriptions of guilt and shame. *Motivation and Emotion*, **7**, 25–39.

Woodworth, R. S. (1938). *Experimental psychology*. New York: Henry Holt.

Wundt, W. (1905). *Grundzüge der physiologischen Psychologie*, Vol. 3. Leipzig: Wilhelm Engelmann.

Wurtman, R. J. (1977). Diseases of the pineal gland. In G. W. Thorn, R. D. Adams, E. Braunwald, K. J. Isselbacher & R. G. Petersdorf (Eds.), *Harrison's principles of internal medicine*. New York: McGraw-Hill.

Index

Page references in italic indicate tables or figures.

The following abbreviations are used: Belg. = Belgium; Fr. = France; G.B. = Great Britain; Isr. = Israel; Ita. = Italy; Sp. = Spain; Switz. = Switzerland; W.Ger. = West Germany.

DATE DUE

ILL 8217156

MAR 2 7 1995